The Elements of Archaeological Conservation

What are the objectives and principles of archaeological conservation? Janey Cronyn sets out, in a lucid and practical manner, to survey the current processes and technologies employed in conservation, to explore the nature of artefacts, their decay, and how they are examined and treated in the laboratory. A general preface to the subject introduces individual chapters investigating the agents of deterioration and preservation, techniques of conservation, siliceous and related materials, metals, and organic materials. The concluding section offers a guide to relevant organizations, training facilities, and publications.

Copiously illustrated with both photographs and line drawings, The Elements of Archaeological Conservation is a unique and valuable reference text for anyone training – or considering training – in conservation or archaeology, as well as for non-professionals such as excavators, finds specialists, archaeometrists, and museum curators.

A freelance consultant, lecturer, and author in archaeological conservation, J. M. Cronyn is a Fellow of the International Institute for Conservation (FIIC), and taught the subject to archaeology undergraduates and to graduate conservators at the University of Durham for fourteen years. W. S. Robinson who has contributed details on marine materials, is a consultant archaeological conservator and an officer of the Nautical Archaeology Society.

To
R.S.O.T.

The Elements of
Archaeological Conservation

J. M. Cronyn

Contributions on marine material by W. S. Robinson

Routledge

910122 B&T 79.95

First published 1990
by Routledge
11 New Fetter Lane, London EC4P 4EE
29 West 35th Street, New York, NY 10001

© 1990 J. M. Cronyn

Typeset by Columns of Reading
Printed by TJ Press (Padstow) Ltd., Padstow, Cornwall.

British Library Cataloguing in Publication Data

Cronyn, J. M. (Janet Margaret)
  The elements of archaeological conservation
  1. Antiquities. Excavation of remains.
  Techniques
  I. Title   II. Robinson, W. S.
  930.1'028'3

Library of Congress Cataloging in Publication Data

Cronyn, J. M.
    The elements of archaeological conservation / J. M. Cronyn;
  contributions on marine material, W. S. Robinson.
        p.   cm.
    Bibliography: p.
    Includes index.
    ISBN 0–415–01206–6. — ISBN 0–415–01207–4 (pbk.)
    1. Antiquities—Collection and preservation. 2. Archaeology—
  Methodology.   I. Robinson, W. S.   II. Title.
  CC135.C76 1989
  930.1—dc19   88–31497
                                                                  CIP

ISBN 0–415–01206–6
ISBN 0–415–01207–4 (Pbk)

Contents

Preface

The aim of this book is to explain archaeological conservation, to describe its principles and objectives, and in so doing to give an explanation of its methodology. By doing this it is hoped that the potential of archaeological conservation, together with the processes which are necessary to maximize it, can be made more readily understandable to all those interested in archaeology. The book, then, is intended in the main for those other than professional conservators who are involved in the understanding and care of excavated materials whether excavators, finds specialists, archaeometrists, museum curators, collectors, or administrators. It can be used both by those who are already committed to archaeology and by those who are studying, taking subsidiary courses in conservation. It will also prove useful to those setting out to train as archaeological conservators since it contains the fundamentals of the subject and, by citing many references, introduces the reader to the literature. Inevitably, when describing the decay, examination, and up-to-date treatment of materials, science is essential to the explanation. The general reader who at some time has had an introduction to chemistry should have no difficulty in following the text where all but the very basic scientific terms are explained. Where an explanation of a process has to be particularly scientific, a summary in lay English follows. The scientific explanations are retained, since they are intrinsic to the subject and will prove of interest to those with a first-level qualification in chemistry.

The book is not intended to be an on-site or museum manual for the non-specialist. As explained in the text, it would be dangerous to produce such a manual in a form which could not be readily updated. No more is it intended to be a recipe book of specialist conservation treatments; thus case studies, which would only mislead more than they would enlighten, are not given. Reference to particular sites or to particular objects is kept to a minimum for two reasons: first, since the book is relevant to archaeology wherever it is practised, such illustrations would be unhelpful to those unfamiliar with the reference; second, if examples were given of all possible types of site, museum, and condition of artefacts, the book would be unwieldy. The scope of the book is limited, however, to portable artefacts; whilst building materials left *in situ* are mentioned, it is recognized that these constitute a separate specialism with its own literature. Specific reference has been made to marine material only when it differs from that of land sites. This aspect of conservation is not to be seen as a separate discipline with different ethics and standards, but rather as yet another category of material an archaeological conservator may have to deal with. Finally, the book does not claim to convey the special fascination of archaeological conservation; this remains to be illustrated by a different type of publication.

Whilst the reader is encouraged to read through the introductory chapter, it should be realized that the book is for reference. The second and third chapters deal with the decay of material and the methods of investigation and preservation, whilst the following three chapters look at both these aspects in relation to particular materials. Considerable use is made of the numbering of small sections of text and of cross-referencing so that the reader can easily turn to the particular sections of the book which are relevant to the problem in hand. Furthermore, a summary of the aspects of conservation which concern the non-specialist is given at the end of every section. These summaries can be used as outlines for practice, but since the subject is continually developing and techniques change, they must be used in conjunction with more up-to-the-minute manuals. What is hoped is that the reader, using the explanations given in this book, will be able to understand and interpret such manuals more successfully. Moreover, by using this fundamental text, all those interested in excavated artefacts should find conservation more coherent and rewarding, and so derive more from that subject which unites us all – archaeology.

Durham
January 1987

Acknowledgements

To collect the information for this book has taken several years, and has been possible only because of the contribution of professional colleagues through conversation, response to specific queries, and conference discussions over this time. A second indirect, but lively, contribution has been from the conservation students I have been lucky enough to teach at the University of Durham. I wish to thank all these usually 'unconscious' contributors and trust that they will be happy to see this distillation of our subject.

I am much indebted to Anna Fedden of Methuen & Co. (now Routledge) who originally commissioned the book. Three valued stimuli have been Ione Gedye, through her initial teaching of the subject, Leo Biek, whose 'forensic' approach to artefacts directed this book towards an explanation of conservation, and Rosemary Cramp, who has always been a staunch supporter of the subject. I am very grateful to Elizabeth Pye (Institute of Archaeology) and Kate Foley (HBMC) for their invaluable suggestions and unfailing encouragement throughout. I would like to thank Kate, Wendy Robinson (my contributor) and Mike Corfield (National Museum of Wales) for their comments on an earlier draft of the whole text, and to the following colleagues who read drafts of particular chapters: Mike Alexander (Dept. of Geography) and Martin Jones (Dept. of Archaeology) both of the University of Durham for Chapter 2; David Scott (Getty Conservation Institute) for Chapter 5; and James Rackham (Museum of London) for Chapter 6.4. Finally, my thanks to Roger Tomlin (University of Oxford) for his comments as a 'non-specialist' in conservation and I am much indebted to him for his assistance with both the first and the final draft of the book.

I am very grateful to the following members of the Department of Archaeology, University of Durham: to Philip Clogg (University of Durham) for making the x-radiographs, for preparing material for photography, and for photographing plates 1.1c, 3.4, and 3.14; to Trevor Woods (and Tom Middlemass) for photographing the remainder of the plates except those mentioned below; and to Yvonne Beadnell for drafting the figures.

I would like to acknowledge permission to reproduce photographs (**p**), or to photograph objects (**o**), kindly given by the following: R. Young (University of Leicester) **p** 1.1 a & b, **o** 1.1c; Dean and Chapter of Durham Cathedral, **o** 2.1, 2.7, 4.2, 4.6 & 6.15; York Archaeological Trust, **p** 2.2 & 6.3; A.F. Harding (University of Durham) **o** 2.3, 2.4, 5.18c & 5.19; Oriental Museum, Durham, **o** 2.6, 2.8, 3.19 & 4.4); C.V. Horie (Manchester Museum) **p** 2.7 & 3.11; R. Janaway (University of Bradford) **p** 5.5; North of England Museums Service, **p** 2.9; C.D. Morris (University of Durham) **p** 3.1, and with Scottish Development Department **o** 5.21b & 5.22; L. Bacon (Horniman Museum) **p** 3.3; W. Robinson **p** 3.6, 5.1, 5.7, 5.8, 5.12 & 6.2; E. Cameron (Institute of Archaeology, Oxford) **p** 3.12; M. Millett (University of Durham) **p** 3.13, **o** 4.16; Museum of London **p** 4.3 & 5.16; Carlisle Archaeological Unit and HBMC **o** 4.5, 5.18b, 6.1 & 6.16; Colchester & Essex Museums Service **p** 4.7; Leicester Museums & Art Gallery Service **p** 4.8 & 4.9; R. Newton (University of Sheffield) **p** 4.11; Roxburgh District Museums **p** 4.14a, **o** 4.14b; V. Fell (HBMC, Manchester Museum) **p** 5.9a; R.J. Cramp (University of Durham) **o** 4.6, 5.3, 5.9b & 5.11; Trustees of the British Museum **p** 5.17; and K. Foley (HBMC) **p** 5.21a.

Abbreviations and addresses

AATA	Art and Archaeological Technical Abstracts (from IIC/GCI)
AIC	American Institute for Conservation
	1400 16th Street NW, Suite 340, Washington,
	DC 20036, USA
CBA	Council for British Archaeology
	112 Kennington Park Road, London SE11 6RE, UK
CCI	Canadian Conservation Institute
	1030 Innes Road, Ottawa, K1A 0M8, Canada
D of E	Department of the Environment (see HBMC)
GCI	Getty Conservation Institute
	4503 Glencoe Avenue, Marina del Rey, CA 90292, USA
HBMC	Historic Buildings and Monuments Commission
	Fortress House, 23 Savile Row, London W1X 2HE, UK
ICCM	Institute for Conservation of Cultural Material
	PO Box 1638, Canberra ACT, Australia
ICCROM	International Centre for Study of Preservation and
	Restoration of Cultural Property
	Via di san Michele 13, 00153 Rome, Italy
ICOM	International Council of Museums,
	Committee for Conservation
	Maison de l'Unesco, 1 rue Miollis, 75015 Paris, France
IIC	International Institute for Conservation of Historic and
	Artistic Works
	6 Buckingham Street, London WC2N 6BA, UK
IIC–CG	IIC–Canadian Group
	Box/CP9195, Ottawa, K1G 3T9, Canada
MASCA	Museum Applied Science Center for Archaeology,
	University Museum, University of Pennsylvania,
	33rd and Spruce Streets, Philadelphia, PA 19104, USA
MGC	Museums and Galleries Commission, Conservation Unit
	7 St James' Square, London SW1Y 4JU, UK

SSCR   Scottish Society for Conservation and Restoration
c/o Department of Archaeology, University of Glasgow,
10 The Square, Glasgow G12 8QQ, UK

UKIC   United Kingdom Institute for Conservation
37 Upper Addison Gardens, London W14 8AJ, UK

UNESCO   United Nations Education, Scientific and Cultural
Organisation
(see ICOM)

Chapter One

Introducing archaeological conservation

During the recent excavation[1] of an Early Bronze Age burial cairn in Crawley Edge, County Durham, the top of an urn is exposed (plate 1.1a). Its texture is that of sticky porridge. The conservator is called in and the whole but badly damaged urn is carefully lifted as a block complete with its contents and surrounding deposit (plate 1.1b). In the conservation laboratory the whole package is x-rayed, revealing that no bones or artefacts are present within the urn. The packing is then partially removed and the conservator, together with the excavator, undertakes a micro-excavation of the urn, its contents, and its surrounding deposit. As each piece of pottery is exposed it is cleaned and consolidated with a water-miscible synthetic resin. All details observed, tests made, and treatments given are recorded; in this instance no evidence for the original contents of the urn is found. For accurate publication drawing, the pottery fragments are reconstructed over a clay core. Later, for display in the local museum, the missing gaps in the fabric are filled and toned in to enable the public to appreciate this rare example of Bronze Age pottery from the north-east of England (plate 1.1c).

On a different excavation,[2] that of the early medieval ecclesiastical site at the Hirsel, Coldstream in Berwickshire, the excavator carefully removes a piece of corroded copper alloy, possibly a coin, surrounded by some fibrous material from the proximity of a burial. The finds supervisor packs the item in silica gel to preserve it and despatches it to the conservation laboratory. Here close examination and cleaning under a microscope show the find to be composed of two coins corroded together and enclosed in the remains of a small bag of woollen weave cloth. After chemical stabilization the item is ready for display or storage in reasonable conditions, dryness no longer being essential.

All the steps described here, even though in themselves rather different, together concern the conservation of archaeological material, that is the preservation and elucidation of artefacts from excavations. Conservation basically aims to prevent objects disintegrating once they have been exposed to the atmosphere and to discover the true nature of

(a)

(c)   (b)

Plate 1.1 The lifting and treatment of an urn. (a) Excavation to reveal top rim of an Early Bronze Age burial urn. (b) Urn being lifted after encasement in polyurethane foam. (c) Urn after micro-excavation, stabilization, and gap filling

the original artefact. Even though these are very wide and somewhat amorphous terms, it can be seen that conservation is part and parcel of archaeology; without it, much archaeological information is lost or left unexploited.

1.1 The processes of conservation

In order to define conservation more closely it is best to examine it in its various processes or stages. At the same time we can look at what happens at each stage if conservation is ignored and at cases where conservation is not necessary, that is where material does not disintegrate and where it reveals its secrets without recourse to special techniques.

1.1.1 Pre-excavation considerations

Even before a site is excavated it is important to consider the conservation requirements likely in order to ensure that adequate facilities and funds are available. In the first instance the level of requirement will depend on the type of site. Thus, for example, a Roman villa would be expected to engender more material for conservation than would a Bronze Age settlement site in Britain; moreover the former could produce iron objects and mosaics, both of which can cause conservation problems not to be found in dealing with the latter site. A second consideration is the demands which will be made upon the artefacts; for example, if in order to establish the construction of a long-decayed coffin it is necessary to study all the nails found by investigative cleaning rather than simply by x-radiography, or if waterlogged timbers are to be displayed rather than stored in water for study purposes only, much more conservation time and funds will be required. This introduces an equally important pre-excavation consideration, that of the burial conditions expected, for these will affect not only the condition of material recovered but also the type of material found. For example, a waterlogged Neolithic site could produce much organic artefactual material whilst a dry one virtually none. This complex aspect is dwelt on at much greater length in the forthcoming chapters.

Without due thought being given to conservation before excavation, disaster can occur on site when unpredictable materials and conditions are found and there is no equipment or personnel available to deal with them; this is especially true on excavations at some distance from a town or even a telephone. In the longer run, both publication and preservation of the excavated archive are in jeopardy if adequate conservation has not been planned.

1.1.2 On-site conservation

On-site conservation is perhaps the most crucial stage of all. But as such it consists in the main of preservation with scarcely any emphasis upon elucidating the nature of the material, which is more loosely called 'cleaning'.

It will be shown that many materials are most in jeopardy when first exposed to the atmosphere after many centuries of burial. They begin to dry out and shrink, react with the air, or crumble as they lose the support of the surrounding soil. Thus on-site conservation begins from the moment of exposure.

First then, for materials at risk, it may be necessary to retain dampness whilst an artefact is still *in situ*; just occasionally, as for soft pottery, it may be the reverse, and drying out *in situ* is important. Next the artefacts must be lifted from the deposit without damaging them or introducing unnecessary adhering supporting materials which are later difficult to remove or which actually harm the finds. In the vast majority of cases no special techniques are necessary, thought and dexterity alone being required. However, fragile objects may need support and where possible this is given by very simple techniques; but in the case of a crumbling mass, such as a totally corroded iron sword in a gravel deposit, more elaborate techniques are necessary.

Once lifted, either by hand or with supports, materials are preserved by good packaging and where necessary controlling their environment. Bad handling/packing is responsible for a great deal of harm to objects which unfortunately are often much more fragile than they appear. In subsequent chapters the damage which can occur by failing to control the environment of materials at risk will be shown; for example, the decorated surface of a waterlogged timber may decay in ten minutes or a copper alloy coin may begin to disintegrate within twenty-four hours if they are not stored correctly. Obviously there are some objects from some deposits such as well-fired medieval earthenware from most types of deposit that do not suffer in these ways.

The other aspect of conservation, that of investigative cleaning, for many materials can only be carried out successfully in a laboratory. To ensure the maximum potential information is obtained, as much deposit as possible is allowed to remain adhering to an object when it is lifted and packed. However, again for certain categories of material/objects, on-site cleaning is possible and even helpful; robust pot-sherds or waterlogged timbers, for example.

Conservation on site may even encompass materials which are not coherent, which do not have a shape. Thus industrial waste in the form of soil discoloration or the stain in a deposit caused by a totally decayed object may fall into the realms of conservation, requiring the nature of the artefactual material to be determined. Further in this vein, conservation attempts to understand how and why materials decay in burial environments. This is not only to assist in devising new cleaning and stabilization treatments but also to attempt to answer problems related to the site rather than the material in question. Thus a particular type of corrosion product found on iron objects could identify the archaeological activity of an area, or the absence of glass artefacts from a deposit could be a result of decay and not an absence of deposition of glass originally.

1.1.3 Laboratory conservation

In the laboratory the real examination of the excavated material begins. Details are given in section 3.3, but in general, using microscopes, artefacts are carefully inspected as the obscuring debris is removed, a process known as investigative cleaning. During this process, aspects of artefacts, such as what they are made of, how they are made, and what they were used for, may emerge. Such questions are as important as the more obvious but fundamental one of 'what is it?'. A great deal of information can be collected in this way and recorded to produce an archive which includes photographs and radiographs.

This aspect of examination is a distinct activity from that of preservation when attempts are made to bring materials into equilibrium with their surroundings. Preservation is achieved either passively by continued control of the environment and supportive packing or else actively, when chemicals are removed from or introduced into the artefacts (section 3.4). These processes are known as stabilization, but it should be realized that in the nature of things such processes will never be capable of succeeding indefinitely.

Whether investigative cleaning is required and/or stabilization is necessary, or even possible, will depend both on the condition of the material and the archaeological questions it can answer. A badly corroded unstable copper alloy coin from a sealed context will require considerable investigative cleaning for a site report and, being a crucial dating tool, it will be stabilized chemically to preserve it. However, a similar routine coin of no archaeological significance may not be cleaned immediately; it will be stabilized passively until required for numismatic study. To be drawn for publication, a fragmented pot may require little cleaning but considerable stabilization in the form of reconstruction; unless the pot is particularly significant, such a time-consuming and expensive practice might not be deemed reasonable, and a drawing is achieved simply by taping together a profile of the pot. Alternatively, a great deal of excavated material cannot be fully investigated until it has been actively stabilized since, like wet glass or leather, it may be too

Plate 1.2 Totally corroded iron stylus where overlying bulky orange/brown corrosion products have been partially removed to reveal original surface with silver inlay retained by dense black corrosion products

fragile to handle. In general, all artefacts benefit from the attention of a conservator even if this is only in the form of a quick examination to ensure that they are stable and that there is nothing on them visible even microscopically which is significant.

A third aspect of laboratory conservation not yet mentioned is that of getting material ready for display. Here objects may require a greater degree of cleaning and/or stabilization than that described above. For example, it is possible to publish significant iron nails after the overlying products of corrosion have been removed from only a part of each one to reveal the section. This together with an x-radiographic plate may reveal significant features for study. However, such an object would look strange (plate 1.2) on display and total cleaning would then be required. Such nails could be stabilized passively in storage, but if required for display adequate environmental control might no longer be possible and so active steps would have to be taken.

Laboratory conservation may also be required for artefacts which are not freshly excavated but which have lain in a museum for many years. These artefacts may well have been treated at some early date and in such cases part of the laboratory investigation will aim to determine the nature of any previous treatments. These may well be obscuring or may have removed, altered, or damaged evidence. Conservation will attempt to distinguish the true original nature of the artefacts and then stabilize this evidence as described above. However, earlier treatments themselves might, without design, make stabilization or retreatment more difficult.

1.1.4 Long-term conservation by control of the environment

This is the prophylactic or preventive aspect of conservation. It is obvious that material which is stable only as a result of the exact control of its environment, for example some untreated iron, must be closely monitored in perpetuity after excavation. Its condition and the variables in the atmosphere surrounding it have to be checked and maintained. However, some degree of monitoring/control of all excavated material, whether it appears stable or has been stabilized actively, must be carried out. This is because all materials, especially those which have undergone some degree of decay, and even modern ones such as adhesives or packaging used, are subject to deterioration over time. Whether this is a matter of weeks or decades will depend on the material and on the environment. Since it is not possible totally to adapt archaeological material to post-excavation environments, it must be the environment which is modified. Thus conservation must continue as long as it is decided that the excavated archive is to be retained.

1.2 Archaeological conservation today

Over the past forty years, conservation has developed from a simple craft into an integrated part of archaeology. It demands not only a high degree of manual dexterity but also an understanding of the processes and preoccupations of modern archaeology, a knowledge of material science and early technology, combined with an aesthetic sense. This evolution is to be found in all fields of conservation, and to clarify the current situation the Conservation Committee of the International Council of Museums (ICOM) has produced a document entitled 'The conservator–restorer: a definition of the profession'.[3]

The development of the investigative aspect of conservation has come about in part from the use of equipment such as the microscope and radiographic facilities. In early days, cleaning tended to be aimed at removing all altered or adhering material from an artefact, leaving only that remaining in its 'original' condition to make it appear as it might have done in antiquity, and as such the methods used were rather harsh whether they were chemical or mechanical. Thus decayed glass surfaces were polished off to expose glass underneath and iron corrosion dissolved away to reveal metal below (plate 1.3). However, when the microscope/radiographs are used, it can be seen that such treatments not only take no account of the original shape and surface details and adhering materials of the artefact but also may alter the original nature of the remaining material. More delicate techniques have been developed to retain this hitherto lost information and in so doing have tapped a whole further pool of data (section 1.1.3). Investigative cleaning offers perhaps the best

Plate 1.3 Iron key stripped of all corrosion products to reveal diminished remaining metal; whilst this is much disfigured, the direction of forging the iron is revealed in the fibrous texture

opportunity for the collection of this information and may be the only occasion when many artefacts are in fact examined in such detail.

Stabilization of materials, whether on site, in the laboratory, or long term, aims to interfere in the least possible way with the archaeological evidence. This means that in order to preserve bronzes, for example, the unstable corrosion is no longer chemically removed as used to be the practice since such treatment tends to leach metal from the remaining alloy core, rendering it useless for analytical purposes. Again, fragile glass is not routinely consolidated with epoxy resins since these cannot be removed at a later date if a mistake has been made, if stabilization is not successful, or if further study of the glass is required. More emphasis is now placed on passive means of stabilization by control of the environment since the methods are often simple but successful, not labour-intensive, and respect the ethic of minimal intervention.

The United Kingdom Institute of Conservation of Historic and Artistic Works (UKIC) has produced guidelines[4] covering the knotty questions of ethics in all fields of conservation. It is realized that no treatment is in the strictest sense 'reversible' but the most important criterion is that the conservator should interfere minimally with the true nature of an artefact. A second important practice is the keeping of records, not only of what treatment is used but also what is observed on an object and what is removed from it. These are kept for several reasons: to record information observed during investigative cleaning; to facilitate further treatment either now or in the future; to record the level of interference for future analysts or finds specialists; and to build up data for the basis of conservation research concerning the success of techniques.

This touches on the final point, that, as pointed out in the Dimbleby Report,[5] conservation engenders its own research problems; problems such as the cause of the break-up of much excavated iron or the development of a suitable synthetic polymer for penetrating a decayed glass crust and sticking to the glass core underneath. Whilst the practising conservator can collect data to analyse such problems, these require corrosion scientists and polymer chemists with relevant equipment to tackle them adequately. Whilst there is indeed some work in such fields being undertaken at present, there is nothing like enough; such a shortcoming means that today archaeological material neither yields up all its information nor is it reliably preserved for future study or display.

1.3 Conservation in practice: a collaborative exercise

Collaboration in conservation is the only ethical approach (see note 4); without it information is lost and time is wasted. The collaboration must be between all those who have an interest in the excavated archive, who in the main are excavators, finds specialists, curators, analytical scientists, and conservators. However, there are many others who could also be named, such as the owners of finds, finds assistants, draughtsmen, exhibition designers, and specialized researchers such as numismatists.

Collaboration begins at the first stage of conservation, that is, before excavation. Not only should the owner-to-be of the finds be established, but also a receiving museum must be alerted, for no curator will wish to take into care a large site archive without early consultation. At this stage too, short-term as well as this longer-term conservation must be arranged. Successful immediate on-site conservation requires the excavator to have obtained advice for the particular site and that there is a conservator who can be called out in an emergency. The excavator should also ensure that adequate conservation material, mainly in the form of packaging, is available and that someone, who is suitably informed, is made responsible for conservation on site. On large excavations it may be worthwhile to plan for a conservator to be on site at all times. A great deal of time and expense at a later date can be saved if, at this early juncture, thought is given to labelling and packaging. If artefacts can be given a robust long-lasting label for both excavation *and* post-excavation data, they need only be labelled once and for all, saving considerable time. Likewise, packaging which is durable should be purchased and where possible chosen to fit into the shelving arrangements of the receiving museum; 2 centimetres could make all the difference.

On site, care of finds requires the co-operation of everyone from the site director to first-season diggers. Artefacts need to be properly treated from the moment of exposure until their arrival at the conservation laboratory. Thus it is important that transport to the laboratory, as well as stabilization, lifting, restricted cleaning, and packing, is catered for. A word here should be said about the collaboration involved in lifting large artefacts such as kilns or mosaic pavements. Here, not only is a conservator involved but also the proposed receiving museum should be consulted, for such artefacts require considerable storage space and display conservation. In some cases the expense of lifting is not justified by the return in archaeological data or display value. However, if left *in situ*, unless given considerable long-term conservation treatment, such artefacts are bound to disintegrate.

Post-excavation is a stage when collaboration is most vital, but when it can easily fail. Attention has recently been focused[6] on this need for collaboration by the suggestion that designs for post-excavation research are as vital as those for excavation itself if archaeology is to maximize its primary data, part of which are represented by artefacts. Post-excavation research designs seek in part to prioritize work on artefacts including conservation. Two categories of study may be recognized, the first being simple identification of materials and artefacts for incorporation into the publication of the interpretation of the site which follows swiftly upon excavation. The second category of study might be a more detailed investigation of an important class of artefact found on the site, which can be seen as crucial to a broader aspect of archaeology than the description of a single site and so might follow this initial report. A different aspect of post-excavation conservation is the extended treatment that is required by objects suitable for display whilst ultimately there is the consideration of the stabilization of the whole site archive. When considering whether this is to be achieved by passive means alone or by active techniques, arguments concerning ethics of minimum intervention, unpredictability of results of intervention, and expense of active treatments will be ranged against those of expense of passive curation, failure of passive techniques, and necessity for intervention, etc. Here too is raised the thorny question of whether the whole archive is to be retained or only certain items selected for retention.[7] If some material is to be discarded, what criteria are to be used for selection? Conservators obviously have a role to play here advising on methods of investigation, recording, and storage.

Before any post-excavation treatment, then, consultation is essential to draw up a conservation strategy: consultation between excavator, conservator, finds specialists, curator designate, and, where appropriate, analytical scientist. The conservation strategy will incorporate an element of selectivity[8] which means that not all artefacts may necessarily receive the same level of conservation (*level* here defining extent rather than worth, for all material should receive the same quality of treatment regardless of its role in archaeology). The material from an excavation then may be divided into five categories, as outlined in the guidelines[9] published by the UKIC Archaeological Section. They are as follows:

1. Display conservation – further cleaning, additional restoration, and cosmetic treatment may be required in addition to category 2.
2. Full conservation – work is understood to include photography, x-radiography, examination and investigation, cleaning, active stabilization, and certain reconstruction. Appropriate analytical information to be provided where required.
3. Partial conservation – will include work in category 4 and a high degree of cleaning with or without active stabilization. This category may include reassembly of broken or detached fragments but not reconstruction of missing areas.
4. Minimal conservation – this category includes 'first-aid', x-radiography and photography, the minimum amount of investigative cleaning, and suitable packaging or repackaging for stable storage.
5. No conservation – no work of any kind is undertaken by the laboratory except for handling and checking.

This system of prioritizing is useful logistically since it enables the many sites excavated annually (producing in Britain alone about 50,000 objects) to be published swiftly; it also allows meaningful programmes of information gathering to be devised and for a small proportion of untreated artefacts to be retained in the archive for future study.

During the publication process, collaboration especially between conservator and finds specialists is continuous.[10] As shown above, conservators are in a unique position to study finds but, like excavators, they cannot be expected to have an in-depth knowledge of every type of artefact. Thus when working on a particular type of find, whether it be a coin, a writing tablet, or a shield-boss, the conservator is bound to call upon the expertise of the relevant specialist. Where a specialist is not available, it has been suggested that data sheets of pertinent information would be useful,[11] but as yet few of these have been drawn up. Of course, over the years conservators will develop a general background knowledge of much of the material they treat, contributing to the planning of investigation programmes, or indeed, they may become finds specialists in their own right. Also during publication, the conservation strategy should ensure that x-radiographs and record cards are presented to the draughtsman before the drawing of the finds so that no information elucidated during the conservation process is now inadvertently lost. It is important that conservators write summaries of their work on the artefacts from a site. These should cover the major pieces of evidence uncovered as well as the criteria used in the selection of material for different levels of treatment and an outline of the treatment itself. Only in this way will information not be lost and will it be possible for those reading site reports to assess the level of information retrieval aimed at.

Collaboration is equally but perhaps not so obviously necessary when material excavated a long time ago is conserved. Often the impetus for treatment is in response to the poor state of an artefact or because it is required for display and not because it is necessary to publish it. If so, the opportunity must be taken to reveal evidence during treatment, and thus once again collaboration with a finds specialist is probably essential; any evidence found must be recorded and the information made available.[12]

For the well-being of materials both on display and in store in museums co-operation between the curator and conservator is essential.[13] As shown in section 1.1.4, there must be continuous monitoring of the condition of artefacts and control of environmental conditions to a level required by the material in question. Monitoring of condition both of artefacts and environment is usually the province of the conservator. In small museums, however, a curator may have to undertake this, calling on the services of a conservator occasionally to review the situation. The methods by which the environment is controlled may vary from simple steps such as choice of storage area or use of a desiccating agent to complex systems involving maintenance of large areas in precise conditions. In this latter case the services of an engineer will be required, for whilst archaeological conservators will be able to define the conditions required, they will not be equipped to devise specialist systems for realizing them.

Whenever a particular exhibition is being prepared, it is essential that the designer and conservator meet at an early stage to discuss aspects such as essential environmental control, choice of display materials, and methods of attaching objects in position. Such aspects cannot be dealt with at the last minute, for the artefacts will suffer whether in the short or long term. Thus leather shoes begin to crack, cheap metal display pins corrode, staining artefacts, or fragile textiles disintegrate under vertical stresses if faulty display techniques are used.

In conclusion, then, conservation can be seen as a practice within archaeology. Like all archaeological practices, whether surveying, excavation, finds research, archaeometry, or curation, its aim is to increase our understanding of the past.

Chapter Two

Agents of deterioration and preservation

2.1 Introduction

The deterioration and preservation of materials depends on two things: the nature of the material, which will be discussed in chapters 4, 5, and 6; and the environment surrounding the material, which is the subject of this chapter. Sometimes it is difficult to separate these two aspects of deterioration/preservation, for the survival of a particular material may be due in part to its resistance to decay and in part to the environment, whether in the ground or in the museum, having been benign. However, some degree of understanding can be gained by trying to identify the factors in the environment which may be affecting either the deterioration or the preservation of artefacts.

In this chapter, after the agents of decay/preservation have been described, their effects on material are discussed. These agents cause decay in two distinct ways:

(a) Physical deterioration: the breakdown of structure of materials, examples being the destruction of stone by frost, the abrasion of soft bone by running water, or the distortion of lead by the weight of overburden.

(b) Chemical deterioration: the alteration of the chemical composition of materials; thus water and air corrode iron, acids dissolve lime-plaster, and bacteria break down leather.

Preservation of material on the other hand may be a result either of an absence of all or some of the agents of decay or of the addition of agents which preserve; thus iron may be preserved where water is absent or phosphates are present, and wood where oxygen is absent or there are copper salts present. Whilst many of the agents of decay/preservation in the environment are familiar, for example temperature, humidity, and acidity, organisms are less so. Thus before embarking upon a discussion as to how these agents which include organisms affect materials, it is important to understand how organisms themselves are affected by the environment whether this is archaeological or post-excavation.

2.1.1 Organisms

Organisms all need some degree of water and so will not tolerate extreme desiccation, nor will they tolerate extreme cold or heat. Many are limited by high levels of salt and by copper and certain complex organic chemicals; these toxins can be used as biocides.

2.1.1.1 Higher animals and plants

Both these types of organism require oxygen for respiration, the release of energy for the activities essential to life:

Respiration: $6O_2 + C_6H_{12}O_6 \rightarrow 6CO_2 + 6H_2O$.
carbohydrate

This oxygen-requiring aerobic respiration means that the organisms cannot function in oxygen-free, that is anoxic, environments. Thus the roots of higher plants will not penetrate anoxic deposits in which earthworms and insects will also be unable to exist. The degree of desiccation/saturation that these macro-organisms can tolerate is extremely varied but sufficient oxygen must be available. Whereas animals ingest their energy stores and building blocks, higher plants must create theirs by the process of photosynthesis:

$$\text{light}$$
Photosynthesis: $6CO_2 + 6H_2O \rightarrow C_6H_{12}O_6 + 6O_2$.
carbohydrate

Green plants, therefore, are also restricted to regions of sufficient light.

2.1.1.2 Micro-organisms

Being more primitive, these organisms are more susceptible to changes in the environment, but certain species have adapted to tolerate great extremes of pH, desiccation, or oxygen privation. The range of temperature and pH at which different species are active varies but this usually covers about 4 pH units for each species. The metabolism of micro-organisms is not particularly efficient and they excrete organic acids which in more efficient organisms would be broken down to provide further energy. Individual organisms are not usually visible to the eye: what is seen is a colony of individuals.

ALGAE. These are in fact extremely simple plants which live in very damp places or in water, both sea and fresh. They can appear as greenish or brownish slimes or suspensions in water; a sudden increase in their numbers gives a dense bright coloration known as a bloom. The large marine types are the seaweeds. Being aerobic and photosynthetic, they are restricted by lack of oxygen and light; in a clear-water ocean this may mean up to a depth of 100 metres, which is reduced to 3 metres in a turbid estuary.

FUNGI. These simple organisms are usually found as long filaments of cells (hyphae). The largest group of fungi involved in material decay comprises the mushroom fungi such as the dry rot fungus, where the mass of hyphae can be seen running through a material or substrate on which the fungus is feeding. Occasionally large, often colourful, fruiting bodies are formed for reproduction. Fungi secrete enzymes which break down the organic substrate into smaller chemical units which can then be absorbed into the hyphae. Whilst there is a wide variety of organic materials used by fungi in this way, particular species often require particular substrates. A second group of fungi, the moulds, are not so efficient in breaking down substrates; they require smaller chemical units as a food source. Unfortunately for artefacts, they produce pigment particles often black but sometimes brightly coloured. All fungi are aerobic, requiring oxygen for respiration; unicellular yeasts alone provide an occasional exception to this rule. For those involved in material decay to flourish, the moisture content of the substrate should be at least 20 per cent and the air damp (relative humidity (RH) > 65 per cent) and the balance between water and oxygen availability is crucial for their activity. In general, fungi can grow in more acidic conditions than other micro-organisms but they flourish at near neutral pH.

LICHENS. These organisms which grow in colonies visible to the naked eye are associations of fungi and algae. This symbiotic relationship means that lichens are able to withstand extremes of dry and wet. Like the individual organisms they are aerobic and secrete a significant quantity of organic acid.

BACTERIA. These constitute a group of single-celled entities only 1–2 micrometres in size; there may be as many as 3 billion per gram of deposit. Their presence may not be visible but they can often be smelt as they give off characteristic odours. When present in large numbers on artefacts, they may appear either as coloured stains, since many produce pigment particles, or even as encrustations or slimes. One group of organisms known as actinomycetes is made up of chains of bacteria-like cells which also produce odours and slimes. Bacteria secrete enzymes to break down a wide variety of organic substrates and, like fungi, are on the whole aerobic. However, there is a subgroup which, unlike almost all other organisms, does not require oxygen for respiration, that is, they are anaerobic. Instead, they oxidize their energy foods by the reduction of inorganic chemicals such as sulphates, nitrates, carbon dioxide, manganese(IV), and even iron(III). This type of respiration is inefficient and the bacteria excrete organic acids instead of carbon dioxide as a result, but it does mean they can colonize anoxic deposits. Only a limited number of these bacteria are involved in the breakdown of organic artefacts but some have an indirect effect on both organic and inorganic materials. Important amongst these in burial are the anaerobic sulphate-reducing bacteria (SRB) such as *Desulphovibrio* spp. They reduce sulphates to sulphides, their activity being readily detected by the smell of 'bad eggs' (hydrogen sulphide) and by a blackening of the deposit caused by the formation of metal sulphides. Whilst bacteria grow in damp deposits, as do fungi, they require a higher relative humidity of 70 per cent to flourish in the atmosphere. They are inhibited by acidity, preferring a pH range of 6 to 8; inhibition may also be caused by either the presence or the absence of light, depending on the species.

2.2 Archaeological environments

In archaeology, most artefacts are extracted from environments in which they have lain for between one hundred and several thousand years. Since all matter is subject to decay (the laws of thermodynamics state that order must decline into chaos), the discovery of an *undecayed* artefact after so long a period of time implies that for some reason expected deterioration has not taken place. This is because either some or all of the agents of decay are absent or because preserving conditions have prevailed.

In other words, it is not so much the speed of action of the agents of decay which is important; it is their presence, absence, or inactivation which must be considered. This consideration is more significant the longer the period of deposition. It is true that immediately upon abandonment or entombment the rate of decay may be fast, but for a particular material to survive this rate must be rapidly reduced to near zero. If this does not happen, the material will alter composition either into something which *is* in equilibrium with the environment, and thus survives, or into something which decomposes completely. Very often the surviving *altered* material retains the original shape of the artefact, a process known as pseudomorphic replacement; otherwise it simply becomes a shapeless mass.

Whilst a small percentage of archaeological objects have remained undisturbed by being sequestered in tombs, the vast majority become buried either deliberately, as in graves, or by incorporation in archaeological deposits, the formation of which are the subjects of other specialized texts.[1]

2.2.1 *Agents of decay in archaeological environments*[2]

2.2.1.1 Water

In archaeological deposits water is found within the voids between mineral particles and organic debris or adsorbed onto the active surfaces of clays and humus. Where water is unable to drain away because of an impervious sublayer or a high water table, and in marine or estuarine deposits, the voids are full of water. Where drainage is possible, the voids of a size greater than about 0.1 millimetres will empty, but water will be retained in micropores because of surface forces known as capillary action. Thus fine-grained materials such as clays and silts retain water. Water will also be held in a very fine layer around individual soil particles (bound or hygroscopic water) after gravity water has drained away.

Whilst water can itself inflict physical and chemical damage on materials, it is known as the 'universal catalyst' since it activates many other agents of decay; thus it facilitates most chemical reactions and enables organisms to flourish.

Where water moves rapidly through a deposit, for example a coarse sand or gravel, it can physically abrade soft materials such as pottery or bone. When artefacts are submerged, abrasion caused by water currents can be severe where these are strong and/or contain abrasive particles like sand. If temperatures fall below zero in a wet soil, where a porous artefact such as stone is wet, the approximately 9 per cent expansion of the water on freezing may cause considerable frost damage. However, it is successive freeze/thaw cycles which really cause noticeable deterioration.

Many organic materials contain water within the structure of their fibres and cells (section 6.1.1) to a level which is in equilibrium with the surrounding atmosphere. When they are subjected to wetter or drier environments, as may occur on burial, they gain or lose water, swelling or shrinking as a result. Water has a very important indirect role in the decay of salt-laden porous materials, as described in section 2.2.1.5.

Water must also be considered as a chemical, for it interferes with the composition of materials. Sometimes, archaeological materials such as glues dissolve in water, but more often leaching of the more soluble constituents of the material only results. Insoluble materials may be chemically broken down by water, that is hydrolysed, to produce other materials which themselves may be soluble or insoluble. Thus many organic polymers are hydrolysed into smaller and smaller molecules which finally dissolve. Water can also combine with chemicals, as when unslaked quicklime in plaster forms slaked-lime, causing blisters (section 4.3.2). Water is an essential ingredient in corrosion and other types of electrochemical reaction involving the movement of electrons. Here the 'universal catalyst' permits chemicals to form solutions of ions which, being charged particles, allow the transmission of electrons and thus the speeding up of chemical reactions.

2.2.1.2 Oxygen

In deposits, oxygen occurs mainly within the voids of the deposit as a gas and thus the amount present is inversely proportional to the amount of pore water present (section 2.2.1.1). In the pore atmosphere, oxygen can vary from 0 to 21 per cent, low levels being a result of displacement by carbon dioxide given out by the respiration of plant roots and soil micro-organisms. High levels exist where oxygen from the air can diffuse through the deposit. Such levels are expected where water content of the pores, is low, where porosity of the deposit is high, this occurring where soil particles are large, and where the depth of overburden is not very great. Oxygen also dissolves to a small extent in any water within the pores, as it does in the sea and in inland waters. Oxygen levels in water are extremely variable but are high in turbulent surface layers and at depths where photosynthetic plants release oxygen or where oxygen-rich currents flow. Oxygen is an oxidizing agent and thus takes part in many reactions; these 'redox' reactions are discussed below (section 2.2.1.4). Moreover, it is the presence or absence of oxygen which has the basic control of organism activity and thus a key indirect role in the decay of materials.

2.2.1.3 Acidity and alkalinity

Since the pH of a deposit describes the concentration of hydrogen ions (H^+) present, it follows that pH is important in environments containing water in which the ions are mobile. Acidity (low pH) can arise for a number of reasons, two of the most straightforward of which are described below:

(a) Where there are few bases (cations) present. Clay particles and humus are negatively charged entities; in the absence of bases (Ca^{2+}, Mg^{2+}, Na^+, K^+) they will be surrounded instead by H^+ causing the pH to fall. Bases are produced when rock particles dissolve, but in areas of high rainfall and low evaporation, these are usually leached out by rain-water, causing acidity to develop. This is particularly pronounced where aluminium ions are also produced since by hydrolysis they may cause a pH of as low as 3.

(b) Where the breakdown of organic litter is incomplete. If oxygen fails to penetrate organic matter during decay, initial aerobic respiration is succeeded by anaerobic decomposition which produces large quantities of organic acids. In areas where these acids cannot be washed away, the pH falls dramatically and organism activity ceases, causing the formation of, for example, the ooze of sea-beds or peat bogs. Alkaline deposits (pH 7–9) are common where evaporation exceeds precipitation, as in arid climates. Here any bases formed from dissolving rock particles remain in the deposit since the upward movement of water by evaporation is faster that the washing out by rain. Thus alkaline deposits of pH 7–9 are found in semi-arid environments.

However, in general the pH of deposits are rarely extreme. This is usually because small charged particles (colloids) of clay or of humus are present: these hold a reserve of base ions which can be released in acidic conditions, preventing the pH falling excessively. This capability varies with each deposit and is known as the base exchange capacity.

Sea-water has a constant pH of 8.2 since it is, as are some land deposits, stabilized by the carbonate buffer. This buffer depends on there being a supply both of bicarbonate ions, which react with any added H^+ to give undissociated carbonic acid, preventing the pH falling, and of weak carbonic acid which reacts with any added hydroxyl ions (OH^-), preventing the pH rising:

$$HCO_3^- + H^+ \rightleftarrows H_2CO_3$$
bicarbonate $\qquad$ carbonic acid
$$H_2CO_3 + OH^- \rightleftarrows HCO_3^- + H_2O.$$
carbonic acid $\qquad\qquad$ bicarbonate

In deposits, bicarbonate may be present from dissolved limestone, chalk, mortar, etc. and in the sea from calcareous skeletons of marine organisms. Where these supplies are adequate, the pH of a deposit may be buffered to between 7 and 8.5.

Whilst the main causes for the overall pH of a deposit have been described above, it is certain that localized variations of pH will occur within it. Such variations may be a result of natural phenomena such as is found around plant roots or where aerobic organisms are active; here respiration produces high quantities of carbon dioxide which reacts with moisture to give carbonic acid (H_2CO_3). Alternatively, the phenomenon may be produced artificially; for example, deposits of wood ash, mortar, or limestone all dissolve slowly, giving localized areas of alkalinity. The study of micro-environments is extremely complex: for further discussion of this, as well as for a fuller description of soil and marine pH, which of necessity has been much simplified in the foregoing, specialist texts must be sought.[2]

The stability of materials is greatly affected by pH: some materials are stable at acid, some at alkaline, and some at neutral pH. For example, either a high or a low pH can speed up the hydrolysis of organic materials, proteins being especially affected by high pH and cellulose by low pH. Calcium carbonate present in a calcite-gritted pot, for example, is more readily leached out at a low pH whilst iron oxide which might be the sole remains of a corroded ironwork in poorly aerated deposits may be precipitated and thus preserved when the pH rises to about 5.5; below this, the iron oxide is mobile and the artefact dissolves away.

2.2.1.4 Redox potential

Whether a deposit is reducing or oxidizing affects the mobility and stability of certain chemicals as well as the activity of bacteria (section 2.1.2). Where oxygen is plentiful, this controls the oxidizing and reducing (redox) reactions involved. Elements will be in their oxidized form, thus any iron present will be oxidized to the iron(III) form. Where oxygen concentration is low, the contribution of minor oxidizing and reducing agents becomes important. As the number of agents involved is usually great, and their interaction complex, the outcome of their activities *in toto* is determined. Thus, for a deposit, the overall figure, the redox potential E_H, is measured. This is given in millivolts and deposits may then be categorized as follows:

Oxidizing deposits	+700 to +400 millivolts
Moderately reducing deposits	+400 to +100
Reducing deposits	+100 to −100
Highly reducing deposits	−100 to −300

From this, the mobility, stability, and colour of chemicals subject to oxidation and reduction can be predicted. For example, where the redox potential is less than 200 millivolts, the stable form of iron, whether this is from corroded metal or simply contamination in the deposit, is black iron(II), whereas if the potential is greater than 200 millivolts, it is red-brown iron(III).

Where the deposit is moderately reducing, manganese is in the form of mobile manganese(II), whilst in oxidizing deposits it is deposited as black manganese(IV). These chemicals not only colour the deposit, they can stain artefacts, especially pale porous ceramics.

It should be noted that the redox potential of a solution is related to pH, since hydrogen ions can participate in oxidizing reactions by accepting electrons. Thus, in theory, if the pH of a deposit rises, the redox potential falls; in practice, since the soil system is so complex, this effect may not be obviously apparent.

2.2.1.5 Salts

Combinations of bases and acids form salts such as calcium carbonate or sodium chloride. When dissolved, they dissociate into separate ions, calcium (Ca^{2+}), bicarbonate (HCO_3^-), sodium (Na^+), and chloride (Cl^-). A common source of ions which form salts in soils is the weathering of rocks; thus Na^+, Ca^{2+}, Mg^{2+}, K^+, Cl^-, SO_4^{2-}, HCO_3^-, and silicates are derived. Further HCO_3^- is present from the dissolution and washing in of atmospheric carbon dioxide and from the decomposition of organic matter. This decomposition also produces organic acids which form more salts. High levels of Na^+ and Cl^- may be present from inundation by sea-water or salt spray. Man adds to these through his activities; the advent of phosphate (PO_4^{3-}) from decomposed dung or bone is familiar, but others are common. Animal/human waste matter also contains Cl^- and NO_3^-, wood-ash contains Ca^{2+}, K^+, Na^+, SO_4^{2-} and HCO_3^-, whilst decaying artefacts produce a wide range, for example, silicates from glass to Fe^{3+} and Cu^{2+} from metals. Modern fertilizers add yet more phosphate, and atmospheric pollution in the form of sulphur dioxide may increase the sulphate (SO_4^{2-}) level. Unlike soils and even inland waters, most sea-water has a constant composition of dissolved salts, with slight variations occurring in land-locked seas. Na^+ and Cl^- are the principal ions but levels of SO_4^{2-} are also high. Virtually every other type of anion or cation is present in the sea to a greater or lesser extent and again, unless they are involved in biological processes, their individual concentrations vary little, both geographically and seasonally.

When an ion pair (cation and anion) reach a critical concentration in water, they will combine to form a solid salt. This critical concentration, known as the solubility of the salt, is reached either by an influx of the ions or else by evaporation of the water. Solubility depends on both the particular anion and cation involved and is affected by temperature, with an increase usually leading to greater solubility. A notable exception is calcium sulphate which is more soluble in tepid water than in hot. All salts have some degree of solubility in water but sometimes this is so slight as to appear negligible and thus they are referred to as insoluble. The following table shows the relative solubilities of salts in relation to the anion involved.

Table 2.1 Relative solubility of salts in water

Highly soluble	Intermediate solubility	Low solubility
Nitrates (all)	$CaSO_4.2H_2O$	Silicates (most)
Chlorides (most)		Oxides (most)
Sulphates (most)		Sulphides (most)
Bicarbonates (most)		Phosphates (most)
Acetates (most)		Carbonates (most)

However, these solubilities are altered by other factors, for example pH. Thus carbonates, oxides, and sulphides are all more soluble at low pH, whilst silicates are more soluble at high pH. Carbonates in particular have increased solubility where carbon dioxide and thus carbonic acid concentrations are high. If the cation of the ion pair is considered, it can be seen that all sodium and potassium salts are highly soluble.

Obvious locations for high salt concentrations are salt mines, marine deposits, and coastal sites, but less obvious ones are cesspits and proximity to corroding metal artefacts. A widespread build-up of salts is common in arid areas where evaporation exceeds precipitation. Here salts are constantly dragged back up to the soil surface by evaporation faster than they are washed down. Since levels of moisture are so low, the salts may have crystallized or precipitated out of solution and may be visible in the soil.

When soluble salts crystallize out as water evaporates, there is a great increase in volume. If this occurs inside a porous artefact, the pressure can disrupt the material. Furthermore, insoluble salts may precipitate over the surface of objects, obscuring them completely. Since the damage is seen most frequently in ceramics and stone, details of it are given in section 4.1.2. But it should be remembered that any porous material such as ivory or corroded iron could be broken up by soluble salts; likewise insoluble salts may build up on any artefact in an affected deposit.

Particular salts are also responsible for the discoloration of materials. Iron and manganese were discussed in section 2.2.1.4, but other important examples are the green discoloration from copper(II) salts and black from many metallic sulphides, notably iron, lead, copper, and silver.

Whilst certain salts when dissolved in water react directly with artefacts, an important role in destruction is that, being charged, they can carry an electric current, that is they are electrolytes. Thus they facilitate electrochemical corrosion of metals (section 5.1.3.2), speeding up the decay of metals.

2.2.1.6 Complexes

Many cations can form complexes with organic compounds, the result of which is that the ions apparently become soluble in conditions in which they would otherwise remain fixed. Such agents when in specific conditions of correct pH and E_H could possibly leach calcium from glass or iron from ironwork, much as similar complexing sequestering agents are used to clean artefacts (section 3.3.2.1). However, the extent of their role in the deterioration of artefacts in the ground is still not clear.

2.2.1.7 Temperature

It is usual that the depth of overburden of a deposit will buffer against changes in temperature of the atmosphere, but surface layers will be affected. Recurrent freeze/thaw conditions will cause frost damage, elsewhere warm temperatures increase the rate of chemical reactions and biological growth. However, the temperature deeper in deposits is considerably below that of the air temperature and problems arise when artefacts are removed from these cooler environments.

2.2.1.8 Overburden

The weight of soil, buildings, etc. over a deposit may well deform plastic materials buried in it. Elastic ones such as leather may reshape on removal, but others such as soft pottery may be permanently deformed.

2.2.1.9 Organisms

The effect of organisms on materials, known as biodeterioration, is most obvious on organic materials since they are part of the natural cycle of decay. They may be broken down to provide a food source for rodents, insects, fungi, etc., to provide a habitat for the marine wood-boring mollusc *Toredo* spp., for example, or they may be chemically weakened by metabolic waste products such as the urine of rats or the organic acids from micro-organisms. The appearance of artefacts can be disfigured by pigment particles produced by fungi and bacteria or by black sulphides resulting from the activity of sulphate-reducing bacteria; surfaces may be obscured by the growth of plants or micro-organisms.

Even though inorganic materials cannot directly provide a food source for organisms, they can be affected in all the ways described above. Certain marine molluscs can bore through stone while metabolic waste products from animals in the vicinity or organisms living on the dirt and debris in the pores of an artefact will obviously have an effect; the staining of pale porous materials is a particular problem.

2.2.2 *Conditions in archaeological environments for preservation*

It is often extremely difficult to identify precisely why material within a particular deposit or micro-environment has been preserved, but some of the more usual and comprehensive causes are discussed below. In some cases they are simply the absence of the agents of destruction of section 2.2.1 but in others the situation is more complex.[3]

2.2.2.1 Absence of oxygen

By this one factor alone a wide spectrum of materials can be preserved partially or *in toto*; the activity of aerobic organisms which destroy organic materials ceases and the corrosion of metals is much reduced in the absence of oxygen. However, as water is almost always present anaerobic bacteria may still be able to flourish and these *slowly* break down organics and corrode iron. This residual activity can itself be reduced; for example, bacteria which break down cellulose are inhibited in pH < 3 or if toxins are present; and corrosive, sulphate-reducers cannot function if the pH is less than 5.5 or the redox potential is too low. The water will also allow dissolution and hydrolysis of materials to continue and so preservation is not absolute unless the condition is allied with desiccation.

In most cases absence of oxygen is caused by the abundance of water (see below) but it is possible to describe other situations in which oxygen has been excluded by other means; for example, a sealed tomb or coffin or a deeply stratified level which lies underneath compacted layers of wet clay or habitation debris. More exotically, oxygen may be displaced by an inert gas such as methane or carbon dioxide, such a condition having been suggested for the preservation of material deposited in limestone tombs.[4]

2.2.2.2   Absence of water

If absolute, the absence of water provides excellent conditions of preservation, except that it causes shrinkage and embrittlement of organic materials by water loss. Whilst in north-west Europe such conditions are rare, they are of course more likely in hotter regions (plate 2.1). However, total continuous desiccation is unusual and some degree of decay is virtually inevitable; insects and dry rot, for example, can function even in very dry conditions. Perhaps the best condition for preservation is that of extreme cold for here, since all water is turned to ice, it is

Plate 2.1   Dry conditions in the tomb of St Cuthbert, Durham Cathedral, have preserved these fragments of Byzantine silk. Here the fragile textile has been conserved by means of couching whereby long threads are applied and caught by short threads onto a backing fabric

inactivated without being lost and so both inorganic and organic materials are unaffected.

2.2.2.3 Presence of water

Paradoxically, the presence of water in abundance is one of the environments which in north-west Europe often produces the best preserved artefacts. Here waterlogging prevents oxygen reaching the materials and thus allows preservation by absence of oxygen (section 2.2.2.1). However, because of the saturation of the materials, hydrolysis is extensive and thus organic materials are much weakened. Fortunately, their form is maintained as water takes the place of the hydrolysed substances. In this way water preserves the shape and dimensions of an artefact by preventing its collapse, although of course dissolution inexorably continues (section 6.1.2).

Anoxic conditions are normally formed by waterlogging where either a deposit is below the natural water-table or where the drainage capacity of the deposit is greatly exceeded by water intake in the form of

Plate 2.2 Anoxic conditions caused by waterlogging have led to the preservation of the wooden lining, bucket, and ironwork of a medieval well from an urban site in York

precipitation or inflow from surrounding high ground. Urban sites in low-lying positions (plate 2.2) and marine silts (plate 3.13) often produce conditions of preservation overall, whilst on a smaller scale waterlogging can occur in individual ditches or storage pits. Because of the efficient mixing process, the sea itself is usually well oxygenated; it is only in deep waters and in the sea-bed itself that anaerobic conditions prevail.

In much drier circumstances, water can be said to aid preservation since its high surface tension may hold fragile material together, as in the case of crumbling pottery or flaking paint (sections 4.5.5 and 4.3.5).

2.2.2.4 Presence of salts and other residues

These may help to preserve organic materials since the growth of micro-organisms is inhibited by high salt concentrations; thus organic artefacts

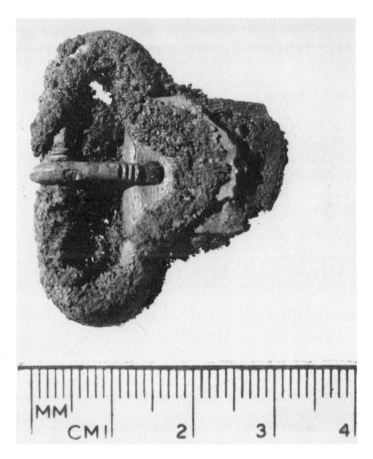

Plate 2.3 Conditions toxic to organisms caused by a corroding copper alloy buckle leading to the preservation of fabric and leather in association with it

are found in salt mines or salty arid soils. Copper ions are especially toxic to organisms and so protect organic materials (plate 2.3). Where these conditions prevail, it is likely that salts will further aid preservation by impregnating organic material and preventing its collapse. An extreme example of this phenomenon is the fossilization of bone in limestone caves. However, it should be noted that salts can cause considerable damage to porous material and metals (section 2.2.1.5).

Polyphenols are residues which too are toxic to micro-organisms. These may derive from the tannins of leather artefacts or more simply from decaying plants, especially bracken. These may contribute to the preservation of organic materials, but possibly also metals since poly-phenols may form protective coatings on them thus preventing corrosion. A similar phenomenon occurs when iron is in contact with phosphates under certain conditions, as elaborated in section 5.2.2.1.

2.2.2.5 Absence of movement/fluctuations

In general, archaeological material is preserved since it is hidden away from gross disturbance. More precisely, in the period after deposition, preservation is enhanced if the artefact is quickly covered and protected from abrasion by wind- or water-borne particles. In fact if water is absent from, or stagnant in, a deposit, this sort of physical damage to soft material is avoided. The deeper a deposit, the less temperature and humidity fluctuations will occur and the cooler the mean temperature will be. In shallower deposits this buffering may occur also where the overburden is compact. As will be seen from the deterioration described in section 2.2.1 this sequestration of material from the variability of the normal atmospheric environment enhances its chances of preservation.

2.2.2.6 Pseudomorphic replacement, chemical traces, and impressions

As explained earlier, part or all of an artefact may be preserved not as the original material but as a pseudomorphic replacement which is stable in the deposit. Thus iron in neutral/alkaline aerated conditions may be replaced by iron oxides (plate 2.4), or wood in wet alkaline deposits may be virtually fossilized by calcium carbonate. An extreme example of replacement is that of soil silhouettes in which there is absolutely no texture of the original artefact remaining but the soil found in its place is discoloured, revealing a trace of the position and in some cases even the shape of the original. A most useful example of this is bone where iron and manganese remain fixed to the phosphatic mineral portion of the decaying bone. Whilst the stain sometimes formed by decaying wooden posts is well known, shadows of other materials such as leather may also occur. Non-visible traces of decayed materials too have been found; phosphate from decayed bones held in a soil by calcium, iron, or aluminium can be identified chemically. Even though the whole area of

Plate 2.4 Knife handle, once wood, now preserved as a pseudomorph composed of iron corrosion products

study concerning the soil around decayed artefacts and the invisible remains of man's activities was identified long ago,[5] there has been little development in available techniques. Recently, steps have been taken in this field and it is hoped that these will enable evidence which has hitherto been unobserved to be revealed.[6]

If an artefact has ceased to exist altogether, occasionally it is recorded by an impression. Thus the weave of a long-vanished textile can be found on soft, damp clay of a deposit or an artefact.

2.3 Immediate deterioration caused by excavation

If materials or their replacements have survived burial or submersion, it is usually only because they have come into equilibrium with their environment. When they are excavated, suddenly this equilibrium is profoundly disturbed as the artefact is introduced into the atmospheric environment. Deterioration will begin again and may be obvious after as little time as a few seconds but may not become apparent for a year or more. If, within a short space of time, a second equilibrium is not reached, deterioration to destruction will follow. Conservation seeks to ensure that this second equilibrium is reached as soon as possible. Excavation not only disrupts the conditions for preservation described above, it may well reactivate many of the agents of deterioration previously discussed; furthermore, the post-excavation environment contains new hazards not present in the archaeological environment. The immediate and most common causes of decay of the post-excavation environment are discussed in this section.

2.3.1 Water content

For many materials the most damaging feature of excavation is the change in the water content of their environment. Those exposed from damp or wet deposits suffer from loss of water and those from extremely dry conditions from the presence of water. More often than not, artefacts lose water to the atmosphere on excavation since air is drier than most deposits; this is compounded by drying wind and sunshine. Only rarely is the post-excavation atmosphere wetter than the burial environment, as for example when a desiccated coffin is opened or material is brought from an arid climate into a temperate one; here the artefact may take up moisture. Whilst the archaeological environment has a fairly stable water content and temperature, after excavation these are likely to fluctuate regularly on a daily and an annual basis and irregularly as the situation alters. Loss of water on excavation can have several deleterious effects. Water within a fragile damp artefact and surrounding soil may be holding

0   M/M   10

Plate 2.5 Crumbling of decayed medieval glass caused by drying out on excavation

it together by surface tension, or within a decayed organic waterlogged artefact water may be preventing its collapse (section 2.2.2.3). Water may be part of the structure of less decayed organics. In all these cases, loss of water leads to falling apart, collapse, shrinking, and warping (plate 2.5). If salt-laden porous materials, especially marine artefacts, are dried out, salts crystallize (section 4.1.2), disrupting the fabric. Surface damage on drying often results when soils, especially clays, are allowed to dry, since they shrink, pulling off paint, delicate surfacings, etc. Furthermore, if damp insoluble salt encrustations dry out, they are usually harder and become much more difficult to remove.

Loss of water on excavation results in lower levels of dissolution and chemical reaction. However, since some reactions, noticeably corrosion of metals, require very little water, the objects must be very dry before the beneficial effect of loss of water is felt.

2.3.2 Oxygen

The level of oxygen in the atmosphere is 21 per cent by volume and thus is considerably higher than that of most deposits. This oxygen penetrates porous material especially when it dries out; it will also dissolve in the water in tanks where waterlogged materials are stored.

This high level of oxygen means that oxidation reactions such as corrosion (plate 2.6) and the fading of dyes can take place and aerobic organisms flourish. All these activities are enhanced by water and can lead to rapid deterioration during drying out or even during wet storage.

2.3.3 Light

The fading of inks or dyes can be the most noticeable type of deterioration seen on excavation, for it can occur in a matter of minutes if not seconds when decayed pigments are exposed to light after total darkness for extremely long periods of time.

2.3.4 Organisms

Within a week of excavation micro-organisms may be visible, indicating that they have been growing throughout this period. Spores in the deposit or from the atmosphere may develop fast in warm damp environments. Over short periods of time, they may have little effect on the strength of materials, but they can cause fouling both of artefacts and packaging; moulds, slimes, or blooms (section 2.1.1.2) may obscure artefacts, even staining them and making labels illegible.

One of the most destructive organisms to excavated material is *Homo sapiens*. The mishandling of material from the moment of its exposure

Plate 2.6 Copper alloy statuette from Egypt showing considerable post-excavation corrosion 'bronze disease' which appears here as pale crystals splitting open the corrosion crust

leads to the loss of much information as well as unnecessary treatment later. One aspect of this mishandling is the failure to retrieve all associated artefactual evidence; thus artefacts are overcleaned *in situ* or later and all-important 'dirt' containing perhaps decayed organic matter or totally corroded metal is lost. Perhaps the greatest problem is the failure to appreciate and to deal with the fact that excavated materials are much weaker than they appear. An object may appear whole but in fact be greatly fragmented, just lying where it broke, or it may be cradled by the deposit and simply disintegrate when lifted. The rubbing of a corroded coin with a thumb and the scrubbing of a soft pot are also manifestations of this problem. Finally, insufficient awareness of the inevitable decay of material after excavation, and how to deal with it, will lead to the loss of evidence which, in almost every case, is avoidable when the correct conservation steps are taken.

2.4 Agents of long-term deterioration to excavated material[7]

Whilst there are many factors in the environment which affect unconserved materials, it should not be assumed that conservation inevitably renders materials immune to the effects of these. Conservation attempts to buffer materials against de+eriorating agents but sometimes even this buffering is not possible. Moreover, conservation treatments may resort to the introduction of new materials into an artefact which themselves are subject to decay. Thus this section is applicable to both unconserved and conserved artefacts as well as to associated labelling and packaging, shelving, display fabrics, etc., and to the written excavation archive. However, only an outline of the latter specialism is given here, and other texts should be consulted.[8]

2.4.1 Water

Water is present in the atmosphere, unlike the normal buried environment, as a vapour dispersed in air rather than as a liquid. In order to determine if air is dry enough or damp enough to affect excavated materials, it is no use measuring the absolute quantity of water vapour present in the atmosphere. This is because at raised temperatures air can take up more water vapour than at cool temperatures; an analogy is that an expanded sponge can hold more water than a compressed one. Thus, if a volume of air and an artefact are sealed inside a plastic bag and that bag is then placed in a hot room, there will be increased capacity of the entrapped air to take up moisture which it will do from the enclosed artefact. If the bag is then put into a refrigerator this capacity is suddenly much reduced and water may be forced out of the vapour phase to appear as drops of condensation. Measurement of dampness in the air which takes note of the ambient temperature will therefore indicate whether water is likely to be removed from or deposited on materials. This measurement is achieved by comparing the actual quantity of water in the air at the temperature in question as the maximum quantity of water the air could hold at that temperature before condensation appears. The first figure in this comparison is the absolute humidity (AH) and the second is the saturation humidity (SH). The comparison between the two is expressed as a percentage and is called the relative humidity (RH):

$$RH\ (\%) = \frac{AH}{SH} \times 100.$$

This means that an RH of 100 per cent indicates that the air is saturated whilst an RH of 0 per cent indicates a complete absence of water vapour. If an RH is 50 per cent, air is holding only half as much vapour as it could do.

If a volume of air and water is enclosed, the AH remains constant but the RH may vary. If the temperature rises the RH *falls*, and if it falls the RH *rises*. Thus the air inside a polyethylene bag, display case, or museum store will become drier as the temperature rises and wetter as it falls. As a rule of thumb, desiccated air has an RH of less than 40 per cent, 'dry' air an RH of 40–65 per cent, and 'damp' air an RH of 65–80 per cent. For more detailed discussion of this topic the reader is referred to other texts.[9]

Many excavated materials are only stable in extremes of RH, whether desiccated or saturated or in very constant conditions. Treatment of such materials attempts to make them stable in RH conditions which are normally found in most storage and display areas. It should be remembered that associated storage/archival material is also affected by environmental RH. Since there is such a range of materials to consider, only a few generalizations can be made here; details are given in the appropriate chapters. Untreated materials in store/display will continue to be affected by RH in the same way as occurs immediately after excavation (section 2.3.1); here only additional problems are considered.

Physical problems caused by unsuitable or fluctuating RH are mainly confined to organic artefacts, even if treated (section 6.1.3.2), and to shelving made of wood, cardboard boxes, paper bags, written archives, various types of film, etc. If the RH is too low these materials lose water, becoming brittle or warped; if the RH fluctuates, frail artefacts may disintegrate or wooden shelving become loose at the joints. If it is too high, gelatin on film/photographs softens, sticking them together if the RH falls again.

Where the RH is particularly high, even active conservation treatments may not be able to prevent chemical reactions occurring, a common source of water for such reactions being condensation (section 2.4.3). The poor quality paper of much of the written archive and of paper-bag containers, is particularly prone to hydrolysis and oxidation at a high RH, resulting in discoloration and weakening.

2.4.2 Oxygen

See section 2.3.2.

2.4.3 Temperature

The temperature of the post-excavation environment is always higher than that of the archaeological environment. It is raised still further by heating systems, sunshine, lights, etc., and is more subject to variation than the temperature of deposits. Thus it can fluctuate irregularly or daily and/or annually, depending on the situation. Also it can fall extremely low, perhaps much lower than that of the original deposit in which an object lay.

Long-term effects of excessively high temperatures are felt by materials such as lead or ancient waxes which soften on heating and become distorted and, in the latter case, tacky. These effects too are felt by certain synthetic adhesives/consolidants (section 3.4.2.2) (plate 2.7) or synthetic finishes on photographs. Tracing films embrittle over time as incorporated materials deteriorate. At raised temperatures chemical reactions are faster and organism activity greater, provided both have sufficient moisture.

Fluctuating temperatures are particularly damaging. One well-known

Plate 2.7 Slumping on an adhesive caused by warm conditons leading to a displacement of part of the restored seventh century wooden coffin of St Cuthbert

cause of decay of wet stone is that of freeze/thaw where the recurring expansion of water as it freezes to ice breaks up wet porous materials. Another problem arises because many materials expand when heated. This expansion is measured by the coefficient of expansion, which is high in materials such as metals which respond considerably to a rise in temperature. Disruption occurs where there are two adjacent materials which have very different coefficients of expansion: one remains static whilst the other expands, resulting in disruption of the weaker. This destruction is felt most where the temperature fluctuates and the process recurs innumerable times.

Finally, since moisture in the air and temperature are intimately linked, the formation of condensation is considered here. If air with a high RH near saturation point comes into contact with a cold material, heat is lost from the air, causing the RH to rise until the air can hold no more water and condensation appears. Metals are foremost in condensation formation since they are good conductors of heat and so cool the air locally. Water droplets can form not only on metal artefacts but also on metal shelving and even glass display cases if the ambient temperature of damp air falls too low. Even if the temperature does not fall low enough for condensation to form, it must be remembered that a drop in temperature causes the RH to rise.

2.4.4 Light

Both visible and ultraviolet light are forms of energy. Since the amount of energy is inversely proportional to the wavelength of the light, ultraviolet light and the blue end of the visible spectrum, being of short wavelength, have the most energy. Visible light is measured in lux (lumens per square metre) using a light or lux meter. Ultraviolet (UV) light is then determined as its proportion in a particular light source, by using a UV monitor. In Britain, sunlight at 12 noon on a clear summer day can exceed 60,000 lux, with a high proportion of UV; on a dull day, even though the light level drops, the UV level remains high since its proportion in an overcast sky rises. With artificial lights the level of light is much lower, being perhaps in the region of 95 lux at a distance of 1 metre from a single 100 watt bulb. Whilst very little UV light is emitted by tungsten lamps, the proportion in most fluorescent lamps remains high. For further information the reader is directed to Thomson.

Since both visible and ultraviolet light are forms of energy they can take part in chemical reactions; these are often enhanced by the presence of moisture. Light energy is absorbed more readily by certain colours and materials; the process is most efficient in yellow dyes/pigments/discolorations which absorb dangerous blue light and in dyes/inks which contain iron and other impurities. The absorbed energy can then oxidize dyes/pigments, altering their colour and normally causing them to fade. Organic polymers are particularly sensitive to oxidation by light which causes these complex reactions. Thus textiles and leather embrittle, cheap papers and wood yellow and embrittle, as do many synthetics used as adhesives and lacquers.

2.4.5 Particulate pollution

A major source of such pollution is the burning of fossil fuels which produces minute fragments of carbon often combined with acids, tars, and metals. Other sources are wind-blown soil particles and simple generalized dust. Pieces up to 15 micrometres in size can remain suspended in air whilst larger pieces are deposited.

Soiling of artefacts is the obvious hazard. The dirt becomes fixed to them by interaction of small electric charges, as with clays, etc., by adhesion due to tarry substances or to tacky lacquers or consolidants, or by rubbing in during handling. Porous pale materials will suffer the most (plate 2.8). Sharp particles penetrating fragile flexible materials such as textiles will cause internal abrasion of the fibres as the material is flexed.

Salt from sea-spray will increase corrosion (section 5.1.3.2) but a more general effect is the 'poultice' role of surface dirt. A layer of dirt absorbs and retains moisture, allowing corrosion, acidic reactions, and even organism growth.

2.4.6 Gaseous pollution

Whilst carbonic acid in rain-water from dissolved carbon dioxide is normal, high levels of sulphuric acid from the oxidation of sulphur dioxide in polluted air are common in the rain-water of cities, reducing its pH to 4. The concentration of sulphur dioxide inside a building is usually half that of outdoors, but in sunlight and in the presence of moisture and catalysts such as iron appreciable quantities of sulphuric acid may be found. Organic acids are given off as vapours from the timber of buildings, show cases, cupboards, etc., especially when made of oak or unseasoned wood, but some poor-quality polyvinyl acetate emulsions (section 3.4.2.2) are also responsible. Volatile sulphides emanate from vulcanized rubber of floors etc., as well as from composite boards and certain textiles.

All these gaseous components enhance the corrosion of all or some specific metals; for example, the blackening of silver by sulphide pollution (plate 2.9). Sulphuric acid is especially damaging to frail textiles whilst papers are attacked not only by acidic pollution but also by acids left within them from manufacturing processes; cheap papers and cardboards

Plate 2.8 Airborne dust particles causing soiling of stored artefacts: a recently removed label on a stone stele reveals the extent of discoloration

are particularly prone to this decay. It would appear too that shell may be attacked by organic acids (section 6.4.5).

2.4.7 Organisms

Biological activity in the atmosphere, unlike in buried deposits, is not limited by lack of oxygen or normally by low temperatures. Here the

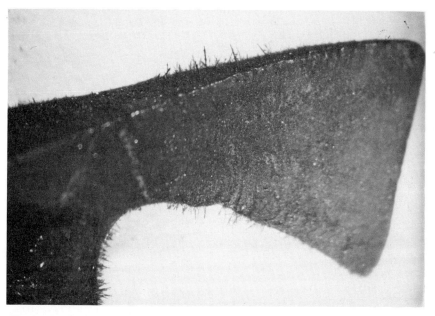

Plate 2.9 General blackening and large sulphide crystals formed on a miniature silver axe whilst on display

chief factor in determining the growth or otherwise of a particular organism, apart from a source of food, is that of humidity. The information presented below builds upon the details discussed in section 2.1.1.

2.4.7.1 Organisms in wet or damp storage

In the case of organic artefacts or indeed archival material, the food source may be obvious, but organism growth may be found on other materials in similar conditions where the food is supplied by adhering soil, accumulation of dust, wrapping materials, etc. In waterlogged conditions or where the RH is greater than 80 per cent, bacteria flourish, producing stains and slimes; they weaken organic materials either by directly attacking them or by producing organic acids which do so. Fungi demanding a slightly lower level of water do similar damage to artefacts but the mould fungi can only attack non-robust organics such as associated debris, applied lubricating dressings, and paper (plate 2.10). Most bacteria and fungi are inhibited by light but some require it.

The light of the post-excavation environment favours the growth of organisms which exhibit photosynthesis. The rudimentary blue-green algae grow in damp conditions, producing slimes over artefacts and packaging. The higher plants follow in drier lighter conditions, breaking up materials by root growth and acidic secretions.

Table 2.2 Agents of decay of particular environments and their effects on materials

	Temperate climates (buried)		Waterlogged urban	Mediterranean climates (buried)			Post-excavation atmosphere
	Non-calcareous gravel	Calcareous		Sea (not sediment)	Semi-arid	Tomb	
Agents of decay							
H₂O	rapid draining	draining	stagnant	moving	wet/dry	very low	drier and fluctuating
O₂	present	present	absent	present	present	√ or ×	very high
pH	acidic	alkaline	neutral	just alkaline	alkaline	—	acidic pollution
E_H	oxidizing	oxidizing	reducing	oxidizing	oxidizing	—	oxidizing
Salts	low	carbonates	± phosphates	high	high	—	sweat, sea spray, etc.
Temperature	fluctuating	fluctuating	stable	fairly stable	extreme high/low	stable	higher and fluctuating
Organisms	aerobes – many bacteria inhibited	aerobes – many but fungi inhibited	anaerobic bacteria only	aerobes – many	aerobes – some	insects only	aerobes – many including humans
Effect on materials							
Siliceous							
Porous ceramics	abraded much softened	good but concreted with insoluble salts	stained or blackened and softened	good but abraded and concreted with insoluble salts	weakened by soluble salts and encrusted with insoluble salts	very good	encrustations harden; sol. salt damage; surface exfoliation or crumbling soiling and breakage

	Temperate climates (buried)			Mediterranean climates (buried)			Post-excavation atmosphere
	Non-calcareous gravel	Calcareous	Waterlogged urban	Sea (not sediment)	Semi-arid	Tomb	
Mortars	very weak	good	as ceramics	weak	as ceramics	very good	as for ceramics
Poorly durable glass	reasonable	poor or absent	blackened; reasonable to poor	reasonable to poor	reasonable to poor and encrusted	very good	as for ceramics
Metals							
Iron	hollow lumps of rust or absent	bulky lumps of corrosion product overlying metal	good ± blue/black; phosphate layer	large often hollow concretions	as for gravel	very good	breaking up of corrosion crust in one year
Copper	distorted and totally corroded	patinated	bright but etched; ± black sulphide	as for calcareous	warty crust ± some metal	very good	bronze disease within 1 hour–several years
Lead	etched or absent	good under white crust	good under black sulphide layer	as for calcareous	as for calcareous	very good	disintegration by organic acid pollution
Organic							
Wood and leather	absent except where near copper etc.; pseudomorphs in iron corrosion products	as for gravel	preserved but in weakened condition; blackened	as for gravel	as for gravel	good except for desiccation and insect attack	waterlogged materials shrink drastically; attack by light and organisms
Bone	abraded and much softened	brittle, powdery, and concreted	good but blackened	abraded, calcified, and concreted with insoluble salts	as for calcareous	good except for desiccation	as for siliceous materials

Plate 2.10 Growth of mould on paper leading to loss of this label

2.4.7.2 Normal or dry conditions

Of the micro-organisms only a few fungi flourish in these drier conditions and so activity is limited to insects, rodents, and man. Insects are discussed in detail in chapter 6 in relation to organic artefacts but they have some effect on packaging and the written archive. Examples are silver-fish devouring thin bleached papers, booklice and cockroaches feeding on glues, and wood-boring insects incidentally making passages through cardboard or paper when seeking out a wooden substrate. The infection of clean material with fungal spores or insect eggs is increased in dusty (food and moisture-retaining) warm conditions.

2.4.8 *Mishandling*

This is a major cause of deterioration of material after excavation (section 2.3.4). Retreatment can be avoided if objects are handled, displayed, and stored with care and knowledge; some simple steps will save much time and money.

2.5 Summary

A summary of the agents of decay in particular environments and their effects on materials is given in table 2.2. It is obviously not comprehensive but is helpful as a guide to this complex subject.

Chapter Three

General techniques of conservation[1]

Whilst for ease of understanding, the deterioration and treatment of artefacts has been divided up in this book into particular materials, there are both general and more specific approaches and techniques of conservation which apply to a great number of materials. Hence they are gathered together in this chapter under headings which refer to the main aims of conservation.

3.1 Retrieval of artefacts and associated information from a deposit

3.1.1 Lifting artefacts[2]

If damage is done to artefacts or they are treated injudiciously at the early stage of removal from their archaeological context, much information is lost and much time wasted in the laboratory.

In the first instance it is important to realize that considerable information may lie in the deposit layer attached to an artefact. This could contain a metallic surfacing (section 5.5.3), food debris (section 4.5.3), or fibres for example. It may also be holding a fragmented object together, and it may be difficult in the field to judge where the soil ends and the object begins. Thus, when artefacts are retrieved, a layer of deposit is allowed to remain adhering to them. For this reason, damage is done if objects *in situ* are overcleaned for photography. Techniques to assist in retrieving materials from the ground can be simple or complex, but before the latter are used it should be ascertained that they are really needed and that the artefact must be retrieved. The most satisfactory techniques of lifting are those which are quick, cheap, protect the artefact from damage without prejudicing future conservation treatments, and which interfere minimally with the surrounding archaeological features and excavation activity. However, a small degree of care at this stage can save evidence and money.

Techniques to assist lifting are designed for a variety of purposes: they may simply add support to a single object to prevent it fracturing; they may hold a mass of indefinable material together so that it can be excavated in the laboratory; or they may hold heavy large complex artefacts together to avoid lengthy reconstruction at a later date. Before lifting large complex items, whether these are kilns or waterlogged timber-lined wells, a thorough investigation must be carried out concerning not only feasibility but also whether removal of the artefact will be useful. Criteria involved will include not only finance and facilities but also whether or not the item can ever be displayed, where it can be displayed or stored, and what archaeological evidence will be retrieved by lifting it which could not be gained from on-site observation. It may be found that dismantling for lifting is preferable or that only sections, such as the jointing of a well-lining, need be retrieved, whilst the rest can be recorded and even moulded (section 3.1.2).

There are three approaches in lifting techniques. In the first a rigid framework is put around the object to prevent it collapsing; in the second a strengthening material or a sheeting to hold fragments together is fixed directly to the artefact; and in the third a synthetic consolidant (section 3.4.2.2) is added to impregnate the object itself before it is lifted. The first method interferes least with the object and so is to be preferred. The second is only used where it is certain that the adhesive is doing no damage to the material and can be removed later, whilst the third is only used when advised in a particular case or for less important items since it interferes greatly with the object. Again it is important to know which approach is being used, for many of the materials used to form a rigid framework in the first method will cause untold damage if they come into contact with the artefact itself.

Once it has been ascertained that some assistance is required to remove an artefact, it is essential that *everything* necessary for the lift is assembled before work begins; many disasters occur for want of a simple item in the middle of the lift. The artefact is recorded as well as possible before lifting; this is a photographic record, but where complex artefacts are involved, planning too is essential.

Where unknown material is lifted and required for identification later, for example the contents of a whole vessel, a sample of the neighbouring deposit is taken for comparison.

It should be remembered that artificially lifted artefacts have to be stored like all other artefacts excavated in controlled conditions (section 3.4.1). Since the materials used in the lift must withstand such storage, information regarding their suitability will also be found in section 3.4.1.

3.1.1.1 Lifting from the ground

MINIMUM SUPPORT. The simplest method of lifting involves the *ready* provision of a horizontal support underneath an artefact. The support in the form of a rigid sheet is either slid into the deposit beneath the object or the object is placed on the sheet just as soon as it is raised from the ground. Thin metal sheets and wooden or perspex boards with chamfered edges are useful for undercutting. Receiving boards are padded with plastic foam or folded acid-free tissue paper before objects are laid upon them. The objects are then tied onto the boards with bandages or netting. For damp/wet objects, only waterproof materials (section 3.4.1.1) can be used for supports, padding, and bandaging.

Objects which can be excavated so that they stand proud of the surrounding deposit, whole vessels for example, can be strengthened as they are exposed by bandaging with crêpe bandages. These must be tied tight enough to prevent any movement but care is taken with soft material such as damp pottery to prevent the imprint of the bandage/net. Here a barrier of a layer of thin material such as polyethylene paper is placed between the object and the support. In the case of whole vessels, soil is not removed from inside, for when balanced against the external support it acts as a support too. After bandaging, the object is carefully lifted and placed inside a well-padded box; alternatively, if further support is needed, a rigid framework can be constructed around the bandages before the object is lifted.

RIGID FRAMEWORKS. These can be used with caution by the non-specialist for objects whose total measurement (length + width + height) does not exceed 500 millimetres. The frameworks are usually formed *in situ* around individual objects by the setting of a variety of chemicals. On no account must the chemicals come into actual contact with the objects for they usually cannot be removed at a later date. A 'release' layer between the chemical and artefact is essential; in simple cases this may be soil but usually a more reliable barrier is needed. Depending on how frail the object is, there are two approaches to forming rigid frameworks. These may be formed either around a block of soil containing very frail objects or directly around more robust objects.

The most simple rigid framework which can be used is an existing one in the form of a tin or plastic box or can. The exposed object is backfilled with about 3 centimetres of soil and then the container is inverted over it and pushed fully into the deposit, so enclosing the object. The container, deposit, and object can then be removed and inverted as described below. This method can of course only be used where the deposit is neither too hard nor too stony. An interesting use of this method on a micro-scale is the removal of samples of apparent organic artefact

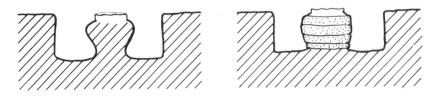

1 Object isolated on platform

2 Platform strengthened with bandages dipped in plaster of Paris

Figure 3.1 Lifting on a reinforced platform

material from a site. Here small cores are removed by using syringes with the ends cut off. Later in the laboratory the samples are consolidated and examined microscopically.[3]

The first method of forming a rigid framework *in situ* is used for lifting small blocks of soil containing frail objects. The object is first isolated in a block of soil, leaving as much as possible of it buried in the soil platform. The edges of the platform are then strengthened and a flat support slid in below the platform to undercut the object. The strengthening is carried out most cheaply by using bandages dipped into plaster of Paris and wrapped around the soil of the platform, taking care not to contaminate the object (figure 3.1).

Alternatively, paraffin wax may be melted and dribbled down the sides of the platform until a rigid framework has been made. Great care must be exercised in heating the wax since it is flammable and can cause bad burns. Synthetic emulsions such as polyvinyl acetate emulsion could be used instead, but they are not very robust. Suggestions have been made that the entire platform could be strengthened by consolidating the soil with synthetic resins. Here great care has to be exercised to avoid contaminating the artefacts.

A second, more elaborate, method of forming a rigid framework *in situ* can be used to lift a block of soil containing either an unidentifiable feature (for later excavation in the laboratory) or a frail or fragmentary object. Here the 'object' is undercut as far as possible using crumpled tissue or bandages to hold the block together temporarily (figure 3.2). This means that now a framework can be formed almost spherically around the block. Soil is left in place where its removal will disturb the object. Bandages soaked in plaster of Paris can be used[4] here too, but *only* after a release layer of wet acid-free tissue has been stippled over the entire object and the edges of the pedestal (figure 3.2). Undercuts or holes in the object are filled with wet tissue to avoid plaster becoming trapped in them. Next the bandages or tissue dipped in plaster are

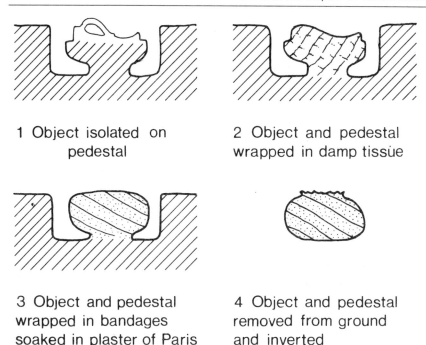

1 Object isolated on pedestal

2 Object and pedestal wrapped in damp tissue

3 Object and pedestal wrapped in bandages soaked in plaster of Paris

4 Object and pedestal removed from ground and inverted

Figure 3.2 Lifting with a cocoon

wrapped around the object and pedestal as completely as possible; only one or two layers are used, as more may make removal in the laboratory difficult. Once the plaster has set hard, a board is slid under the cocoon which if necessary can be quickly inverted to avoid soil being lost through the open end of the pedestal.

Setting materials other than plaster of Paris have been used in a similar manner; especially where lengthy damp storage follows, plaster of Paris is not sufficiently durable and casting tapes, prepacked bandages soaked in a resin which hardens when exposed to air, have been used in its stead.[5] A third choice is polyurethane foam; its advantages are that it is very light in weight, easy to remove in the laboratory, and can either be used on its own or to reinforce other setting materials. However, its disadvantages are its expense and its toxicity (see below). The foam is a two-part liquid which when mixed foams up *in situ* and hardens to make a cocoon. If it is used as the sole support, then any frail surfaces must be protected by padding with soil or polythene bags filled with it. The release layer for foam is made from kitchen clingfilm or aluminium foil. An external former for the foam support is constructed. A collar of corrugated cardboard is placed around the pedestal, leaving a 20 millimetre space and standing 20 millimetres or more proud of the upper surface of the

Plate 3.1 Lifting using a cocoon of polyurethane foam. (a) A very frail corroded copper alloy object is revealed on excavation. (b) The object is isolated in a platform of soil on a pedestal. A release layer of 'clingfilm' and a collar of cardboard are set in place. (c) Using strict safety precautions the polyurethane foam is made *in situ* to fill the cardboard collar

object (plate 3.1b). Earth is thrown around the outside of the collar to ensure no gaps between it and the ground are present. When everything is ready, the liquid is mixed according to its instructions, but it must be stressed that fumes given off at this stage are toxic;[6] the mixing must take place in the open air and goggles and a fume mask must be worn. One of the components of the mix can also cause dermatitis and thus rubber gloves *must* be worn during mixing and pouring. The liquid is poured into the base of the former as it begins to foam (plate 3.1c). It is allowed to harden (approximately five minutes) and the process repeated until the former is filled. In cold weather, foaming is reduced. Once complete and hard, the cocoon is treated as was the plaster of Paris one (figure 3.3).

As mentioned before, polyurethane foam can also be used to strengthen other support materials, for example, plaster of Paris bandages. The foam support can be built in two halves by placing a cardboard divider across the former which, when constructed on a large scale, is made from wood rather than corrugated cardboard. A good separating layer of aluminium foil over the bandages and the former means that this secondary foam support can be readily removed at a later

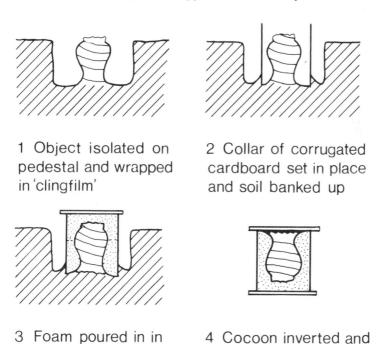

1 Object isolated on pedestal and wrapped in 'clingfilm'

2 Collar of corrugated cardboard set in place and soil banked up

3 Foam poured in in stages and stopped with plywood lid

4 Cocoon inverted and exposed soil enclosed with lid

Figure 3.3 Lifting by the formation of a polyurethane foam cocoon

Plate 3.2 Lifting using a directly adhering support. (a) Cotton sheeting is stippled onto the surface of a mosaic with polyvinyl acetate emulsion. (b) After the adhesive has set the reinforced mosaic tesserae are lifted from their bed of mortar onto a ready-made frame

date. Because polyurethane foam is light, it can be used to lift large objects such as kilns. However, these large lifts which engender their own problems are only attempted after considerable planning and with great expertise.[7]

Another approach to the use of rigid frameworks is where an object can be excavated so that it stands proud of the soil but is not robust enough to lift;[8] examples here could be a weakened long-bone or a pot on its side. Here the upper half of the object is exposed, all soil being removed. After undercuts have been padded a release layer is put in place before plaster of Paris bandages or casting tape is applied. Then half the object is undercut, reinforced as described, and the upper and lower halves of the framework are tied together with bandages. The process is then repeated on the other horizontal half of the object.

DIRECTLY ADHERING SUPPORTS. Unlike the types of support described above, these are stuck directly onto the object. This means that great care must be taken that they are only used for artefacts from which they can be removed and to which they do no damage. Also the choice of adhesive is problematic and thus this method is only used by specialists. An example of a direct support is in the lifting of a mosaic where the robust surface of the tesserae can be stuck directly to a fabric; polyvinyl acetate emulsion and cotton sheeting are used (section 4.3.6.2) (plate 3.2). If this same technique were used on a bone comb, for example, disastrous disruption caused by shrinkage of the support might result (plate 3.3).

CONSOLIDATION. In this method a synthetic consolidant (section 3.4.2.2) is dripped onto the artefact, hardening it so that it can be lifted out of the ground. There are dangers here of using an unsuitable consolidant, of failing to get penetration which can result in the surface falling off and the core collapsing (plate 3.4); it may also prejudice future conservation treatments and cause unwanted soil to adhere to the object. This method should only be used under specialist advice; it could be recommended for lifting a fragmented unworked bone, for example, to ensure all pieces are retrieved for later reconstruction and identification (section 6.4.1).

Some years ago, Swedish workers[9] overcame many of the drawbacks of on-site consolidation by using a system which does not introduce alien material into an artefact. Instead, the water already existing in the surrounding soil and artefact was simply frozen *in situ* with dry ice, and the hardened material lifted and immediately stored in freezing conditions until it could be treated in a laboratory. They in fact lifted whole spreads of artefacts, graves in particular, in this way, carrying out

Plate 3.3 Wrong use of a directly adhering support: here the shrinking adhesive has caused the disintegration of a frail ivory comb

the excavation of the spread in the laboratory. More recently the technique has been tried out in the north of England.[10] Whilst it has proved extremely useful to lift very fragile, wet spongey bone, more research into possible drawbacks is required (plate 3.5).

3.1.1.2 Lifting from underwater sites

It need hardly be said that working underwater is much more complicated than on land, not only because of the obvious hazards involved but because thought processes become dimmed and even the most simple task will require considerable mental effort. Recovering material from underwater sites must therefore be left to people with a wide experience of working underwater and of handling delicate archaeological finds. This is one of the few instances where it is preferable for an experienced underwater archaeologist to be responsible for lifting tasks rather than a land-based conservator, although the latter is always forewarned whenever underwater finds are to be raised. Nevertheless, special care is required if finds are to survive the perilous journey from the sea-bed to the surface intact and without being dropped, and from the sea to the atmosphere without collapsing under their own weight. The usual practice is to use mesh 'shopping baskets' for small items and for larger ones metal or plastic crates which can then be winched or air-lifted to the surface.

Plate 3.4 Poor application of a consolidant for lifting purposes: the consolidant has failed to penetrate this prehistoric pottery, resulting in the collapse of the vessel when lifted

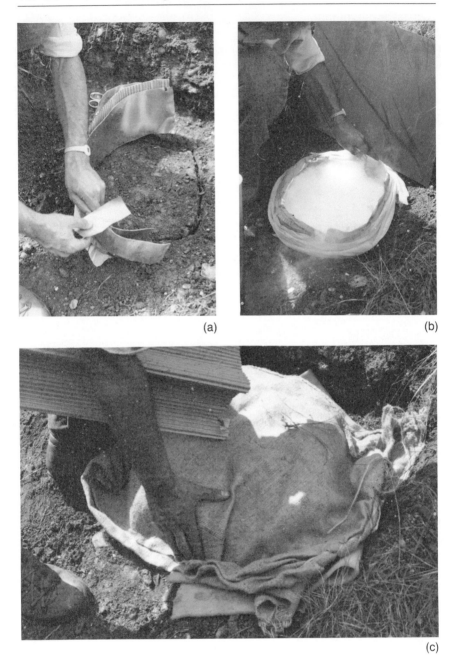

(a)

(b)

(c)

Plate 3.5 Lifting by freezing *in situ* water. (a) A thermally insulated barrier is placed around the object. (b) Using adequate safety precautions, the barrier is infilled with dry ice and wrapped in more insulation. (c) Insulation is placed over the ice whilst the water freezes.

(d)

(e)

(d) The barrier is removed and the frozen wedge levered from the ground. (e) The wedge is settled into a bed of vermiculite for support and insulation

Plate 3.6 Lifting from an underwater site: objects are winched up in a box of sediment

Small and delicate finds of wood, rope, leather, etc. are packed in fine sediment for protection, placed individually into boxes, and then sealed before lifting (plate 3.6).[11] Plaster of Paris and polysulphide rubber could probably be used to encase fragile materials and insubstantial mineralized remains before raising, especially on shallow-water sites where diving operations are less complicated.

3.1.2 *Moulding* in situ[12]

Since the lifting of large objects, especially from the sea-bottom, is a costly process, recording the shape of objects by moulding is becoming more widespread, the objects being left in the ground. Plaster of Paris has been widely used on land but it can be used underwater too. More recent developments have been in the use of polysulphide rubber for wet-site wooden hurdles and marine timbers, and of aerosol polyurethane foam. On dry sites, rubber latex can be used to record surface details such as inscriptions on stone, but since this material shrinks the mould has a short life. Surprisingly resilient records can be made by impressing wet filter paper into an inscription, which is known as making a squeeze; such a method is inexpensive and quick.

Moulding may be carried out on a large artefact such as a boat so that reconstruction at a later date is simplified. Of course moulds, and later casts, can be made of standing monuments and excavated objects; this is a specialized field and will not be developed here.[13] Suffice it to say that in these cases great care has to be taken to avoid any surface damage to the object such as the dislodging of a flaking surface by the moulding materials.

3.1.3 Measurement of the conditions of burial

Conservation is concerned not only with preserving existing materials but also with attempting to understand why materials decay sometimes to a state of unrecognizability. To do this it is necessary to correlate burial conditions with the state of a material in, or its absence from, a deposit. Thus conservators are measuring agents of decay within deposits, agents whose interactions remain enigmatic (section 2.1). However, it would seem that in general water content and redox potential (section 2.2) are two of the most important variables for study. Both of these alter as soon as the deposit is exposed to the air. Thus when measuring water content a soil sample is quickly sealed in polyethylene bags whilst redox potential is best measured by a special electrode device pushed into a deposit before it is excavated. If particular materials are under study, then those agents of decay deemed most important in their preservation/deterioration are measured.

3.2 Marking and labelling artefacts

Techniques for marking individual types of material are given in subsequent chapters but the aim in general is to ensure that whilst the mark survives not only handling but also conservation treatments, it can be removed if required. This is especially true of material which is ultimately used for display.

Tagging or labelling is often a more satisfactory method of identifying artefacts since the information does not disintegrate if the material decays, and the artefacts are not adversely affected by the practice. Endurance is all important and thus tags and labels associated with wet or damp storage must be of a rot-proof character. Spun-bonded polyethylene labels secured with terylene twine are useful here. Alternatively, or in addition, polyethylene bags with opaque bands for marking are reasonably durable if they do not suffer excessive handling/rubbing. The medium of the message must also be enduring, especially against fading: materials are recommended elsewhere[14], but it is important to use a permanent, black, spirit-based waterproof marker or *good*-quality ball-point pen. Even so, they will be affected by light in the long term.

It is important that, in order to save an extraordinary amount of 'hidden' time in the future, a label which can encompass site as well as conservation and even museum information should be used so that relabelling is avoided.

3.3 Examination and cleaning

Examination of excavated materials is fundamental to archaeological conservation; it aims to identify the nature of artefacts both for recording and for treatment purposes. The conservator looks at any remaining original material together with its deterioration products and any adhering associated material. In order to understand what he/she is looking at, a conservator must have a good knowledge not only of materials and how they decay, but also of technology of the past. During this examination, which for many artefacts is the only time when they are looked at closely, fine details of shape and construction may be observed; these could include alloy constituents, tool marks, remains of solder, textile fibres, or wear patterns, for example. This information is then used not only to determine the mode of treatment for the artefact but also to unravel how it was made originally, what it was used for, and even the significance of the context in which it was found; examples of this are given throughout the following chapters, but here one could instance the blue coloration of corroded iron (section 5.2.2.1) indicating high levels of phosphate in the burial environment. Furthermore, if at this stage unknowns are not identified, they may be misinterpreted both by conservators and by finds specialists, both then and in the future; such unknowns may easily be lost either in treatment or by decay and attrition. Where feasible, examination in the first instance, at least, is carried out without intervention, that is, without disturbing anything, much as geophysical survey is used prior to excavation. However, just as such surveys only reveal a certain level of information regarding a site, destructive excavation normally following, so normally irreversible investigation of artefacts must follow preliminary non-destructive examination.

3.3.1 Non-interventionist methods

3.3.1.1 Visible light

Before any other method of examination is carried out, it is normal to examine artefacts by eye. However, by using magnification provided by either a simple glass ($\times 3$) or a binocular microscope (greater than $\times 6$) (plate 3.7), the yield of information is enormously increased. Information such as the distinction between soil and corroded artefact or textile fibre and peat simply cannot be made with the naked eye alone.

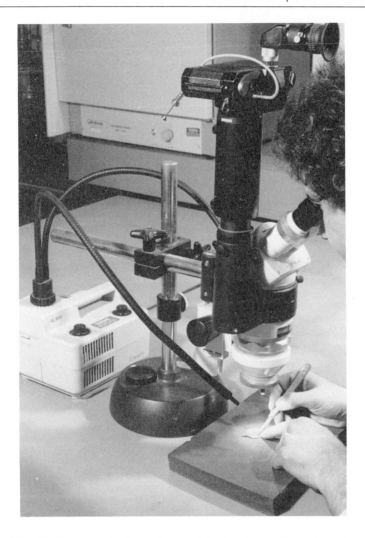

Plate 3.7 Routine examination of an artefact using a binocular microscope which has facilities for photographic recording

3.3.1.2 Infrared and ultraviolet

If visible light is substituted by other electromagnetic waves of more or less energy, further information may be forthcoming. Wavelengths at the red end of the visible spectrum lengthen and have less energy, finally becoming infrared (IR) rays which are not visible. Such longer waves are scattered less efficiently than is visible light, by small particles such as are found in adhering soil encrustations. Thus if infrared rays are directed towards a soil-encrusted painted surface, they will penetrate the obscuring crust and be reflected back by the paint. The reflected infrared rays also are not visible and so they are 'visualized' either by exposing a sensitive film or by using an electronic image converter. At the opposite end of the visible spectrum, the wavelengths shorten, becoming more energetic until forming ultraviolet (UV) rays. These can be used to distinguish between materials in the following way.

Certain molecular structures absorb UV energy and re-emit it as visible light, a phenomenon known as fluorescence. Old organic substances are particularly liable to fluorescence if irradiated with UV and thus a very thin resin coat on corroded metal or fragmented bone within a soil lump may be distinguished.

3.3.1.3 Radiography[15]

By far the most important use of wave energy for examination of metallic artefacts is x-radiography. X-rays are of even shorter wavelength than UV and thus are even more energetic. Therefore they are able to penetrate materials which are opaque to both visible light and UV. But just as visible light is absorbed by opaque materials but passes through transparent ones, so x-rays are absorbed by or pass through various substances. Thus a metal is more dense to x-rays than its corrosion products; lead corrosion products are more dense than iron metal; silver metal is more dense than iron metal. A thin piece of silver may be of a similar density to a thick piece of iron. To record these phenomena and make them visible to the eye, shadow radiographs (figure 3.4) are produced on a film which is very similar to photographic film. An object is placed between an x-ray source and a film plate and the source turned on to irradiate the object. The film then receives only those rays which manage to penetrate the object and so when developed, in a similar manner to photographic film, reveals areas of different density to x-rays within the object. Radiographs are studied by placing them on a light box; much information is lost through using a poor or uneven light source. Areas on the film which have received x-rays are black and those which have not are white. Thus thick parts of an object and those materials which absorb rays appear pale (plate 3.8a).

Many conservation laboratories have small, self-contained, x-ray units which look rather like ovens whilst others have lead-screened rooms with more powerful x-ray sources (plate 3.8b). With both these facilities, there are several ways of improving radiographs. The choice of voltage at which the x-rays are produced, the type of film, and the duration of exposure are all important. Other techniques include the use of lead screens to absorb scattered x-rays and filters to cut out unwanted rays. Radiographs give two-dimensional images of whole objects, of which the surface touching the film is best in focus. With certain manoeuvring more details can be obtained; these include varying the distance between the x-ray

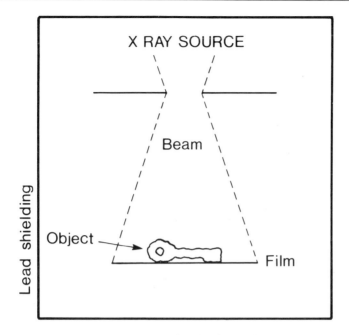

Figure 3.4 The production of a shadow radiograph

source, the film, and the object; tilting the object; and bending the film. Pairs of radiographs to be viewed on a stereoscope, to visualize an object three-dimensionally, can be made fairly simply by moving the object a few centimetres between shots. However, the final interpretation of even routine radiographs and the information they contain are both problematic and limited, as discussed in the following chapters.

In the past five years, conservation has made considerable use of much more sophisticated techniques of radiography available in industry and medicine. Industrial high-density radiography is extremely useful for revealing fine detail since a small area can be magnified radiographically without any loss of definition. There are also techniques available for radiography of a curved surface which cannot be carried out successfully with conventional devices. However, the cost of using such a facility is high and a much simpler and cheaper device has been developed for use within a conservation laboratory; it has been used to visualize an inscription on the lip of a metal bowl.[16] The medical technique whereby it is possible to focus the x-rays on a point within an object – tomography – has been used to interpret the contents of large archaeological artefacts. More exotically, the facilities of body-scanners (computerized axial tomography, CAT) have been made available to conservation to solve crucial problems.[17] Here x-rays are focused at very small intervals throughout a

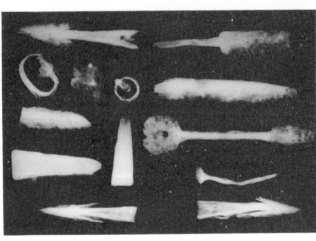

Plate 3.8 Examination using shadow x-radiography. (a) Shadow x-radiograph of corroded iron artefacts. (b) Typical x-radiographic facility found in many conservation laboratories

'body' and the results sorted by computer; however, even these are difficult to interpret.

In certain circumstances even shorter and more energetic gamma-rays can be useful for examination purposes. They may be produced by decaying radioactive isotopes and so can be used where electric power to produce x-rays is not available. Gamma-rays have been used to produce shadow radiographs of very dense artefacts where x-rays have proved inadequate. X-rays, and even more so gamma-rays, are extremely damaging to health and are only used where subject to stringent safety protection and monitoring.

A third type of radiography using a source of neutrons rather than electromagnetic energy has a unique role in examination. Since metals are more dense to x- and gamma-rays than are organic materials, it is not possible to visualize organic material within or beneath a metal covering using these energies. In contrast, neutrons will pass through metals only to be absorbed by organic materials. Thus radiographs showing wood beneath a copper surface, for example, could be made by establishments such as the Atomic Energy Authority at Harwell, where controlled neutron sources are available. Unlike x-rays, neutrons can penetrate lead and so neutron radiography is also used in the examination of lead and lead bronzes.[18]

Like photographic negatives, radiographs are subject to deterioration; they adhere together if damp and slowly fade in the light especially if not rinsed correctly during processing. Ideally they should be stored in individual non-acidic envelopes, stacked on edge, and kept cool, dry, and dark (section 2.4).

3.3.1.4   Chemical analysis

There are a small number of methods of chemical analysis which do not require samples to be taken and thus can be considered non-interventionist. Such methods range from specific gravity measurements to use of x-ray fluorescence and are dealt with adequately in other texts.[19] More usual, and where quantitative information is required, is the use of methods of analysis which require a sample to be taken (section 3.3.2.2).

3.3.2   Interventionist methods

3.3.2.1   Investigative cleaning

Just as excavation is destructive, so is the removal of soil, encrustations, and decay products from artefacts; the process is interventionist and cannot be reversed. Investigative cleaning is 'micro-archaeology' – the removal of material only after careful recording, to reveal structures below. These structures may be part of a discrete object or they may be associated material, and decisions have to be made as to what is to be exposed and what must remain. The criteria involved arise not only from the artefact itself but also from the type of information required or whether or not display is envisaged. This leads to a variation in degree or level of cleaning but not of course in the standard of cleaning. Thus material for publication may undergo minimal cleaning whilst that for display, total cleaning.

Wherever possible, investigative cleaning is carried out mechanically since in skilled hands these methods are the most controllable and they do not introduce chemicals into the artefact. Small hand-tools of a wide range to provide versatility are used (plate 3.9). Needles held in pincers, scalpels, and dental picks provide hard edges and points whilst softer ones are given by wooden modelling tools, bone points, or plastic probes. Brushes range from the softest squirrel to hard glass bristles. To avoid marking the artefact, the tool should be softer than the material being cleaned but care is taken to avoid using such tools which when abraded could adhere to the material; thus brass brushes are not used to 'brighten' bronze coins. Abrasive powders too are used, but here again great care must be taken to choose a powder which is softer than the material of the original surface so that it does not become scratched. These powders range from the softest gum to the hardest carborundum.

Plate 3.9 A selection of small hand tools used in the investigative cleaning of artefacts

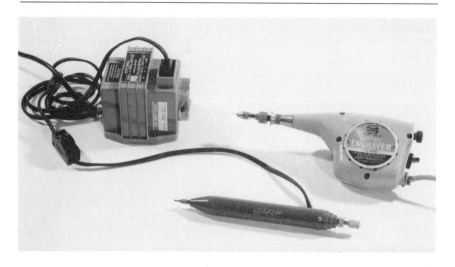

Plate 3.10 Two electrically powered needle points used in the investigative cleaning of artefacts

Tools powered by electricity, compressed air, or ultrasonics are useful (plate 3.10). The hand-held electric engraver usually with a needle fitted instead of the engraving point, or the lighter, quieter electric stylus have been widely used; in both these tools the working point vibrates in and out in a movement which dislodges overlying debris. Small revolving electric motors can be fitted with a variety of grinding wheels. Perhaps the most useful air-tool, apart from a simple vacuum cleaner, is the air abrasion unit (figure 3.5). Here abrasive powders of a variety of hardness are directed in a fine jet of air accurately onto the artefact. These give a high cleaning power but minimal stress and vibration to the object as a whole, but the abrasive powder can remain trapped in the interstices of porous material and could cause problems in the future. Ultrasonic vibrations can be used either distributed from small mobile heads as in dental descaling units or in tanks into which objects are immersed in a liquid. Many other tools are available but it is not within the scope of this book to describe them.

The two main types of chemical cleaning of archaeological artefacts involve either dispersion by surface-active agents or dissolution by particular reagents.[20] In the first type, dirt which does not dissolve easily in water is removed by the addition of a detergent (or surface-active agent) which links both to the dirt and to the water, allowing the former to become dispersed and lifted off into the latter. To prevent damage to the remaining artefact, neutral (i.e. neither acid nor alkaline) detergents are used. In the second type of cleaning, obscuring deposits or crusts are broken down chemically to soluble materials which are then washed off.

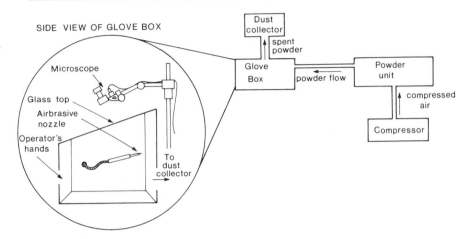

Figure 3.5 An air-abrasive investigative cleaning unit (schematic)

The simplest agent to use is water itself, but for many operations stronger chemicals are required. Alteration of pH of the washing solution by the addition of alkalis or more usefully acids often facilitates dissolution of obscuring debris but they are liable to attack the artefact too.

A useful group of cleaning agents are the sequestering agents. These are ions or molecules which form soluble complexes with metal ions, especially transition metal ions such as iron and copper. They remove these ions from solution, thereby allowing more to be dissolved from a solid and preventing the dissolved ions from reacting further. For example, the disodium salt of ethylenediaminetetraacetic acid (EDTA) sequesters iron(III) ions in particular and so allows deposits of iron oxides to dissolve. Great care has to be exercised in their use, to prevent sequestering and therefore the leaching of ions from artefacts themselves.

Organic solvents, such as alcohols, may be used instead of water to remove dirt from delicate surfaces where the high surface tension of water is too destructive. Usually they are found to be of more use in dissolving oils, brown organic colorations, old repairs, etc.

Apart from these groups of chemicals for cleaning there are many others which can be used for specific cases where there is a knowledge of exactly what is to be destroyed and what to be retained; some of these reagents are described in later chapters. Bleaching reagents, even hydrogen peroxide, are rarely used on archaeological material unless to remove stains from previous treatment or storage, since unrecognized evidence may be lost by their use.

In general, however, chemical cleaning is difficult to control, the agents often penetrating micro-cracks to reach the weakened artefact. Washing must of course follow the use of aqueous chemicals to remove not only the added chemical but also the soluble product it now carries; failure to

Plate 3.11 Use of a paste pack over a release layer to clean a stone object: as the reagent dries, dragging the dirt into the pack, the powder crumbles

do this can lead to breakdown of the artefact in the future.

The method of wet chemical cleaning varies with the problem in hand. Waterlogged artefacts or dry robust materials may be soaked; as long as the water in the baths is changed regularly, running water is not necessary. However, more often than not, it is unwise to immerse porous dry materials since surface debris is immediately carried by the agent into the centre of the object. Preferable is the use of packs of absorbent materials such as paper pulp or hydrated magnesium silicate powder (Sepiolite) which are soaked in the reagent and applied over a release layer of soft tissue paper (plate 3.11) to the artefact. The material to be removed is then drawn into the pack as the chemical evaporates and the pack dries out. The process is repeated until the treatment is finished. In a similar way, discrete areas of the surface of dense artefacts can be treated by applying the chemical in a gel such as Laponite, a synthetic inorganic clay. The use of electrolysis for cleaning is a technique only applicable to metallic artefacts and so is discussed in section 5.1.4.

3.3.2.2 Microscopy and chemical analysis

In order to identify materials and determine their degree of decay, if non-destructive methods (section 3.3.1) are not found to be helpful, samples for microscopy or analysis may have to be taken, the size of the sample depending on the technique being employed. Organic fibres may be mounted whole and examined in a transmitted light microscope; wood

Plate 3.12 A scanning electron microphotograph showing wood replaced by iron corrosion products

samples are sliced and their sections examined microscopically; samples of stone or ceramic are mounted, polished, and viewed with a petrological microscope whilst metals, similarly treated, are examined with a metallurgical microscope. For looking at the physical structure of materials at very high magnification, scanning electron microscopy (SEM) has proved extremely useful both for identifying material and determining its degree of decay (plate 3.12). Not many conservation laboratories will have all of these facilities but access to them is essential.

The chemical nature of material can be looked at by simple wet chemical techniques, but access to more sophisticated physical methods of analysis such as spectrometry, electron probe, neutron activation, x-ray diffraction, or chromatography, described well in other texts (see note 19), is essential to cope with tiny samples and the vast range of possible unknowns.

3.4 Stabilization

This aspect of conservation is a distinct activity from examination and cleaning; it aims to make excavated material stable both physically and chemically. It can be approached in two ways: the first is non-interventionist or passive, attempting to create acceptable physical and chemical equilibria simply by manipulating the normal constituents of the environment without adding alien chemicals to the material; and the second is an active interventionist approach, attempting either to remove destructive agents from the material with chemicals or to introduce preservative compounds into the material.

3.4.1 Passive techniques

It was shown in section 2.3 that upon excavation the environment of materials alters considerably and it is this alteration which causes the loss of much artefactual evidence. More often than not the aim with freshly excavated material is to maintain it in an environment similar to that in which it was found. However, it is not feasible to maintain all the variables in the environment at the levels obtaining during burial. Thus reproduction of the environment is normally restricted to one or possibly two factors such as humidity and temperature, which means that stability is not assured. Whilst in some cases it is known which environmental factors must be controlled in order to optimize stability, in others either this, or the level at which they must be kept, are still not clear; it is this area of conservation which at present is undergoing considerable research. A different line can be taken with metals where, rather than an attempt being made to mimic the burial environments, corrosion is prevented by storage in extreme environments either of desiccation or removal of oxygen.

In the longer term, such techniques impose limitations on study and display and often do not totally prevent deterioration. So active techniques of stabilization are practised. However, even after an object has been treated in this way, it will not be able to survive the full range of conditions found in the atmosphere and thus storage and display environments will have to be controlled, albeit to less exacting levels than before. This is an expanding activity in conservation with more resources being put into the care of materials in this way and less emphasis being put on active treatments which interfere with the materials; such a shift in direction is beneficial both ethically and financially. It should be noted that much research is still required in this field before passive stabilization is more reliable and practicable. Methods for immediate passive stabilization are given in 'first-aid' manuals[21] whilst many of the long-term requirements and techniques are discussed by Thomson, Stolow, and others.[22] However, as stated earlier (section 1.3), the designing of complex systems of control is the province of the engineer rather than the conservator.

3.4.1.1 Humidity

Incorrect humidity in both the short and the long term (sections 2.3.1 and 2.4.1) is perhaps the major cause of deterioration of artefacts. Since the relative humidity (section 2.4.1) of the environment can be controlled in discrete areas at crude levels fairly easily, this is an important aspect of passive stabilization. In the chapters which follow it will be made clear at what level the RH should be maintained for particular materials; in this chapter the techniques for obtaining particular RHs will be discussed.

CONTROL OF HUMIDITY UPON EXCAVATION. Preventing water loss from materials will in part depend on the ambient environment of the excavation, matters being worse on a hot, sunny, windy day. Simple steps such as covering the material *in situ* with polyethylene or damp foam sheets may suffice, but spraying and more sophisticated techniques (section 6.2.8) could be needed (plate 3.13). Once lifted, sensitive material has to be put into the correct storage RH; drying out at this stage could be catastrophic. More robust material, however, may be

Plate 3.13 Exposed timber being kept wet on site using farm sprays and sheets of plastic foam; Iron Age logboat from Hasholme, East Yorkshire, preserved in the anoxic conditions of an estuarine deposit

allowed to dry out and so equilibrate with the ambient RH. Drying out is always monitored so that, if any damage ensues, drying can cease forthwith. Heat from the sun or artificial sources is never used, but the process should not be too slow in case micro-organisms develop. Thus a warm area with a good current of air is used. If drying is too fast, it can be slowed down by covering with a polyethylene sheet or clean damp sand, providing a watch is kept for the growth of micro-organisms.

Marine finds are particularly sensitive to drying out (section 2.3.1) and great care must be taken to have tanks/containers available for immediate storage (see below).

WET AND DAMP STORAGE. Much of the deterioration of waterlogged and wet excavated material can be easily prevented by simple but immediate storage in correct conditions. Thus decay is readily prevented if the material/artefact can be immersed in water, here called 'wet' storage, either in small containers or else in large temporary tanks described elsewhere.[23] Where this is not feasible or where the material is too frail to survive movement within a body of water, the different and often less satisfactory method of 'damp' storage is used. When material is not immersed it can readily lose water and then perhaps regain it repeatedly as the ambient relative humidity of the atmosphere changes. Thus in damp storage, attempts are made to maintain this RH at 100 per cent by sealing materials in polyethylene bags or polyethylene boxes. If bags are used, as much air as possible is squeezed out and a small quantity of free water added before sealing. Since no bag is truly sealable, each bag is placed within two further sealed bags in an attempt to prevent water loss (plate 3.14). If boxes are used it must be remembered that if they are stored in a warm environment the RH within the box could fall as the air heats up, and thus either a considerable quantity of water, loose or absorbed in a plastic sponge etc., must be incorporated or else the air in the box must be displaced by solids such as soil. This is extremely heavy and for this and other reasons experiments are in hand to determine the possibility of using artificial soil in boxes.[24]

In this context, the description 'damp' is applied to any excavated material except that which is from extremely dry environments. Whilst the burial environment may not be saturated, the chances are that it will have a much higher moisture content than the air. Whilst storage conditions of 100 per cent RH may be excessive, there must be sufficient water sealed in the storage containers to maintain a reasonably high RH even when they are placed in a warm room.

For both wet and damp storage, waterproof materials must be used. These are detailed in site manuals, and include polyethylene labels, terylene string, and waterproof inks.

Whilst the maintenance of materials in these damp conditions preserves

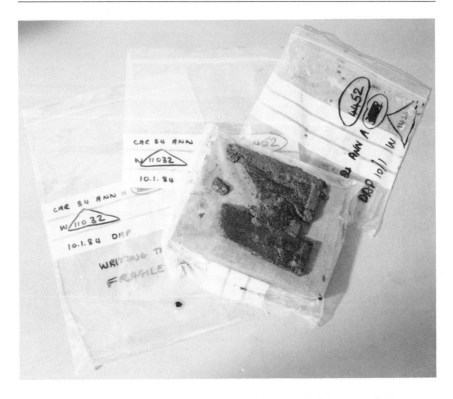

Plate 3.14 To maintain a damp storage environment, it is essential to use a triple layer of sealed polyethylene bags

them structurally, it will of course expose them to the other effects of water, both chemical and biological (section 2.2.1.1); attempts are made to control these in the ways described below, but as yet the results are not always satisfactory or reliable and so wet and damp storage can only be temporary.

DRY STORAGE OR DISPLAY. Such conditions require an RH of anywhere between 65 per cent (damp) and 40 per cent (desiccated). This upper limit is set to prevent the growth of micro-organisms not only on organic artefacts but also on the soil adhering to artefacts and on their packaging. Thus before any material is stored in this way, it must be dried out as described above or else the RH inside the packaging will rise above 65 per cent.

Below a figure of 40 per cent RH organic packaging (and of course artefacts) become brittle, inorganic material may crumble, and no improved stabilization is achieved. RH requirements for particular materials involve not only levels but also whether the level must be prevented from fluctuating; materials can in general be divided into 'bulk store' and 'sensitive store' materials.[25]

Some materials, such as salt-free ceramics, survive a wide range of RH with no necessity for constancy. They may be kept in containers which allow for the movement of air such as perforated polyethylene bags or cardboard boxes which prevent localized build-up of humidity. The containers are housed in areas in which the RH conforms to this undemanding range. Much more difficult to deal with are 'sensitive store' materials, for here the RH range is limiting, but what action has to be taken will depend on the RH demanded and the particular area to be controlled.

Full-scale air-conditioning is not necessarily the answer; it is extremely expensive to install and maintain, and there have been many problems with it in museums. It is much simpler and cheaper to attempt only to regulate discrete areas such as small rooms or showcases, for if things go wrong here material can be moved out or extra machinery brought in. Whilst there are available commercial humidifiers and dehumidifiers to control the RH of stated volumes of air, small units have been designed specifically for display cases.[26] Machinery can be avoided altogether for showcases and plastic storage boxes, a particular RH being achieved by using conditioned silica gel (figure 3.6).[27] Sufficient water vapour is added to the silica gel such that, as the ambient RH changes, water is drawn from or taken up by the gel so as to mask the variations and prevent movement of water in and out of the artefacts. For maximum stability with minimum attention, in all these systems, the room, showcase, or box

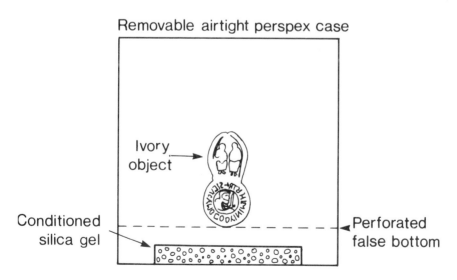

Figure 3.6 Display case to provide stable relative humidity conditions

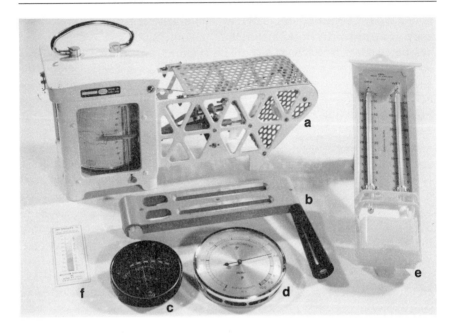

Plate 3.15 Hygrometers used for the measurement of relative humidity: a, thermohygrograph; b, whirling hygrometer; c, paper hygrometer; d, hair hygrometer; e, wet and dry bulb hygrometer; f, humidity strip

must be sealed as well as possible, but in every case monitoring is essential.

Monitoring of RH can be done by means of hygrometers (plate 3.15). These can be small devices which are placed in display cases or small storage areas and inform the observer of the ambient RH at the moment of reading. They are not particularly accurate and require calibrating at least once a month. More useful are recording hygrometers which trace out the ambient RH on a graph over a day, a week, or several weeks; these too must be calibrated at intervals. Either the machine is placed where the measurement is required or, with the more expensive equipment, a small sensitive probe may be put in a display case and connected to the machine elsewhere. Calibration is best achieved by means of a whirling hygrometer which can be used to measure the RH of a room at a given instant. Apart from these instruments, RH may be measured by the use of humidity strips.[28] These are paper/cardboard strips which incorporate salts which change colour as the RH changes. They are relatively cheap and so can be put in individual storage boxes or cases. After positioning hygrometers and humidity strips, an interval of a few hours is allowed to elapse before a reading is made, to allow the device to equilibrate to its new surroundings.

DESICCATED STORAGE OR DISPLAY. Such conditions of very low RH may be required to prevent chemical reactions occurring and are usually restricted to metals. Whilst dehumidifiers could be used to achieve these low levels, more economic is the use of a desiccating agent, usually silica gel. The gel extracts water vapour from the air into its extraordinary system of micropores until the quantity of absorbed water is in equilibrium with that in the surrounding atmosphere. Thus in order for the gel to maintain the ambient RH at very low levels, sufficient quantities of gel must be present and the area to be desiccated must be enclosed as well as possible from the rest of the storage/display area.

Sealed containers or display cases are essential; polyethylene boxes are far preferable to polyethylene bags which are bound to leak (figure 3.7).

Whilst sealed display cases are extremely expensive and rarely totally efficient, the smaller the volume the easier it is to control. There should be approximately 1 kilogram of gel for every 0.012 cubic metres of volume to be desiccated.[29]

In a well-sealed container, sufficient gel should be able to maintain the RH at about 10 per cent, which can be monitored using humidity strips. A salt indicator, cobalt chloride, is often added to silica gel itself. This changes from blue to pink as the RH rises over about 40 per cent, and thus is only useful where desiccation to below this figure is required. As soon as the colour of the humidity strip or the self-indicator changes to show a higher RH than required, the gel must be replaced by dry gel and the removed gel desiccated by heating in an oven at 105°C for a few hours. The more often the container is opened the more frequently the gel must be changed but, in general, if well sealed and unopened, a change should not be required more than biannually.

3.4.1.2 Temperature

Since temperature is intimately linked with relative humidity, it is always considered when controlling RH, but its regulation will stabilize materials

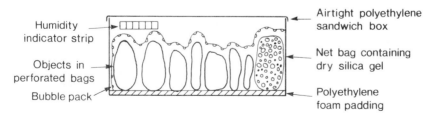

Figure 3.7 Packaging of a storage box to ensure condition of physical stability and of desiccation

for other reasons too (section 2.4.3). Fluctuations in temperature can be prevented by storing materials away from sunshine and intermittent spotlights, in rooms with few external walls, and by turning off *intermittent* central heating or other types of heating. Cool conditions are preferable; special filters can be applied to lights to cut out this major source of heat. However, in cool conditions care is taken to avoid condensation and growth of micro-organisms. Temperatures of 4°C may be useful to slow down the chemical and biological attack of wet artefacts, but freezing to −16°C is the only way of really ensuring preservation. This of course introduces the problem of disruption of saturated porous artefacts when water freezes and expands its volume by 9 per cent. Certainly it is damaging when it occurs in stone by accident when artefacts are left outside, but it is hoped that further work already underway in this area may result in methods whereby deliberate deep freezing can be used safely. They would of course be of great use in the field of underwater archaeology.

3.4.1.3 Oxygen

Oxygen enhances many chemical reactions and allows the growth of most organisms (section 2.1); to reduce these activities its level in the surrounding environment could be lowered. This can be done simply in solution by using boiled water which contains low levels of oxygen and in which artefacts can be immersed. Uptake of oxygen by storage water can be slowed down by excluding air from the system simply by filling tanks full and using close-fitting lids or by squeezing the air out of polyethylene bags before they are sealed. Oxygen can be excluded from within damp storage polypropylene boxes by filling them with soil, but more complicatedly it can be removed from these and from solutions by the addition of chemicals known as oxygen scavengers; their use with archaeological materials is still experimental.

Alternatively oxygen and humidity may be removed from the environment of an artefact by displacing the air with inert nitrogen.[30] The object is put into a sealed container with a small outlet; nitrogen from a cylinder is then discharged into the container in a continuous stream.

3.4.1.4 Dust

For preservation of artefacts (section 2.4.5) good housekeeping, that is a programme of dusting and airing stores, is essential as is the prevention of gross contamination of the air, by boiler flues, etc. Where there is no air-conditioning, artefacts must be covered. This means that they are either boxed or else covered by cloths; these are more suitable than polyethylene sheets which pick up dust and prevent circulation of air. If boxes are airtight, it must be ascertained that the contents are not damp

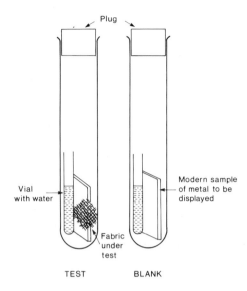

Plug

Vial
with water

Modern sample
of metal to be
displayed

Fabric
under
test

TEST   BLANK

Figure 3.8 Testing display material to determine if gases given off by the fabric corrode the metal to be displayed

before sealing. Also the amount of dust in a storage area can be lessened by sealing windows and putting dust excluders on the doors.

More problematic is the presence of salt in the air in maritime regions. Here a system of air filtration is essential when the salt levels and size of collection of metallic artefacts are high.

3.4.1.5   Gaseous pollution

Only in large heavily industrialized towns are attempts made to reduce the sulphur dioxide levels for archaeological collections. This is most successfully achieved by air-conditioning but, failing this, individual display cases may be fitted with air filters and sulphur dioxide absorbers. Sealed storage containers will keep internal levels of the gas low. Where vulnerable materials are to be stored or displayed, great care is taken not to introduce any local sources of pollution in the form of unstable packaging or display fabrics etc. (section 2.4.6). On these occasions all introduced materials are first tested to ensure that they give off no harmful gases (figure 3.8).[31]

3.4.1.6   Light

On the whole, stabilization by control of light is more important to other museum objects than to archaeological material and details can be found elsewhere.[32] However, some general points relevant to the entire excavation archive are made here. To protect boxes and labels, daylight is excluded from stores since it contains high levels of UV and is often present when in fact light is not required. Tungsten lights emit less UV than fluorescent strips and should be fitted with handy switches. On display, moderately sensitive materials should be restricted to 150 lux and very sensitive ones to 50 lux, with any UV filtered out; in storage they should be boxed or covered.

Control of light is not particularly helpful in preventing the growth of organisms; some insects, fungi, and bacteria in fact thrive in dark conditions. However, the growth of photosynthetic plants and algae is halted by shutting out light, which could be helpful in controlling the fouling of wet storage tanks.

3.4.1.7 Organisms

The control of activity of organisms as shown in the preceding sections is mainly carried out through control of other factors, namely humidity, temperature, dust, and light. However, there is one type of passive control not yet mentioned and that is what is known as biological control of pests. In this method, organisms are introduced to the environment to prey on the pest. The best example of this is in the use of fish to control slimes in wet wood tanks (section 6.2.6.1), but other systems could perhaps be developed.

3.4.1.8 The human factor

Much damage can be avoided to artefacts if they are handled properly.[33] Many archaeological artefacts are much weaker than they appear even after conservation and if lifted by one end will fracture; objects should be lifted on a support whenever possible. Moreover, they may be much more brittle than they seem and on no account should be dropped or roughly handled. Bright or patinated metalwork should be handled with gloves to avoid contamination by sweat and grease, and clean hands are required for pale porous materials such as painted wall plaster or ceramics. Even 'experts' can be guilty of causing damage whilst handling objects, but any person new to dealing with archaeological artefacts should be warned of their fragility.

During transportation, such as from an excavation to a laboratory, adequate packing is as important in the preservation of artefacts as is control of relative humidity. Individual wet/damp objects can be wrapped in fine plastic netting/sieve to hold them together if necessary. Padding can be given by shredded polyethylene sheeting, soft polyether sponge or harder more durable polyethylene foam, plastic bubble pack, or even moss (figure 3.7). Support may be given by polyethylene corrugated board, polystyrene blocks cut to shape, perspex sheets, plastic trays, or polypropylene boxes. Packing must be firm enough to prevent any movement of the objects in their containers; packing in boxes of soil is

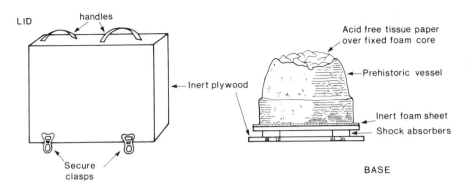

Figure 3.9 Packaging of a ceramic vessel for storage and transport

useful but heavy. If objects are to be moved whilst still immersed, movement within the container must be prevented by adequate padding.

Dry packaging can incorporate any of the materials mentioned above but to these may be added acid-free tissue and corrugated cardboard. Cotton wool must not be used as it catches on the surface of artefacts. As above, movement of artefacts must be prevented at all costs. It is safer to make pads to surround individual objects than to wrap them in sheets of tissue; in this latter case, damage can be done in the unwrapping process.

Even in store, packaging must be adequate to prevent objects rubbing against one another or their containers when boxes are moved or accidentally knocked. Here, cut-away shapes in long-lasting polyethylene foam are particularly useful; soft polyether sponge degrades readily and polystyrene is not robust (figure 3.9).

Details of packaging materials for archaeological collections can be found elsewhere[34] and a new publication is forthcoming.[35]

3.4.1.9   Categories of storage

In order to ensure that unstable material is well looked after whilst robust artefacts are not unduly cossetted, artefacts are divided up according to storage requirements.[36] The most unstable materials (category A) require stringent control and monitoring of environmental conditions which is usually achieved by storing them in specific micro-climates in small enclosed areas or containers. The second and less vulnerable group (category B) can be kept in open stores where there is a lower degree of environmental control, whereas the third group (category C) of robust material can withstand a wider range of environmental conditions. In category A, ironwork and ivory in particular are often found, whilst stabilized copper alloy and bone, for example, are in category B.

Category C will normally contain stone and ceramics. But of course some ironwork is very stable, and some stone exceedingly fragile; thus categories vary for each collection being stored.

3.4.2 Active techniques

3.4.2.1 Removal of agents of deterioration

WATER. Once it has been determined to remove water from a material to enhance its survival this can be done either passively as in air-drying described earlier (section 3.4.1.1) or by intervention as described below.

Water has a high surface energy which leads to the phenomenon of high surface tension demonstrated by the way in which a thin film of water will hold two sheets of glass together. This phenomenon is important in conservation since this high energy holds water in micropores and capillaries within artefacts. Air-drying alone will only remove some water, leaving moisture retained in pores. For some materials where water is part of the structure, namely organic materials, it is important for the maintenance of the structure that held water is not removed; thus air-drying can be useful. For other materials, namely metals, it is important that all water is removed in order to prevent chemical reactions, and thus air-drying is not thorough enough. A second result of this high surface tension is that, as water evaporates from large capillaries, the receding water front pulls the surfaces of the capillary together. If the walls are frail, collapse will follow as is seen notably for decayed organic materials (section 6.1.2.2). Thus other methods of removing water must be sought.

Solvent drying counteracts some of the drawbacks of air-drying. Here, a solvent with a low surface tension displaces the water and is allowed to evaporate off, resulting in a greater degree of water removal and avoidance of capillary collapse.

A third method of water removal is that of freeze-drying.[37] Here the water is frozen and the object placed in an atmosphere which contains very few water molecules such as that which can be produced in a vacuum chamber. If enough energy is present in the form of heat, water molecules will pass directly from the solid to the vapour state without becoming liquid. The vapour is given off into the surrounding atmosphere and is trapped by freezing it on a cold external condenser (figure 3.10, plate 3.16). Thus the material is dried without the problems of surface tension. The degree of water removal is extremely high but a complication arises in this method; the increase in volume of water as it freezes prior to drying could cause damage (section 2.2.1.1).

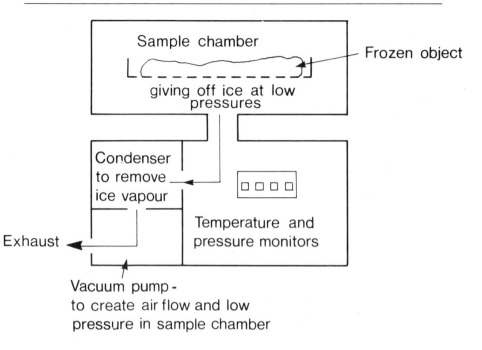

Figure 3.10 The functioning of a freeze-dryer

SOLUBLE SALTS AND CHEMICALS. 'Soluble' in this context implies those that have a high level of solubility in water. Salts may be present from the burial deposit (section 2.2.1.5), or from reactions with chemicals which have been added in conservation treatment to remove insoluble materials. After any treatment involving the use of chemicals, traces of these will remain in the artefacts and must be removed to prevent long-term decay. The simplest method of removing salts is to soak the material in less contaminated water. In this way the concentrated salt solution within the material diffuses out into the less concentrated solution in the washing tank. As the concentration of salt in the material diminishes, so must that in the tank. Thus the water must be changed and later replaced by a pure wash such as distilled or deionized water to allow diffusion of the final salts from within the material. When removing sea-water from porous material, several changes of water in a soaking tank are necessary to ensure the bulk removal of salt. The end point can be monitored by measuring either the conductivity (which is dependent on the salt concentration) or the chloride ion content of the washing water.

It would seem that the removal of soluble materials is not speeded up greatly by running water as long as the volume of water in the washing tank is adequate, and a degree of heat simply assists by expanding

Plate 3.16 Freeze-drying facility: a large vacuum chamber is supported on a freeze-drying unit

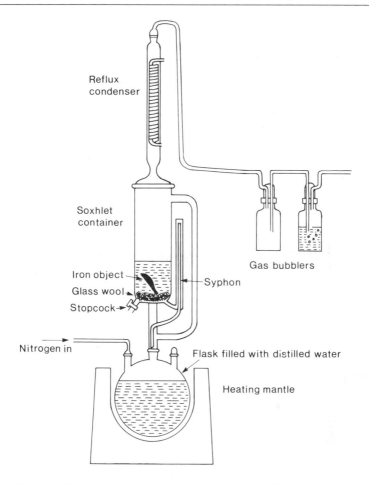

Figure 3.11 A Soxhlet extractor used under inert conditions; a corroded iron object is desalted under nitrogen gas (after Scott and Seeley: ref. 38, chapter 5)

capillaries in the artefact to release trapped salts or chemicals. If heat is useful, a Soxhlet apparatus has the bonus of avoiding having to change washing water. In this standard device, a small artefact is placed over boiling water. The steam passes through it and is condensed, falling back through the object and carrying the salts into the water below where they remain, only water re-vaporizing (figure 3.11).

It would seem that if an electric field were placed around a salt-laden object, removal of salt into the washing tank would be speeded up as the soluble ions migrated to the electrodes; in practice such a technique may not be particularly useful.

Where an object is too large to be immersed in a washing tank, soluble salts or chemicals are removed by the application of wet paper pulp poultices to the surface. The process, if repeated several times, can be extremely effective and less damaging than immersion in water. However, desalting is a topic which warrants further research for reliable results to be achieved.[38]

ORGANISMS.[39] This section describes the removal, or rather the destruction of organisms in artefacts without leaving chemicals behind, and thus is distinct from the use of biocides described in section 3.4.2.2. This destruction is carried out by gases and so can only be used for dry porous materials; it is called fumigation. Fumigation is commonly used for ethnographic collections and for archives, but archaeological collections could require fumigation either where organic artefacts, archive material, packaging or shelving have become infested by insects, or mould. In these cases, specialist apparatus is needed to pass a toxic gas such as methyl bromide through the infected material, thereby killing the organisms but leaving no residue and thus no protection against future attack.

3.4.2.2 Addition of stabilizing materials

BIOCIDES. The addition of biocides to control organism growth should only be tried where passive techniques have failed. There are numerous criteria involved in the choice of biocide, but the primary one is that it should not be toxic to humans, either the conservator or people who curate/study the artefact in the future. This is virtually impossible, for all biocides will have some toxicity to humans, however slight. Secondly, the biocide must not harm the artefact. Both these criteria can be difficult to judge in the short term. Also, before a chemical is chosen it must be ascertained exactly what type of organism is to be controlled and for how long. Because of these problems non-specialists should seek professional advice before using a biocide; products change and research continually pinpoints new hazards.

There are two types of biocide relevant here: the repellants and the remnant action type. The repellants only act for short periods since they work by bombardment of a dry artefact by a vapour given off by a solid. The solids have low vapour pressures and their effect lasts as long as solids remain to vaporize, therefore their action is prolonged if they are sealed with the artefact in a container. Many repellants such as paradichlorobenzene (PDCB or mothballs) which were used in the past are no longer permitted and even the more recent dichlorvos-impregnated strips hung in the atmosphere to protect wool, fur, and feathers from insect attack are no longer deemed safe where workers are repeatedly exposed.

More widely used are the remnant action biocides. These are applied to dry or damp artefacts as a liquid, or are dissolved in the water surrounding immersed materials. Dry artefacts may need to be protected against insects as well as micro-organisms, whereas damp or waterlogged materials are only attacked by insects when the packaging has failed and the RH has fallen. However, marine timber can be attacked by wood borers (section 6.2.5.2). Brief reviews of biocides for use with waterlogged wood are available[40] but at the present time one of the most widely used is dichlorophen (Panacide, Preventol), which affects fungi and bacteria. For marine wood a buffered boric acid solution is another choice. Alternatives are sodium *ortho*-phenylphenate (Topane WS, Dowicide A), a fungicide, and pentachlorophenyl laurate (Mystox LPL), a bacterio/fungi/insecticide. Occasionally the surfactant quarternary ammonium compounds (Tego 51B, Benzalkon B) are used to control algae. All these are used according to supplied instructions, usually in the order of 0.01–2 per cent weight to volume in immersion tanks, and slightly higher when sprayed on damp objects. For dry organic artefacts dichlorophen, pentachlorophenyl laurate, or calcium propionate (a fungicide) could be sprayed on, whilst as an insecticide pyrethrins/ pyrethroids are to be preferred.[41]

The danger to health inherent in the use of biocides cannot be reiterated too many times. Research into less toxic but effective products continues and it is imperative that anyone contemplating using biocides seeks advice first.

CONSOLIDANTS.[42] Consolidants are chemicals which are designed to harden inside a porous material, making it more robust. They are composed of extremely large organic molecules which, being formed by the linking together of a great number of identical small molecules termed monomers, are called polymers. The polymers are applied to the porous material as liquids which then set *in situ*. They can be liquefied either by being melted or else by being dissolved in water or, more usually, in an organic solvent. The former melt–freeze consolidants set by cooling whilst the latter, solvent consolidants, set by loss of water or solvent. Once set, both types are resoluble in an appropriate liquid and soften on heating; they are known as thermoplastics.

In contrast to these resoluble thermoplastic consolidants, there is a second group which set *in situ* as a result of a reaction between two molecular species. These chemicals can be applied undiluted or dispersed in organic solvents, but the polymers once formed are neither resoluble nor soften in heat, and are called reaction consolidants or thermosets.

Whilst organic solvents are used widely in conservation, no more than a passing introduction is given here. This is because the topic is extremely complex and because any encouragement in their use without adequate understanding is to be discouraged, since in the main they are toxic and flammable. Organic solvents vary enormously chemically, offering a wide variety of properties which can be useful in conservation for cleaning (section 3.3.2.1), drying (section 3.4.2.1) or, in this case, dissolving consolidants (or adhesives; section 3.4.2.4). They vary in their ability to dissolve different materials, in their volatility or rate of drying, and in their miscibility with water. A mixture of solvents may meet specifications which a single solvent cannot. Organic solvents must be treated with due respect for the health of both the operator and the artefact.

In the consolidation of artefacts there are two main dangers. The first is that the consolidant will only penetrate the outer layer of the material, and so when it is handled this tough zone which contains surface detail will fall off the friable unconsolidated core of the artefact (plate 3.4). The second is that on setting, or over a long period of time, the consolidant will shrink; this causes the whole internal structure of the artefact to collapse (plate 3.17). Overriding the whole process of consolidation is the conflict with reversibility towards which conservation treatments aspire. If reaction consolidants are used, there is no possibility of reversing the process, but even if the less strong thermoplastic polymers are used, the process is almost impossible to reverse since the dissolution of the consolidant within the friable material will almost certainly cause irreversible damage.

When choosing the method of application of a consolidant the main feature to be considered is the size of the molecule to be introduced. Being large molecules, polymers, when melted or dissolved, form very viscous liquids which do not easily penetrate the micropores of the fragile material. There are several approaches which can ease this problem, one being to avoid using melt–freeze consolidants such as beeswax, since they tend to be particularly poor at penetration. Much the best penetration is achieved by dissolving a polymer in a low surface tension organic solvent which produces a low viscosity liquid. This then sets by loss of solvent; unfortunately problems can arise. One problem is that loss of solvent may lead to shrinkage; another that, since the solution was dilute in the first place, little actual consolidant remains *in situ*; and a third that the evaporating solvent drags the consolidant out of the centre of the material, leaving it in the surface layer only. By judicious choice of solvent(s) some of these drawbacks can be mitigated.

For dry material, another way of aiding penetration is to use a partial vacuum to extract the air from porous materials, thereby enabling a solution to enter the pores (plate 3.18). Heat too can lower viscosity and assist penetration, but care has to be taken, for organic solvents are flammable.

Emulsions and dispersions are potentially very useful in conservation. They are milky in appearance, being colloids; that is, they are suspensions of particles of non-water-soluble consolidant in a mixture of water and solvent, dispersions simply having smaller size particles than emulsions. They tend to have lower viscosities than comparable solutions

Plate 3.17 Crack in a low-fired ceramic caused by shrinking of gap-filling materials. The arrow shows where pottery has adhered to gap fill pulling away from body

of consolidant, and so higher levels of consolidant can be deposited in the artefact. Since emulsions and dispersions contain water, they can be diluted with water and used on damp material. Once set, it must be remembered that the consolidant is only resoluble in a solvent, not in water. Their notable drawbacks are that they also contain other chemicals which stabilize the colloid but decay relatively quickly, and that they often form soft films which pick up dirt readily.

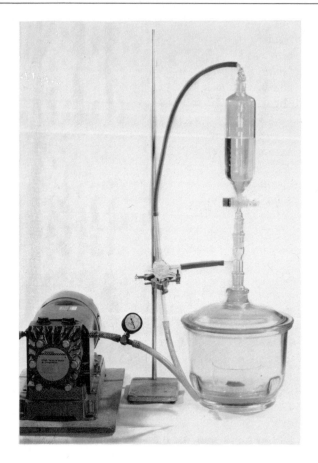

Plate 3.18 Vacuum impregnation facility: a glass vacuum chamber is first evacuated by a vacuum pump, then consolidant in the funnel is dropped onto the artefact in the chamber

There is yet another way in which better penetration of a consolidant can be achieved; this is by forming the polymer *in situ* from monomers with low molecular weights, which can easily impregnate porous material. Polymerization is achieved by applying a source of energy such as gamma-radiation or heat, but whilst such consolidation may achieve great depths, damage may be caused to the artefact in the polymerization process.

A second major consideration when consolidating material is its water content. Where this is high, normally either a water-miscible consolidant is used or else the water is removed first by drying or displacement. If such steps are not taken, the consolidant will fail to penetrate and an opaque surface deposit of polymer will result. Water-miscible consolidants are those which can be dissolved in water, those which are formed into emulsions or dispersions, and those reaction polymers which actually utilize water in their setting reaction. A novel suggestion has been to consolidate damp porous surfaces; a consolidant is applied in a completely non-water-miscible solvent which displaces the water without causing a disfiguring white deposit of consolidant to form.[43]

Turning now to specific polymers for use as consolidants, there are two main groups – the natural and the synthetic. Some of the natural ones such as dammar resin are very stable but in most cases synthetic ones are preferred; batches are more uniform, they are not subject to biodeterioration, and properties can be matched to requirements. The most useful group of resoluble synthetics for consolidants are the acrylics, many of which show very good ageing characteristics. Paraloid (or Acryloid) B72 (polymethyl acrylate/polyethyl methacrylate copolymer)[44], which is soluble in a variety of organic solvents but not water, is widely used. Polyvinyl acetate (PVAC) (see note 44), both when dissolved in an organic solvent or dispersed in an emulsion, has been the stand-by in conservation for many years; whilst still useful, it has an unfortunate property of becoming tacky at raised temperatures and absorbing dirt into any surface film. There is now a considerable case against using the thermoplastic soluble nylon[45] once popular in conservation; this includes its dirt pick-up and long-term shrinkage, but of more particular concern is its rapidly developing insolubility. Unfortunately, when considering damp or wet material, the choice of suitable water-soluble consolidants is limited. The most useful is polyethylene glycol (PEG).[46] This comes in a choice of molecule size, the smallest being liquids which are replaced by soft waxes as the molecular weight rises to about 1500, and thence by harder waxes at 4000. Amongst emulsions and dispersions, the acrylic-based dispersions are currently seen as having advantages over PVAC emulsions.[47] If resort has to be made to reaction consolidants, a group which exhibits excellent penetration are the epoxy resins. They have an unfortunate tendency to yellow, but when used as consolidants this drawback may not be too marked. Another group of reaction polymers are the silanes[48] which, since they react with water, have been used on damp material. They are only really successful at consolidating material which is crumbling, and best results are sometimes achieved when they are used in conjunction with a more adhesive consolidant such as an acrylic resin. They are less successful at reinforcing weakened structures such as the cell walls of plants.

BACKING MATERIALS. Extremely frail artefacts such as a badly corroded metal bowl or a decayed textile may require additional support in the form of supporting materials known as a backing. In the case of items such as wall paintings and mosaics which have been lifted from their original positions, the need for such support is obvious. There are two problems: one being how to bond the backing to the object; the other resulting from the covering up of one face of the artefact by the backing. To some extent this can be minimized by choosing transparent materials where possible. Where this is impossible, attempts could be made to provide voids at strategic points in the backing, but it can never be entirely avoided. Adhesives are usually employed to affix a backing, in which case great care is taken in their choice to avoid irreversibility and shrinkage. Alternatively, mechanical means such as threads can be used for very frail artefacts (plate 2.1). The backing material itself must be chemically inert but must expand/contract in a similar manner to the artefact. It can be either flexible or rigid, depending on the problem in hand.

3.4.2.3 Chemical alteration of archaeological materials

In odd circumstances it has been felt that the only means whereby an archaeological artefact can be stabilized is to change its constitution. Examples are the firing of unbaked clay (section 4.5.6.2) and the reduction of corrosion products to metal (section 5.2.6.2). In these cases the shape and original surface of the artefact is preserved, but any future analysis of the materials would not be helpful archaeologically. Careful recording before treatment is essential, and such techniques should only be used where their full impact is realized and discussed.

3.4.2.4 Reconstruction and gap filling

Reconstruction may be required simply to be able to understand and record an object or else in the longer term, to hold it together during storage or for display. Wherever possible, pieces must be bonded reversibly so that they can be taken apart at a date in the future; more accurate reconstruction, examination, or the availability of an improved adhesive all require this. Adhesives, being polymers, are[49] similar chemicals to consolidants (section 3.4.2.2), and whilst many polymers can be used as either, some have little adhesive power and others make poor consolidants. Like consolidants, some adhesives are resoluble, setting by loss of solvent (thermoplastics), whilst others are not since they set by a chemical reaction (thermosets). For most porous materials, solvent adhesives are suitable and adequate; they are usually supplied in organic solvents, but water-based ones and emulsions are available too. On dense materials, especially where surfaces are smooth, solvents are unable to evaporate from an adhesive and the polymer finds difficulty in adhering to the joins. Here adhesives that set by chemical reaction have to be used which, although insoluble, can be swollen by applying solvents. Since the fabric is not porous, this swelling does no damage to the object but enables the adhesive to be picked off; thus the adhesion is reversible. Another important consideration is that the adhesive should not be stronger than the fabric to be joined (section 4.5.7), but it must adhere sufficiently well to the fabric. Where this is rough, much adhesion is obtained simply by keying, whereby adhesive and fabric interlock. Where surfaces are smooth, or a stronger join is required, the adhesive must be matched in molecular charge to that of the fabric; thus a polar material requires a polar adhesive. There are numerous other points to take into account when choosing an adhesive and they cannot all be explored here. Below are a few of the most available adhesives, with an outline of their drawbacks.

The most easily available resoluble adhesive in a handy tube is cellulose nitrate (HMG waterproof adhesive, Durofix, Universal cement, Duco cement, UHU Hart) but unfortunately it has some unwanted properties.[50] An alternative is solvent-based polyvinyl acetate (e.g. UHU), but this has a tendency to allow joins to sag or to run out of a join in hot weather and to pick up dirt (plate 3.19). More recently, attention has turned to using acrylic resins as adhesives[51] and one in particular (Paraloid B72) is now becoming more readily available in handy tubes. As with consolidants, these solvent-based adhesives will not adhere to wet or damp materials, and in such cases must be replaced by emulsions or water-based adhesives. In the past, white polyvinyl acetate emulsion with all its drawbacks (section 3.4.2.2), and animal glue (gelatin) which tends to shrink badly on drying, have been widely used. Details on how resoluble adhesives are applied are given for ceramics in section 4.5.8.3, but these apply to most archaeological materials.

The epoxies form one of the largest groups of commercially available reaction adhesives (Araldite, Ablebond, Plastogen EP, Epotek, Thermoset). Polyesters comprise a second group whose members, like the epoxies, vary enormously in physical characteristics and ageing qualities. Before any is used, advice should be sought from a specialist.

Gap filling may be an essential part of reconstruction, simply in order to get pieces to hold together. Suitable agents for gap filling are given in the following chapters in relation to specific archaeological materials. It is a difficult task to carry out well, and should only be practised where absolutely necessary either to make the reconstruction possible or to make the object stable for handling and storage. Gap filling for display is discussed below (section 3.4.3).

3.4.3   Presentation for display

Conservation for display requires time; it involves some further techniques not required for publication and storage, and is carried out only after the type of consultation described in chapter 1. The level of cleaning and gap filling required becomes apparent only when it has been ascertained *why* the artefact is to be displayed. Is this for aesthetic reasons, to illustrate a type, to demonstrate a technology, to provide

Plate 3.19 Pick-up of dirt demonstrated by an adhesive: note intense darkening where adhesive is smeared over the surface of a stone stele

atmosphere for a complex display, or what? At this stage it is as well to remember that decayed archaeological material can rarely be cleaned to appear as it did originally, whether 'originally' is taken to mean when newly made, when in use, or prior to being discarded. If accretions of decay are removed, the remaining core is usually disfigured, miscoloured, and blurred in detail. Moreover it must be remembered that, if encrusting salt deposits or corrosion crusts are removed, this entails loss of evidence for future study as well as possible leaching of chemicals from the original fabric. Not only does 'overcleaning' affect the aesthetic appearance of an object, so can its finish. A smooth surface reflects light evenly and thus appears shiny; also its colour is often more obvious as the discontinuities in the surface which diffuse the light are obliterated. In archaeological conservation, such a finish is rarely made by polishing since this interferes with the original surface, but it may be achieved by adding a resoluble lacquer containing a matting agent to reduce glare.

Where gaps are to be filled, care is taken regarding the visual effect of the filled area. There should be no attempt to deceive the close observer as to which areas have been filled, but in general a fill should not detract from the overall unity of an object when viewed at a short distance. Thus the general tone and light reflectance should be similar, but more precise matching will depend on the nature and role of the particular artefact and on the ethical and aesthetic judgement of those involved with the display.

Before deciding how artefacts which are to go on display are to be stabilized, the environmental conditions prevailing are discussed; if the materials involved are particularly sensitive, then the conditions will have to be controlled, a demand which must be realized at an early stage of exhibition design. Attention is paid not only to relative humidity, temperature, light, and dust, but also to gaseous pollution which could arise from fumes given off by display materials such as paints and adhesives (section 3.4.1.5). At an early stage the method of fixing objects in their display positions is discussed in order to minimize stresses on the objects or to provide them with extra support where necessary.

Since archaeological material rarely appears as it may be supposed to have looked during use, it is more satisfactory to build a replica of the artefact at this stage in its existence than to attempt to 'restore' the original to this appearance, thereby grossly interfering with artefactual evidence. Another reason for the manufacture of replicas is that it assists in the interpretation and understanding of the technology of ancient artefacts.[52] Care must be taken when a replica is placed too near an original, for the new material may often detract wildly from the appearance of the old and vice versa. On occasions replicas have to be substituted for an original, for it may be impossible to control the environmental conditions sufficiently to display the latter; the demands both on control of conditions and security made by a polyester/fibre glass or electrotype replica are much less than those made by an original. Such a substitution should always be declared.

3.5 Composite artefacts

Sometimes archaeological artefacts requiring treatment are made of two contrasting materials, such as an iron knife with a bone handle or a glass window quarry with a lead came attached. Very often these contrasting materials require very different methods of cleaning but more especially of stabilization. In some cases the artefact can be dismantled into the two

93

parts which are then treated separately. More usually this is impossible, or would destroy information, and the materials have to be treated together. A decision has to be made as to whether a compromise is attempted or whether one material, being the more sensitive, must be stabilized correctly and the other one must suffer the same treatment. It is hoped that if composites are retrieved on excavation, with the information contained in this book the correct decision for immediate passive stabilization can be reached.

3.6 Recording

Any treatment given to an artefact, however apparently trivial, is recorded; this includes details of lifting methods, methods of examination together with observations, methods of cleaning together with what is removed, and finally stabilization and restoration. Techniques which have failed must be recorded as well as those which succeed.

There are three major reasons why records are kept. The first is to provide information for archaeological/scientific study of a particular artefact both for current publication and future research. Good recording makes explicit the nature of the evidence which is crucial if it is to be queried in the future. The second concerns the conservation of the individual artefact. Details of environmental requirements are given to promote its long-term care but, more importantly, a description of the condition of the artefact, both before and after treatment, is included so that its stability can be monitored. Also recorded is the treatment the artefact has received in the event of it requiring re-treating in the future. The third reason is that if conservation is to continue to develop beyond a craft, it must have records. Without such a database it is not possible to draw inferences upon which to build new approaches and techniques. Therefore, not only are recording systems necessary but information retrieval systems too should be developed.

It can be seen then that records during publication, need to be available to three groups of workers, namely the archaeologist, the scientist, and the finds researcher. In the future, the curator who must care for the material, and the conservator, as well as these workers, will all require access. Information retrieval is best achieved by computerization, and in conservation in Britain steps towards this are being taken.[53] However, important study remains to be done to determine which features of an artefact and its treatment it is crucial to record and how this is best achieved using computerization. Thus record cards/envelopes are likely to be used for some time to come. Such cards are kept with the objects at all times whilst the laboratory which performed the treatment keeps a copy.

The record of treatment of an object includes a description of it and details of its condition before treatment; a photograph of this state can often prove extremely useful as treatment proceeds. Next are details of examination and observations, preferably illustrated with photographs or at least diagrams. Methods of investigative cleaning detailing what has been removed and techniques of stabilization follow. Next a note on the appearance and condition of the object after treatment and finally details of the requirements for environmental control, including handling, are given. If artefacts are treated in the field either by basic lifting techniques, cleaning, or stabilizing procedures then these *must* be noted and the record handed on to the treating laboratory; damage can ensue, techniques fail, or evidence be misinterpreted if early treatment is not known.

3.7   New directions

Working in archaeological conservation, it often seems as though in the past ten years more techniques of conservation have been dismissed than have been developed. This is a result of the changing approach to the specialism and the lack of resources for research into new methods. To compound this, before new methods of conservation can be researched the reason why a material has decayed or is decaying must be investigated; it is here that at present the most effort is being made. Moreover, new techniques may be at the mercy of the manufacturer, for whilst it may be possible to detail the requirements of a consolidant for a particular job, for example, more often than not it is not financially rewarding to a company to manufacture it, demand being so comparatively slight.

Whilst some strides *have* been made in the recent past, radiography and freeze-drying for example, new techniques for lifting, investigation, cleaning, and stabilization are desperately needed. Ideas may come from the fields of polymer chemistry, civil engineering, radiation physics, soil biology, materials science, amongst many others, but all must be tempered by the fragility and the uniqueness of the material of archaeology.

3.8   Summary of the tasks of the non-specialist in conservation

This summary draws together information from the general chapters 1, 2, and 3, as well as problems related to specific materials described in later chapters. From these chapters it extracts current instructions for the non-specialist, but of course some of these instructions could become outdated as techniques develop.

3.8.1   Pre-excavation

3.8.1.1   Liaison (section 1.3)

The director of a planned excavation should make arrangements beforehand with the conservation laboratory that will treat the materials, the owner of the finds, and the museum that will be responsible eventually for the finds. At the planning meeting the following should be brought to the attention of those concerned:

(a)   the nature of the site;
(b)   the type of material likely to be excavated;
(c)   the volume of material likely to be excavated;
(d)   the condition of material likely to be excavated;
(e)   the type of long-term-storage facilities to be made available;
(f)   the proposed long-term owner of the finds and requirements for display;
(g)   any published material available from earlier excavations;
(h)   guidelines for on-site conservation techniques relevant to the planned excavation.

3.8.1.2   Personnel (section 1.3)

Where there is no conservator on the excavation, one person, ideally the finds assistant, must be made responsible for on-site conservation. This conservation supervisor should have a basic knowledge of conservation and, before departure, should liaise with the conservator who will supply detailed on-site conservation instructions.

Arrangements should be made for a conservator to attend the excavation in an emergency or full-time if the planning meeting decides that the site warrants it.

3.8.1.3   Conservation materials, services, and space requirements

For all sites (including wet sites and marine sites):

(a)   Equipment to maintain dampness of materials still *in situ* (section 3.4.1.1).
(b)   Simple lifting equipment (section 3.1.1.1).
(c)   Cleaning/washing equipment for robust materials, mainly ceramics (sections 3.3.2.1 and 4.5.8.1). An area for this must be allocated and a reasonable supply of water arranged.
(d)   Marking equipment (section 3.2).
(e)   Reconstruction materials for ceramics (section 4.5.8.3) plus bench space and light.
(f)   Protected area for storage of packed artefacts and flammable

conservation materials such as adhesives, solvents, and some lifting materials.

(g)   Packing materials. Packing should aim to provide:

a high degree of protection so as to preserve the *chemical* and *physical* stability of the excavated artefact whether dry, damp, or wet (section 3.4.1);

a system which is robust and long-lasting (section 3.4.1), and which can continue to be used both in the laboratory and during long-term storage (section 1.3);

a label which is also robust and long-lasting (section 3.2) and which can be used for *all* excavation and post-excavation data (section 1.3).

(h)   If silica gel is to be reactivated for desiccated storage (section 3.4.1.1), an oven heating to 105°C will be required.

(i)   If finds are to be stored damp on-site for several weeks, access to a large refrigerator is useful (section 3.4.1.2).

(j)   If a conservator is on site full time he/she will require bench space with good light and storage space for conservation materials. He/she will also probably need an electricity supply to illuminate a microscope; batteries or a generator might prove sufficient.

(k)   Recording system for information concerning the on-site treatment of artefacts (section 3.6).

(l)   Suitable transport for packed materials to a laboratory should be planned.

For sites expected to produce waterlogged organic materials (section 2.2.2.3):

(m)   A more elaborate system to maintain dampness *in situ* (section 6.2.8).

(n)   A good supply of water and space for washing finds and for filling storage containers (section 6.2.8).

(o)   If large waterlogged timbers are expected, temporary tanks should be planned on site if possible (section 6.2.6.1).

(p)   Equipment for recording waterlogged timbers (section 6.2.8).

For marine or salty sites (section 2.2.1.5):

(q)   Specialized lifting equipment for marine sites (section 3.1.1.2).

(r)   Tanks for desalting and for storing waterlogged materials (sections 3.4.1.1 and 3.4.2.1).

(s)   A good supply of water fresher than that of the burial deposit for washing and desalting.

(t)   Equipment to test for end point of desalination (section 3.4.2.1).

97

3.8.2   On site

3.8.2.1   Liaison and safety

The conservation supervisor (section 3.8.1.2) should oversee the day-to-day retrieval, treatment, packing, and final transport of artefacts; and should liaise with the conservator, calling him/her out when necessary. If a large complex artefact is uncovered, a meeting of all those interested (sections 1.3 and 3.1.1) should be arranged.

All personnel on site should be made aware of the requirements for *in situ* conservation; delay between the exposure of material at risk and its delivery to the finds processing area should be minimized (section 3.4.1.1).

Attention must be paid to the health and safety warnings which accompany certain conservation materials both when these are in store or in use (e.g. sections 3.1.1.1, 3.4.2.2, 3.8.1.3, and 4.5.8.3).

3.8.2.2   *In situ* processes

(a)   On land sites, where necessary, the maintenance of dampness of exposed materials immediately and continuously (section 3.4.1.1).

(b)   Retrieval of finds with reasonable amount of deposit adhering to them (section 3.1.1); that is, not brushed or rubbed clean.

(c)   Simple lifting techniques (sections 3.1.1.1 and 3.1.1.2) for fragile or complex artefacts.

(d)   Retrieval of soil samples for comparison with vessel contents etc. (section 3.1.1).

(e)   Recording of complex finds prior to lifting (section 3.1.1).

(f)   Maintenance of water content of material at risk between removal from the deposit and delivery to the finds processing area (section 3.4.1.1). At marine sites there must be no delay between retrieval and storage immersion.

(g)   Measurement and recording of conditions of deposits for use in material decay studies (sections 1.2 and 3.1.3).

3.8.2.3   Preservation processes (section 3.4.1)

Stabilization of material to prevent its disintegration, by correct storage controlling the environment of the material, must begin as soon as possible after retrieval; this applies to artefacts lifted with simple techniques as well as without. Discussion of the requirements for storage for particular materials is given in the following chapters and the details of technique to achieve these can be found in section 3.4.1. But since badly controlled storage can be worse than no control at all, storage techniques *must* be properly carried out; a résumé of the methods most commonly advocated today is given below.

MARINE FINDS. All materials in the first instance must be stored by immersion (see wet storage below) but attention must be paid to the salinity of the preliminary storage bath (section 4.5.8.2).

WET STORAGE. Material is immersed in water in rustproof containers with close-fitting lids (section 6.2.6.1). These containers may be large temporary tanks with polyethylene sheeting skimming the surface or small polypropylene boxes with lids which are readily portable. Biocides may or may not be advised. Labelling must be with good-quality waterproof materials.

DAMP STORAGE. Material is *sealed* in watertight containers ·with or without excess water added. Containers may be in the form of a triple layer of polyethylene self-sealing bags, polyethylene tubing, heat-sealed or hermetically sealing polypropylene boxes. The essentials are that the container *must* be watertight and rustproof. Before sealing excess air must be displaced from the containers which should then be stored in a cool place or in a refrigerator. Before a biocide is used, a conservator should be consulted.

DRY STORAGE. Here no attempt is made to retain moisture in the material. Damp material is allowed to dry in air and then placed in *unsealed* containers such as loosely closed polyethylene bags, linen bags, or cardboard boxes to allow dry air to circulate. They must be stored in a *dry* area or they will take up moisture again.

DESICCATED STORAGE. All water is removed from the material by use of a desiccating agent, normally silica gel. To prevent the gel taking up moisture from the air it must be *sealed* together with the material in an airtight container such as a hermetically sealed polypropylene box; polyethylene bags are not suitable here. Care must be taken to ensure that the gel is dry in the first instance and is exchanged for fresh gel when it has taken up moisture. This change is usually monitored by a colour change from blue to pink but is better measured by humidity strips. Damp gel is reactivated in an oven at 105°C.

PADDING AND LABELLING. To prevent physical disruption, materials must be well padded especially during transportation. In the case of wet/damp storage, padding must be rotproof as must the label. Inks for labelling in all types of storage must be non-fading. The type of material (namely iron, ceramics, etc.) should be clearly recorded on the containers to avoid unwanted opening, to aid sorting, and to make sure that they are correctly stored/treated.

3.8.2.4   Other processes

(a)   Further stabilization. Marine finds (and those from salty sites) may be desalted on site and then stored damp, dry, or desiccated for transportation.

(b)   Cleaning. This is restricted to robust ceramics and some waterlogged materials, especially timbers. On no account should metals be cleaned on site (section 5.1.4).

(c)   Marking should be discreet and non-destructive to the artefact (section 3.2).

(d)   Reconstruction of ceramics should only be practised *if essential*, and if done well; otherwise damage is done and time wasted at a later date (section 4.5.8.3).

(e)   Recording. Any treatment carried out on an object should be recorded (sections 1.3 and 3.6). Large waterlogged timbers should be examined and recorded after cleaning but before storage (section 6.2.8).

(f)   Transportation of material to the conservation laboratory should immediately follow the end of the excavation. Where the season is long, an intermediate delivery should be made. Any records should accompany the material.

3.8.3   *Post-excavation*

(a)   Liaison (section 1.3). Maximum discussion between excavator, museum curator, finds specialists, and conservator should be sought before and during conservation treatment. Agreement about the date when materials are required for illustration and when publication is planned must be reached at an early stage.

Material is categorized, by collaboration, according to the levels of conservation required. Whilst this process is in itself time-consuming, it maximizes resources in the long run.

The conservation record card, radiographs, and photographs should be made available to all those involved in publication, e.g. illustrator, finds specialists, etc.

(b)   Care of material. During the publication process, material not as yet stabilized by active techniques must be given the greatest care; all who handle it must be made aware of its inherent instability and ensure that the correct environment for the material is maintained. This material should be checked at regular intervals by both the finds supervisor or the excavator and the conservator.

(c)   Publication. Illustrations should note how they have been arrived at (i.e. with/without radiographs, if wet or dry (e.g. sections 5.2.3

and 6.3.3)). Reference should be made to conservation work (section 1.3) in the publication.

3.8.4 Long-term storage and display

See sections 1.3 and 3.4.1.

(a) Before a museum receives archaeological material, its storage must reach certain standards.

(b) Before material is deposited with a museum, it should have been divided into storage categories by a conservator.

(c) Early consultation between designer and conservator is essential when an exhibition or a new storage area is planned.

(d) Material must be handled with care to avoid a loss of evidence and/or a waste of money.

(e) Resources must be found for continuing monitoring of material both in storage and on display.

Chapter Four

Siliceous and related materials

4.1 General

Materials as diverse as glass and painted plaster are grouped together in this chapter; they are basically inorganic compounds derived from the minerals of the earth's crust. Since silica forms 28 per cent of this crust a high proportion of silica is found in these materials. Artefacts can be made simply by shaping the raw materials or more elaborately with the use of heat or chemical reactions. Even after such treatment the materials are chemically and physically similar to the naturally occurring minerals, and so weather and decay as these do.

4.1.1 Nature of materials

Materials in this group are crystalline and/or glassy and are brittle; they range from extremely porous to exceedingly dense and from soft to very hard. The materials can be subdivided by composition into two groups: those based on silica and those based on calcium.

Silica is the dioxide of silicon (SiO_2); it occurs in a variety of mineral forms both crystalline (quartz and cristobalite) and, with water, cryptocrystalline (flint, chalcedony, agate, onyx, etc.). With the oxides of the alkali metals, alkaline earths, and some metals amongst which aluminium is of prime importance, silica forms both crystalline silicates, such as the clay minerals, feldspars, garnets, etc., and manufactured and natural glasses (obsidian). The two most important compounds based on calcium are its carbonate, which can form the mineral calcite ($CaCO_3$), and its sulphate, forming gypsum ($CaSO_4.2H_2O$).

As raw materials, these minerals are found as undefined masses known as rocks. Rocks may be composed simply of one mineral such as quartzite (quartz) or marble (calcite) or of a mixture of minerals, for example granites, clays, sandstones, limestones, etc.

If these raw materials need to be heated to make artefacts, dehydrated forms, altered crystal formations, glasses, or decomposition products, stable or otherwise, are produced, all of which have similar forms to naturally occurring materials.

4.1.2 Deterioration[1]

Since many of these materials when shaped into artefacts are unaltered from the state in which they have existed in the earth's crust for thousands of years, whilst others which have been heated form similar materials, it is not surprising that relatively little deterioration during burial occurs. However, because they are often buried in environments which are very different from those in which they were formed and since natural geological weathering will continue, decay of some sort takes place.

Many of these materials are chemically stable, so the main type of decay is physical with perhaps breakage due to their brittleness being the most obvious. Probably the most notorious damage is due to soluble salts. Since many of the materials in this group are porous, when a soil dries out, they retain water within their capillaries long after it has left the bulk of the soil and so dissolved salts tend to concentrate in the bodies of these materials. When the solution in the pores finally dries out either during burial or after excavation, the salts crystallize (plate 4.1). Damage occurs where the salt solution is so concentrated that the crystals fill up the pores exerting, as they grow, enormous pressure on the walls of the pores. Greater and even more damaging pressure occurs if the humidity now rises again, for the salts hydrate, taking water into their crystal structure without dissolving. This volume increase produces pressures of hundreds if not thousands of atmospheres. Such damage may be very rapid, for example Na_2SO_4 hydrates to $Na_2SO_4.1OH_2O$ in twenty minutes, needing only a very slight rise in relative humidity. If the RH now drops slightly, the water given out by the dehydrating crystals can also cause pressure damage. If the RH fluctuates, these pressures are recurrent and very damaging. The build-up of salts and ensuing damage tends to occur at the surface of material since each time the air dries, the salts are dragged to the surface in the retreating capillary front. Surface damage is even more marked where there is a moisture barrier, whether a burnished surface, paint, or glaze on pottery, or a paint or wax layer on plaster or stone. Here exceedingly high salt concentrations build up under these layers as they are unable to move out onto the surface. In fact, if all salt is brought out *onto* the surface, as may happen in slow drying of a very porous material, the crystals may cause no damage.

While salt damage could occur during burial, it is more likely to be excessive after excavation when the ambient RH falls and is allowed to

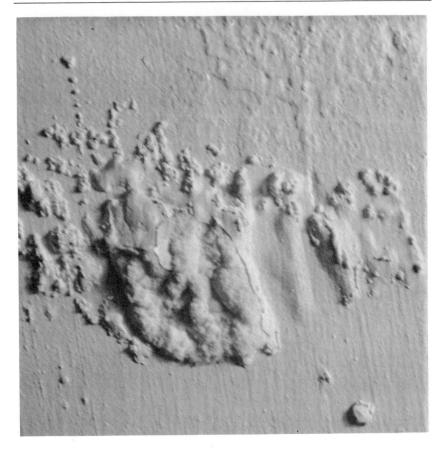

Plate 4.1   Crystals of soluble salts pushing off a surface layer of paint

fluctuate more widely than usually occurs in the ground. High levels of salt may not only result from salt-laden soils, they may develop after excavation by exposure to sea winds, cleaning chemicals, or contact with the ground during storage, etc.

Similar damage is caused by the expansion of water as it freezes inside porous materials exposed to frost. This only occurs where the fabric has large pores and is nearly saturated; ice will not form in tiny capillaries and, unless reasonably wet, the ice expansion is absorbed by the unfilled portion of the pores. Again, damage is worse where the expansion is recurrent as in a freeze/thaw climate.

These siliceous and related porous fabrics are liable to become encrusted with white/grey insoluble salts (section 2.2.1.5), normally

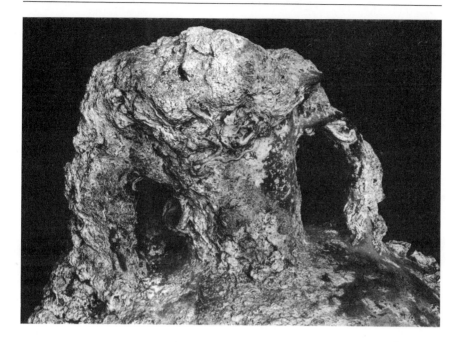

Plate 4.2 Encrustations of calcium carbonate on an amphora formed by organisms and chemical precipitation in the sea

calcium carbonate, sulphate, or silicate, during burial. Several factors contribute to this: as shown above, the surface of a porous body in the soil is the last refuge for water in a drying soil and so salts barely in solution in the soil will precipitate here, causing a crust to build up; leached calcium from a deteriorating artefact may be reprecipitated here as it encounters the soil water/air interface; furthermore, a glaze provides a cool surface within the soil which could allow dew to form, leading to localized dissolution and precipitation of salts. Obscuring encrustations are also likely on artefacts from warm seas where calcium carbonate precipitates (see below) and marine organisms flourish (plate 4.2) (section 4.5.2). Finally, if material is very decayed, water may in fact be holding it together. This is especially true of frail painted surfaces and soft pottery. Drying out on excavation may lead to powdering and crumbling of such materials compounded by the compacting of drying clay (section 4.3.1.1).

Chemical decay of silicates is usually slow, being restricted to dissolution, which is enhanced by alkaline conditions. Calcium carbonate too dissolves only slowly but this is greatly enhanced by cool temperatures and by a low pH or high carbon dioxide levels (section 2.2.1.3).

$$\text{normal conditions} \quad CaCO_3 \text{ (s)} + H_2O \xrightarrow{\text{slow}} Ca^{2+} + HCO_3^- + OH^-$$
$$\text{low pH} \quad CaCO_3 \text{ (s)} + H^+ \rightarrow Ca^{2+} + HCO_3^-$$
$$\text{high } CO_2 \text{ levels} \quad CaCO_3 \text{ (s)} + H_2CO_3 \rightarrow Ca^{2+} + 2HCO_3^-$$

Biological attack is usually slight except where the roots of higher plants damage porous materials into which they penetrate.

4.1.3 Conservation

The original surfaces of artefacts made from these materials are retained either in the original material or as a weathering crust; cleaning involves the removal of soil and encrustations. Chemicals for cleaning are avoided wherever possible partly because the materials are often so similar chemically to the encrustations that they would be damaged by the treatment and partly because the dissolution of encrustations and the application of the chemicals themselves introduce soluble salts into the porous fabrics. Dry, porous, but dirty fabrics are never soaked in order to clean them since this drives soil etc. into the core of the fabric from whence it is difficult to remove. Care is taken to avoid trapping any cleaning agents, whether these be cotton wool fibres or absorbent pack materials (3.4.2.1) such as Sepiolite, on rough surfaces; when applying Sepiolite, a release layer of soft tissue is used. Stabilization to prevent damage from soluble salts can be carried out by environmental control, but if active treatment is required it is necessary to reduce the level of salt contamination by desalination techniques (section 3.4.2.1). Consolidation of weakened fabrics is often carried out and reconstruction of broken artefacts, notably pottery, is probably where 'conservation' historically began.

4.2 Stone

4.2.1 Nature of materials[2]

Stone artefacts are cut from rocks which are usually hard, reasonably inert, and with a varying degree of porosity. They are classified by their manner of geological formation which gives some idea of the degree of this hardness, stability, and porosity.

Igneous rocks are formed when molten material cools down, producing dense networks of crystals. They take many centuries to weather, being relatively inert. The most important minerals involved are quartz (SiO_2) and the complex silicates of feldspars, hornblende, and micas, all of which except for the latter are very hard. They are found either pure as in precious gems, for example amethyst (SiO_2) and garnet (alumino-silicates), or in mixtures of intermeshed crystals, for example granite and basalt. If the molten material cooled quickly, glass such as obsidian or pumice might have formed.

Sedimentary rocks consist of individual minerals which are caused to cohere, either by pressure which welds them at their surfaces, or by cementing material deposited around them. They are thus less dense than igneous rocks. Sandstone, for example, consists of quartz and feldspar welded together and cemented by silicates, carbonates, or iron oxides. Limestone is extremely variable, consisting of either inorganic calcite or organic carbonate from shells and skeletons, welded and cemented together with further calcium carbonate, magnesium carbonate, silicate, or clay. Alabaster is a form of gypsum ($CaSO_4.2H_2O$) and flint is minutely crystalline silica (SiO_2). Clays are composed of decomposed feldspars and, because water can penetrate between the crystals, they become plastic when wet (section 4.5.1.1). Shales on the other hand are made of similar minerals which remain non-plastic when wet. They are all relatively soft rocks.

Finally there are the metamorphic rocks which are sedimentary rocks that have been altered by extremes of temperature and pressure; these cause recrystallization resulting in an intermeshing of crystals and thus less porous rock. Quartzite is metamorphosed sandstone, marble is from limestone, and slate from shales and calcareous clays; as such, they are reasonably dense hard rocks. The exception is steatite or soapstone ($Mg_3[Si_4O_{10}]OH_2$) which is very soft but can be fired rather like clay.

During manufacture into stone artefacts, rock is simply shaped; the exception is clays, which are dealt with separately as ceramics.

Stone in buildings is usually associated with adhesive materials (section 4.3) such as mortar and plaster. In other artefacts, for example mortaria or statuary, metals may be associated in the form of old mends or dowels deep inside the object. Painting or gilding of statuary and even walls is common; this can be directly upon the stone or after a coat of size, red or white lead ground, gesso (section 4.3.1.2), or lime for example. Marble statuary may even be waxed to give an impression of flesh. In the case of gems, weapons, and tools, traces of the adhesives by which they were fixed to brooches, hafts, etc. may remain. Tiny traces may remain of how stone artefacts were used, for example, metal filings trapped in the surface crevices of a hone stone.

4.2.2 Nature of decayed stone[3]

The scope of this book is restricted to excavated artefacts and to movable ones at that, so the decay of stone in exposed standing buildings is not considered.

DETERIORATION BEFORE BURIAL. Marbles and to some extent even limestones can obtain a translucent white/tinted patina by long exposure to rain; carbonic acid from the carbon dioxide in rain-water slightly dissolves the surface calcite which then recrystallizes, giving a glossy surface. Such patinas on marble statuary are much prized. Great heat can cause marble to distort as a result of uneven crystal expansion or even begin to crumble into 'sugar' as the calcite crystal network is destroyed.

It is well-known that stone often appears red when burnt. This is a result of the oxidation of iron, present in many rocks, to form red haematite (αFe_2O_3).

GOOD CONDITION. It is not surprising that many stone artefacts appear to be and are in extremely good condition upon excavation, since they are relatively dense and inert. However, some stone may appear to be in good condition but in fact be much decayed. Shale from waterlogged deposits is a case in point. Apart from compressed clay minerals, shale often contains calcite, pyrite (FeS_2) and carbonaceous organic material, the particles being deposited in layers. During waterlogging there is a leaching of constituents which is masked by the presence of water.

Flints during burial in a variety of deposits may develop transparent patinas but in deposits of pH > 10, a white crust forms.[4]

POWDERING OR CRUMBLING OF STONE OFTEN OF THE SURFACE ONLY. This is akin to geological weathering, being a result of frost action, salt infestation, and dissolution (section 4.1.2). It is a common problem in relatively unstable, porous, sedimentary rocks. Only in very salty dry sites will crystals of salt be visible upon excavation and then they may be actually holding the decayed stone together.

A low pH will attack carbonates and iron oxides and leach feldspars; thus marble may become roughened, sandstone fall into sand grains, limestone and steatite soften. Calcareous stones are also attacked by high carbon dioxide levels (section 4.1.2) and so become roughened in soft ground waters. Pyrite or marcasite (FeS_2) found in shale and in other sedimentary stone may oxidize in damp oxygenated deposits, causing the pH to fall and thus endangering other components of the stone.

Since iron expands when it corrodes, the presence of any ferrous dowels within statuary will cause shattering of the neighbouring areas of stone as the iron reacts with air and water.

DISCOLORATION. Pale porous stone, especially marble and alabaster, is readily stained by copper, iron, or organic oils from a deposit. In deposits with low redox potentials, it is possible for the pink coloration of stone given by iron(III) to be reduced to the grey coloration of iron(II) on exposed surfaces.

DETERIORATION IN MARINE CONDITIONS. In addition to the types of deterioration described above, stone from marine sites may have surfaces which have been severely abraded owing to erosion by sea-water and particles such as sand grains. Such exposed stone may provide a substrate attractive to encrusting organisms like bryozoans and barnacles. Most of these are harmless but some, such as the stone-boring clam and the stone piddock, attack soft and calcareous stone, causing damage similar to shipworm attack in wood (section 6.2.2.4).

4.2.3 Examination

Before any small stone artefact is washed, it is examined minutely for any trace of associated material (section 4.2.1). Likewise, statuary and building stone, especially carved pieces, are examined for limewash, paint, gilding or gesso before and during cleaning; the use of UV light or IR photography can be helpful here (plate 4.3). UV light also helps distinguish modern from ancient breaks in marble and this can be useful in reconstruction. X-radiography will reveal the presence of dowels and cracks and the extent of any marine borer or insect damage. Visual examination will give some idea of the state of deterioration of the stone but it is difficult to obtain an objective measurement of this without taking a sample. However, sampling of a small artefact is not possible and

Plate 4.3 Paint and gilding found on a fragment of medieval stonework during cleaning

for a larger one it can be unrepresentative. The use of the scanning electron microscope, measurement of water absorption, and comparison of the specific gravity (SG) of a sample against expected SG of the rock in question all give some idea of the state of decay of the sample. Measurement of the thermal or electrical conductivity indicates the moisture/salt content of a damp artefact.

Calcareous stone can be identified quickly since it effervesces with dilute acid and an expert can identify other types by surface examination and hardness determination; more precise description requires the preparation of thin sections.

4.2.4 Cleaning[5]

The important features of cleaning stone are first to avoid forcing dirt further into the core and second to avoid introducing yet more soluble salts into it (section 4.1.3). When dry, then, stone is cleaned wherever possible mechanically, especially with the aid of a controlled vacuum cleaner. Where dirt is particularly ingrained, wet methods have to be employed. In these cases, care is taken never to soak objects in water which drives dirt into the core; instead absorbent wet packs are applied to the surface, drawing the dirt into these. Unless carried out over the whole surface, wet cleaning is likely to result in unsightly patchiness. In the case of blackened crusts of calcium sulphate (section 4.2.5) it may be necessary to apply absorbent packs loaded with a particular chemical, for only in this way may the crusts be dissolved without damaging the stone (plate 3.11). Before it can be wet cleaned, decayed stone which is held together by water-soluble salt crystals (section 4.2.2) must be stabilized in some way (section 4.2.6.2). Chemicals and bleaches are only rarely used on stone, for they are likely to attack components of most rocks, producing soluble salts.

4.2.5 Deterioration upon excavation

POWDERING/CRUMBLING WITH POSSIBLE APPEARANCE OF WHITE EFFLORESCENCE (plate 4.4). This type of deterioration caused by soluble salts has been described in section 4.1.2 and occurs either when wet salt-laden stone is dried, or when dry salt-laden stone is subjected to a fluctuating relative humidity in poor storage. The problem is worse where an impervious layer prevents the salts moving onto the surface; the build-up of a sulphate crust (section 4.2.5) or early consolidation treatments with wax exacerbate this problem.

LAMINATION. Damp clay-rich sedimentary stone is prone to laminate on drying, shale being particularly liable (plate 4.5). During burial,

Plate 4.4 A sandstone stele many years after excavation crumbles as a result of salt action

Plate 4.5 A Roman shale ring laminating on drying out after excavation from a waterlogged deposit

cementing compound are destroyed and their place is taken by water. On drying, as for clay (section 4.5.1), shrinkage occurs which the weakened structure cannot counteract; cracks occur along the bedding planes.

SURFACE SPALLING OR DEEPER CRACKING. This may occur where wet porous stone is affected by frost (section 4.1.2). In wet conditions corrosion of iron dowels when deep inside statuary will cause splitting of the surrounding stone. The roots of ivy penetrate porous stone, expand, and crack surrounding regions too.

SURFACE ROUGHENING. Limestones and marbles will be dissolved by

Plate 4.6 An early medieval limestone baluster shaft showing blackening caused by display in a polluted atmosphere

acid (pH 4–7), polluted rainwater (section 4.2.2) roughening the surface; likewise organic acids secreted by lichens will etch.

DISCOLORATION. Previous injudicious washing may have carried surface dirt into the core of porous stone from whence it is impossible to remove. Sticky dirt and soot are not easy to remove from a surface and may actually become bonded to it; in heavily polluted environments limestone and marble react with the sulphur dioxide in the air, producing crystals of calcium sulphate which trap soot particles in a blackened surface layer (plate 4.6). Sandstones may form black siliceous layers similarly; these crusts are worse where the sandstone contains calcite as a cement. In store, stone is readily stained by corroding metal artefacts in contact with them, whilst in extremely damp environments moulds can stain and algae obscure.

4.2.6 Stabilization (see note 5)

4.2.6.1 Passive

Control of ambient relative humidity will prevent damage by soluble salts (section 4.2.5). When stone is wet, the RH is kept high to prevent crystallization of saturated solutions, and when it is dry the RH is kept low to prevent hydration of existing crystals; but most importantly it is prevented from fluctuating since it is this that causes the worst damage. Lamination of damp sedimentary stone is prevented by keeping it damp. Frost damage, surface roughening, spalling, and discoloration can all be prevented by adequate storage conditions which demand comparatively little effort.

4.2.6.2 Active

SOLUBLE SALTS. As shown in section 4.1.2, when stone has high salt concentrations damage occurs; desalination attempts to remove these salts. Since by definition such salts are soluble in water, this is the medium used to remove them, either by soaking or by use of paper pulp poultices.[6] However, problems arise where the stone is flaking or powdering and more especially when the salts are actually holding the stone together (section 4.2.5), for any dissolution will lead to crumbling of the object. This hazard would be overcome by consolidating the stone prior to soaking, but in the past this has led to salts becoming sealed in. It is to be hoped that the recently introduced silanes (see below) can be used more successfully for this purpose.

CONSOLIDATION. The main problems in achieving consolidation of stone lie in the difficulty of getting satisfactory penetration of the consolidant. This is because stone is, fundamentally, a dense material and objects are normally massive. Also the consolidant used must be very strong since stone is so heavy. Many types of consolidant have been used, one group being inorganic compounds; one recent controversial idea which appears to precipitate calcium carbonate in decayed calcareous stone is being subjected to much scrutiny.[7] Other types used include monomers polymerized in situ, epoxies, and now silanes.[8] This last group precipitate silica, itself a stone-forming mineral, within decayed stone, and have proved successful for both limestone and sandstone. It is an irreversible technique, but in reality this drawback is common even to resoluble resins when used to consolidate stone (section 3.4.2.2). Research in this area is one of the most exciting fields in conservation today.

To prevent lamination of wet shale on drying, it has been successfully consolidated with polyethylene glycol[9] but it is doubtful if this material would be any use for more dense laminating sedimentary stone. Further research on shale is to be expected in the next few years.

JOINING. Stone may be difficult to join because it is too dense to allow solvents in adhesive systems to evaporate and because the pieces are often extremely heavy and so require enormous strength in the joint. Whilst resoluble adhesives (section 3.4.2.4) may be suitable on some occasions, very often stronger chemically-setting polyesters (epoxy resins soak in too readily) and even dowels[10] have to be used. As with all adhesives, since they must not be stronger than the material they are joining, they must not be used on crumbling or powdering stone prior to its consolidation.

4.2.7 Summary

On lifting, soil or sediment is allowed to remain in contact with artefacts likely either to have been painted or gilded, or to have been used to abrade (section 4.2.1). Only hard, non-porous, undecorated stone is washed on site; any other cleaning, joining, or consolidation must be carried out in a laboratory.

Damp stone, except if it is painted or if it is shale or other clayey sedimentary rock, usually dries out safely if it is from a deposit low in soluble salts. If an artefact is in one of these restricted categories, then it is stored damp (section 3.4.1.1) until treated. It is essential that stone from marine waters is not allowed to dry out; it must be put directly into containers of water after which the process of desalting begins. In fact, desalting of damp/wet non-porous hard stone can be carried out simply by soaking in a few changes of fresh water. For softer more porous stone this is not so easy and a lengthy process may be involved in which the extraction of salts has to be carefully monitored.

Dry stone from salty deposits presents different problems; if it is held together by salt crystals, wetting will cause it to disintegrate. In this case it is *essential* that it is stored in a low, non-fluctuating RH (section 3.4.1.1).

Robust stone, and most stone that has been treated, will be able to survive long-term storage over a reasonable range of ambient relative humidities. Fragile, salty, or crusted stone, shale, and pyrite will all require closer control both of RH and temperature. Storage of all stone should be dust-free; simple draping in lightweight porous fabric is adequate for large objects.

4.3 Cementing materials and their composites

This section includes inorganic materials which act as cements and so enable mortar, plaster, stucco, concrete, mosaics, etc. to be made. Whilst the materials themselves can be defined, the composites in which they are incorporated are less precise and tend to reflect the use to which they are put rather than their composition.

4.3.1 Nature of materials

4.3.1.1 Cements

These are divided into two groups of adhesive materials: the non-hydraulic cements which only set in air, and the stronger hydraulic ones which can set under water and are therefore insoluble.

Once set, non-hydraulic cements are not absolutely water-resistant but the degree to which they are affected by water varies considerably. Clay (section 4.5.1.1) is a crude cement; upon air-drying, clay particles move together and because, being flat plates, they have enormous surface areas for their size, they adhere together. Gypsum ($CaSO_4.2H_2O$) is a stronger cement. When it is heated to about 150°C for three hours, it becomes plaster of Paris ($CaSO_4.\frac{1}{2}H_2O$). If this is mixed with water it rapidly produces small intertwined crystals of gypsum and sets to a hard mass. If gypsum is burnt to 600°C it becomes 'dead', giving a very slow-setting cement found in Parian or Keene's cement ($CaSO_4$). Lime gives a harder and much more water-resistant cement. It is burnt to 900°C to give quicklime (CaO) which is then carefully combined with water in the absence of carbon dioxide, preferably in a pit for several years, to give slaked lime ($Ca(OH)_2$). This sets first by loss of water to give intertwined crystals of $Ca(OH)_2$ and then combines slowly with CO_2 to give $CaCO_3$ again:

$$\underset{\text{lime}}{CaCO_3} \quad \overset{900°C}{\rightarrow} \quad \underset{\text{quicklime}}{CaO} \quad \overset{H_2O}{\rightarrow} \quad \underset{\text{slaked lime}}{Ca(OH)_2 \text{ paste}} \quad \overset{-H_2O}{\rightarrow} \quad Ca(OH)_2 \text{ crystals}$$

$$\overset{+CO_2}{\longrightarrow} \underset{\text{lime}}{CaCO_3}$$

Hydraulic cements are a group of hydrated calcium silicates/alumino-silicates formed slowly from water, lime, and finely divided silica or alumina; for example, $3CaO.2SiO_2.3H_2O$ (Tobermorite) and $2CaO.Al_2O_3.SiO_2.nH_2O$. The finely divided material can be found naturally in volcanic earths such as pozzolana and trass, and is present in burnt clay (section 4.5.1.1) and shales. If these are mixed with slaked lime they will give a mixture of hydraulic and non-hydraulic cement. A mixture of up to 50 per cent of the former is termed semi-hydraulic. A similar mixture results when clayey grey chalk or argillaceous limestone is burnt at 900°C. Cements containing more than 60 per cent of hydraulic material are formed when lias limestone or chalk marl is calcined (burnt).

4.3.1.2 Composites

MORTARS, CONCRETES, AND PLASTERS.[11] As noted above, the distinction between these composites is more one of the use to which they are put than of composition. Thus mortars can be seen as materials which embed more resilient ones, whilst plasters cover or protect an exposed surface. A further distinction is made: mortar should only contain inclusions of less than 5 millimetre diameter whilst concrete will have larger inclusions. Mud mortars or plasters are based mostly on clay but will probably contain some dissolved calcareous matter which will crystallize as calcite on drying. Because of their position, wall and ceiling plasters may contain fibrous matter to assist in maintaining a vertical or suspended adhering mass; daub (clay) may contain straw, and weak lime-plasters are made more resilient by the addition of hair. These and other additives such as sharp, pointed sand give body and strength to, and prevent cracking of, the cement on setting. Fast-setting plaster of Paris is often used for casting but the addition of size (gelatin) produces a harder and more waterproof surface known as gesso. In fine lime-plasters, sand is replaced by marble dust. Very often lime-mortars/plasters are semi-hydraulic either because the lime contained some clay or because pozzolana, burnt shale, or crushed/powdered tile have been added, the latter giving it a pink hue. But a well-made pure lime-plaster can itself withstand considerable wetness. When incorporated deep within a structure such as a thick stone wall, slaked lime may fail to form calcium carbonate since air is absent.

PAINTED PLASTER.[12] The plaster to which paint is applied is termed the ground which is in turn applied to the support, that is the wall, stone, etc. The ground may be homogeneous or it can be built up laboriously in several layers of diminishing coarseness until a flat surface is produced. Pigments are applied either to wet plaster (fresco) or to dry plaster (secco). In this latter case, bonding of the pigment to the plaster is achieved either by transparent organic adhesives (known as tempera) such as egg, honey, or size (gelatin) or by the use of a suspension of lime water which sets as does lime-plaster (section 4.3.1.1). Clear, robust painting on lime, true fresco, can be achieved by applying pigments to freshly applied wet plaster so that the colour is incorporated into the lime

Table 4.1 Examples of some common paint pigments

Yellow/reds/browns/purples	iron oxides	stable
Red	cinnabar/vermilion (HgS)	may go black in sunlight
	red lead (Pb$_3$O$_4$)	often browns in light
Red/purple	madder (dye)	colour affected by pH and light
Blue	indigo/woad (dyes)	colour affected by pH and light
	azurite (2CuCo$_3$.Cu(OH)$_2$)	stable except in acidic pH
	lapis lazuli	stable except in acidic pH
	Egyptian blue	very stable
Green	green earth (iron silicate)	very stable
	malachite (CuCO$_3$.Cu(OH)$_2$)	stable except in acidic pH
	verdigris (copper acetate)	unstable, may blacken
Blue-black	charcoal	very stable
Black	lampblack	very stable
White	lime white (CaCO$_3$)	stable except in acidic pH
	lead white (2PbCO$_3$.Pb(OH)$_2$)	unstable if impure or in acidic pH

crystals as they form when the plaster sets; details in tempera may be painted over this. It is probable that pigments applied to the walls of limestone caves are bound by a natural mechanism similar to the fresco technique.

Pigments obtained from organic sources, especially purples and blues, are discoloured in an alkaline pH as occurs in true fresco. Other pigments discolour for a variety of reasons. There is no intention here of giving an exhaustive discussion of the composition and range of pigments for there are numerous texts on this topic,[12] but table 4.1 indicates some of the limitations of common pigments.

FLOOR MOSAICS.[13] Whilst mosaics can be found on walls, they are more common as pavements. For a tesselated pavement to remain intact as the subsoil compacts, it must have good foundations to absorb this movement. Improved weathering is achieved by using semi-hydraulic adhesives and thus crushed tile is usually added to the grouting and mortar. The top surface may be finally polished, for it is extremely important that the surface be smooth since uneven tesserae wear badly. Of course, actual construction can differ widely from the theoretical (figure 4.1). Many tesserae used in floor mosaics are varieties of stone which give a range of colours. However, earthenware (terracotta) (section 4.5.1.1) and glass are other materials commonly used.

TILED AREAS. This section covers ceramic tiles set into a mortar; whilst the materials involved are similar to those of floor mosaics, the construction is usually far less complex and the tiles may well be glazed.

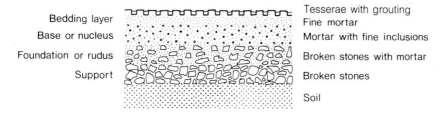

Bedding layer	Tesserae with grouting Fine mortar
Base or nucleus	Mortar with fine inclusions
Foundation or rudus	Broken stones with mortar
Support	Broken stones
	Soil

Figure 4.1 Theoretical structure of a mosaic pavement

4.3.2 *Nature of deteriorated material*

CRUMBLING/POWDERING. In damp soils it is extremely likely that cementing materials will soften. Clay absorbs water, gypsum and slaked lime dissolve slowly, whilst lime and alumino-silicates are very slowly decomposed, all leading to a powdering or crumbling of the composite. Hair and straw will rot out, weakening plasters. If a composite material was poorly made initially, deterioration will be more obvious; if a sand in plaster is too fine or smooth there will not be enough bite and crumbling results; likewise if an aggregate is too large and the cement cannot cover it; if slaking was incomplete, blisters caused by $Ca(OH)_2$ formation may occur. Plaster or mortar burnt *in situ* can lead to quicklime formation if the temperature was high enough; the subsequent slaking can be disruptive. Mosaics lying a few centimetres beneath the ground are particularly sensitive to stubble fires where the heat breaks up the tesserae and cement. Since most of these composites are porous, damage by soluble salts or frost may occur (section 4.1.2).

CONCRETIONS. Coatings of insoluble salts (section 4.1.2) which may even have been formed before burial are often found over the surface of paint or mosaics; decaying calcareous mortar/plaster contribute to these.

HARDENING. Burning prior to or during burial will 'fire' clays, turning them into ceramic; daub when covering wattle is particularly prone to this. Insoluble salts (section 4.1.2) may deposit within the base or foundation of a mosaic, acting as a cement and making them harder than before.

DISCOLORATION. Before burial, pigments may discolour in light (section 4.3.1.2) turning them lighter or darker, and during burial further discoloration by dissolution, chemical reaction, fire, or pH change may occur. Tempera pigments are likely to become dislodged by abrasion or even soluble salts, leaving a thin trace on the plaster beneath; in fact a whole thin paint layer can easily be lost. Staining of these pale porous materials by iron or bacteria is likely.

SETTLEMENT. If the ground underneath a mosaic pavement falls away by the collapse of pre-existing post-holes for example, the mosaic will settle into it, becoming distorted but remaining coherent unless the mortar is too brittle, in which case cracking results (plate 4.7).

4.3.3 Examination

Visual examination will reveal much concerning the condition of the material and the presence or absence of paint. A raking light, UV light, or IR photography may assist in locating the position of lost tempera. Examination of the reverse of plaster and daub is extremely important, determining the type of wall/ceiling to which it was affixed, and to assist in reconstruction if this is required. Analysis for conservation in the case of painting will involve determining the method of paint attachment; this may include identification of the type of ground and pigments used. This can be done to some extent by simple wet chemical analysis and visual inspection of a section of plaster under a microscope. This visual analysis will also assist in determining the inclusions added to a cement, but for precise identification it may be necessary to make thin sections for petrological examination or to take samples for destructive physical/ chemical analysis.[14] For comparative study of plasters and mortars, it is still not clear as to what exactly are the best parameters to measure; straight chemistry does not distinguish cement from additives and dissolution during burial will also obscure the original recipe. Thus most work is carried out on the acid-insoluble portion of composites (alumino-silicates, silicates, clay, heavy minerals).

4.3.4 Cleaning

Dirt and salt encrustations are much easier to remove from these materials whilst they are still damp; once they dry out, the dirt and encrustations become very hard and may pull off a surface. Except with great care, chemicals cannot be used to remove encrustations since the chemicals will dissolve the cementing material as well as the encrustation, both of which are very similar chemically. Salts therefore are normally scraped off mechanically. Cleaning a flaking tempera paint surface is a highly skilled job requiring a steady hand, magnification, and patience.

Plate 4.7 Settlement of a Roman mosaic pavement caused by collapse of the subsoil

4.3.5 Deterioration upon excavation

CRUMBLING, FLAKING WITH/WITHOUT APPEARANCE OF WHITE EFFLORESCENCE. Since the materials are porous, when removed from a salt-laden soil, destruction by soluble salts may follow (section 4.1.2). This is particularly noticeable in painted tempera plaster because the salts may force the whole paint layer off; terracotta tesserae in mosaics are also vulnerable, being soft and porous. Where a composite has been badly weakened during burial, on drying it can crumble, revealing this damage; salts may not necessarily be involved.

HARDENING. As damp material dries out it may harden; this can be beneficial, but if it is accompanied by hardening and shrinking of dirt or encrustations over paint, it is to be avoided.

DISCOLORATION. Again, pigments now perhaps made even more vulnerable by decay in the ground, when exposed to light may fade or darken, especially if accompanied by pollution in the form of sulphur.

COMPOSITES LEFT EXPOSED *IN SITU*. It cannot be expected that these materials, having suffered deterioration during burial, will survive the rigours of long-term exposure; painted wall-plaster and mosaics, probably not having been made for external walls/floors in the first instance, are particularly vulnerable. Wind, rain, and frost are all damaging whilst wear and tear on incomplete mosaics and plant growth (roots and acid secretion) also contribute to decay. The pulling out of weeds, however, can be even more destructive.

Soluble salts are a particular problem: as the surface of the porous materials dry in the wind and sunshine, more water together with dissolved salts is drawn up from the underlying ground. The salts crystallize as the water evaporates and disrupt the exposed faces, causing damage associated with rising damp.

Paint on the walls of limestone caves and even paint on the walls of buildings may become covered by a thin layer of calcium carbonate. This occurs where ground-water rich in carbon dioxide and dissolved lime comes out into the air of an opened cave, for example; the carbon dioxide escapes and calcium carbonate is precipitated (section 4.1.2). However, bacteria too may have a role to play here. The surface of a painting may also become obscured by the growth of algae in damp corners.

4.3.6 *Stabilization*

4.3.6.1 Passive

Damage upon excavation caused by dehydration and light can be prevented simply by controlling these elements immediately. If lifting followed by continued control is not envisaged within a matter of months, the site must be backfilled to prevent inevitable deterioration. The materials used in backfilling should allow the passage of water vapour but not liquid or else moisture damage will occur. Furthermore, they should prevent frost damage and erosion by the weather. Thus polyethylene sheeting is avoided and an inert material such as vermiculite (expanded mica) weighted down by clay and soil is suggested (figure 4.2). In the case of wall-paintings in caves, any artificial alteration of the atmosphere can lead to disastrous consequences and so much preliminary study is essential prior to intervention.[16]

Because painted plaster, stucco, and mosaics are part of the architectural scheme of a building, it is preferable to leave them *in situ*. Where this is feasible, preservation by passive techniques alone is not possible and often the greater success is achieved by lifting the materials completely, actively stabilizing them, and then returning them to their original positions protected by damp-proof courses, shelters, etc.[17]

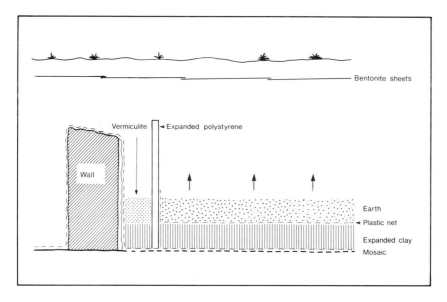

Figure 4.2 Suggested method for backfilling a mosaic pavement[15]

4.3.6.2 Active[18]

The consolidation of small plaster artefacts or pieces of soft/crumbling mortar/plaster/stucco/daub involves many of the same problems and techniques as for ceramics (section 4.5.6.2), but mosaics and large spreads of painted plaster, whether *in situ* or fallen, which are to be lifted, require specialist techniques. To maintain the coherency of these during lifting, a temporary support or facing in the form of a woven material stuck on with a resoluble adhesive is applied to their exposed outer or upper surfaces (plates 3.2 and 4.8). There are considerable problems with and variations in the removal of *in situ* wall-paintings; these arise from the type of painting (fresco/secco), the condition of the paint surface, the condition of the plaster layers, the adhesion of each of these layers, the curvature of the painting, and the choice of adhesive. By variation of technique it is possible simply to remove the paint layer (*strappo*), useful where other paint layers are hidden underneath. More usually, the paint layer plus top plaster layer (*stacco*) is removed, but occasionally the whole wall (*block*) is lifted. Large mosaics can be lifted whole by applying the facing fabric with a strong pliable adhesive and then rolling the mosaic up as a carpet, whilst other experts prefer dividing them into sections and lifting each one flat. Whichever technique is used is tricky: it may take six months to plan how to lift a mosaic but only six

Plate 4.8 Painted plaster *in situ* can be lifted by first adhering a facing fabric and then dislodging areas of plaster

Backing part of a mosaic pavement

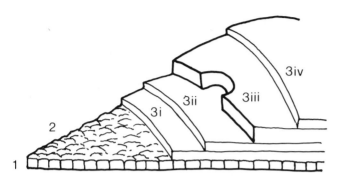

1 Facing of hessian and animal glue (removed when backing completed)
2 Tesserae
3 Backing
   i   Layer of sand (face down) and PVAC emulsion
  ii   Layer of glass fibre mat and polyester resin
 iii   Layer of precast polyurethane foam
 iv   Layer of glass fibre mat and polyester resin

Figure 4.3 Backing part of a mosaic pavement (after Sturge (1987))[18]

hours to do it. Spreads of wall-painting fallen face up (or even down) are lifted with similar adhesive supports. Here the dangers of injudicious choice of facing are noted. Where the artefact is crumbling or flaking, unless it is first consolidated, the facing support will only stick to the surface and more damage will be done than if it had not been used. Where a surface is dirty or an adhesive does not set or is too weak, disaster may occur when the artefact is in the process of being lifted and the adhesion fails. If too strong an adhesive is used, it may shrink pulling off the surface before laboratory treatment has been carried out.

Once back in the laboratory the painting/mosaic is laid face down and the back examined, cleaned, and, if necessary, consolidated. A new support made of very strong light materials such as masonite, expanded aluminium mesh, foaming epoxy resin, or honeycomb glass fibre is stuck to the back so that the temporary facing support can be removed (figure 4.3).

Where plaster has not been lifted in a spread, its reconstruction is aided not only by examination of the paint, brush strokes, scoring marks, and inclusions, but also by close examination of the marks on the reverse where it was fixed to the wall. The pieces are then joined by adhesives and given an overall support as for spreads. For display, gaps are made up, normally with synthetic materials, and then painted. The way in which 'reintegration' of a design is achieved by painting in missing areas varies considerably and is a matter of ethics and aesthetics.

The active stabilization of materials *in situ* is not discussed here but it should be noted that considerable damage can ensue where this is attempted and where the environment remains uncontrolled. For example, continued rising damp will build up behind a consolidated surface ultimately causing the whole surface to exfoliate.

4.3.7 Summary

The most important step in retrieving the maximum information from painted wall-plaster and mosaics is the lifting from the ground; unless this is done correctly not only is information lost but also much time is wasted.

Small isolated pieces of plaster which may or may not be painted are best lifted individually, ensuring that soil remains attached to the surface (plate 4.9). 'Damp' packing (section 3.4.1.4) which must also prevent abrasion is used.

Spreads of fallen plaster and tiled areas require preliminary planning. It is vital that the spread/pavement is first recorded both in plan and photographically. The orientation of fallen plaster must be noted to assist in determining from whence it fell. If help is not available it is best to lift pieces or tiles individually (as above) and to place them on a previously drawn paper template.[19] Pieces can then be numbered and packed as above. It is essential that white 'unpainted' pieces of plaster are lifted as well as those with polychrome, otherwise reconstruction at a later date is greatly hampered. If the plaster or tiles are too weak to lift as individual pieces or if a mosaic or wall-painting *in situ* is uncovered, specialist help must be sought as soon as possible. In the meantime, the finds should be kept damp by covering with polyethylene sheets, preferably black, to cut down sunlight.

Painted plaster is never cleaned on site; other robust materials could be gently swabbed but are never immersed in water. Pavement tiles from salty sites could be desalted on site as described for ceramics (section 4.5.8.2). Packing for all materials must prevent abrasion.

If the material is to be left *in situ* specialist help should be sought. Backfilling probably will be suggested but this is successful only when correctly carried out.[20] Incorrect procedures can lead to a build-up of water with all its concomitant problems or disintegration of the site by bad weather.

During storage treated material should be kept free from dust. The

Plate 4.9 Small areas of plaster which have fallen painted surface uppermost can be lifted by simple means

relative humidity is maintained below 65 per cent to prevent growths of staining fungi and bacteria.

4.4 Glass[21]

4.4.1 Nature of materials

4.4.1.1 Glass[22]

Silica (SiO_2) is the basic 'former' of glass but whereas in quartz and flint it is in a strictly symmetrical crystalline arrangement, here it is randomly arranged in a three-dimensional network. When molten material is cooled down too quickly for a strict arrangement of atoms to align themselves as it sets, a random network forms instead. This gives the resulting glass some fluid-like properties and an imprecise melting point. The melting point of pure silica glass is about 1700°C but if other elements, modifiers, are introduced into the glass, this point falls to less than 1000°C. Monovalent basic oxides (R_2O) such as soda (Na_2O) or potash (K_2O) modifiers behave as *fluxes* by interrupting some of the silicon–oxygen bonds and so breaking the continuous network. The unattached oxygen atoms become negatively charged and loosely hold the monovalent cations in the spaces of the network (figure 4.4):

$$- Si - O - Si- \quad \xrightarrow{R_2O} \quad - Si - O^- \quad \begin{matrix} R^+ \\ \\ R^+ \end{matrix} \quad O^- - Si -$$

This bonding is weak and the cations can migrate out of the network in the presence of water, making these glasses water soluble. To overcome this a second type of modifier, *stabilizers*, divalent oxides (RO) such as lime (CaO) or magnesia (MgO), must also be added. Being doubly

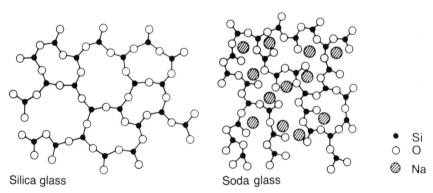

Silica glass   Soda glass

- Si
- ○ O
- Na

Figure 4.4 The arrangement of elements in glasses

charged they are more tightly held than the monovalent ions and so hold the fluxes within the network.

The content and balance of silica:flux:stabilizer (SiO_2:R_2O:RO) in a glass is critical in determining its melting point and character. An average soda–lime glass of 73% SiO_2:22% R_2O:5% RO has a melting point of about 725°C whilst a similar potash glass will harden at a higher temperature and more quickly. The former is more lustrous than the latter, whilst the substitution of some of the silica by lead gives lead crystal which, being soft, is easily cut to show great brilliance. Lead is also used to make the fusible glass required for the manufacture of enamels (section 5.1.2.6).

Colour in glass is usually given by transition metal ions held in the network like the modifying ions. The final hue[23] depends on the redox condition in the glass, the mixtures of ions present, and very precise concentrations of ions; thus it may be dangerous to speculate on the ions responsible for a particular colour. Colour may be extinguished by additives. Thus the blue-green hue of reduced iron is diminished by the introduction of pink manganese ions; the iron is oxidized to a yellow colour which, when viewed with pink from excess manganese, appears colourless. Some metal compounds can opacify glass but it may also appear opaque from large quantities of gas bubbles.

Glass for artefacts may be manufactured in one place and shaped in another. This latter activity is enormously varied, from the chipping and grinding of solid blocks of glass, to the bending of softened glass requiring temperatures of only 500°C, to the blowing of molten glass which requires much more heat (about 1000°C). Each technique of shaping leaves its own clues both in the overall shape of the object, its chemical composition (some glass being more suitable for cutting and some for blowing, etc.), and small visible traces such as bubbles and tool marks.

4.4.1.2 Associated materials

As is discussed elsewhere (section 5.1.2.6) metals may be enamelled[24] with glass which softens below the melting point of the metal, which flows to cover the metal, which adheres to it, and which has a similar coefficient of expansion to the metal; heavily leaded glasses often fit these requirements. Glass may also be inlaid into plaster in a technique known as *opus sectile*. Glass objects may be decorated by firing on powdered glass, metallic lustres or gilding, or by unfired paint applied in lacquer, varnish, or oil. Gold can be applied in the gold sandwich technique, when a design in gold leaf is sealed onto a glass object by a second thin layer of glass. Window glass is painted by enamelling, firing on a mixture of powdered glass and iron oxide, or stained yellow with silver by firing with silver sulphide. Window glass may be found in association with its cames, usually lead, its frame which may be iron, wood, or plaster, and even its putty.

4.4.1.3 Glass-like materials[25]

This category covers materials which may appear glassy but in fact are not, and those which are made of glass but in a debased form. If a mixture of a source of modifiers, sand and copper oxide, or malachite is fired at temperatures about 1000°C, faience is formed. This appears as a pale-yellow body of sand grains stuck together with glass with a bright blue skin of applied or self-formed glaze. On the other hand, if powdered blue glass plus lime paste is fired at about 850°C, a fine-grained chalky (not glossy) object results which is pale blue throughout. This is 'frit' and may contain the crystalline phase $CaO.CuO.4SiO_2$. Glass in the form of pale-grey/green opaque slag is formed as a waste or accidental product from a variety of activities such as glass-making itself, overfiring of clay, burning fuel, or even haystacks. This fuel-ash slag occurs wherever the common raw materials of glass are found in association, and temperatures over about 800°C have been reached. Dark-coloured metal-working slag produced by the non-metallic impurities in metal ores may well be glassy to some extent; thus slag produced by the smelting and smithing of both iron and copper is mainly a mixture of crystalline fayalite ($2FeO.SiO_2$) and glass.

4.4.2 Nature of deteriorated material

The deterioration of glass[26] is a function of its composition, its firing history, and the burial environment and duration. Glass can appear in extremely varied states of decay, and since so many factors are involved it is sometimes dangerous to assume the composition of a glass from its condition. In general, glass with too little silica in it is not stable to moisture, and if there is less than or more than the optimum of 10 per cent lime (RO) there is also instability. Soda glass is almost twice as durable as potash, possibly because the potassium ion being larger than sodium, its loss during burial causes greater damage. A small percentage of alumina (Al_2O_3) increases stability. Scratches and flaws on glass enhance decay and may even appear to be deliberate engraving. Whilst there has already been considerable research into the deterioration of glass there is still much to be done especially in the area of predicting likely decay. The decay dependent on the environment is discussed below, but the overriding factor is that of moisture. Decay is known generally as 'weathering' and decayed areas of glass as a 'weathering crust'.

4.4.2.1 Appearance

GOOD CONDITION. If the composition of glass is exact for stability or even if it is slightly unbalanced, with water absent from the environment glass can be in perfect condition after even thousands of years of burial. It is more usual that these conditions are not met with and, whilst the glass seems to be in good condition, it has in fact deteriorated minutely. This is because the surface has dissolved as described below, but the weathering products have been lost and so the glass appears glossy. If glass is wet, it may in fact be even more badly decayed than this, its true state being masked by the water.

IRIDESCENCE/DULLING (plate 4.10). When glass is in contact with moisture, the alkali metal ions (R^+) are slowly leached out to be replaced by protons (H^+) from the water. The surface layer loses its glassy nature and characteristic refractive index and so appears dull or iridescent. Just as a thin skin of oil on water appears iridescent, so can the translucent decayed surface of glass when it is less than 0.9 micrometres thick. However, if a liquid such as water is introduced into this weathered layer, the inconsistencies of refractive index are obliterated and the decay is not visible. Thus, on excavation, such damp glass may appear in better condition than it actually is. An iridescent surface may in fact be composed of a large number of very thin weathered layers.

It is not yet clear exactly what causes glass to decay in layers; it could be that as large sodium or even larger potassium ions are replaced by protons the physical stress on the structure causes the leached surface layer to split. Water can now seep through to attack fresh glass underneath, repeating the process again and again.

OPAQUE SURFACE POSSIBLY LAMINATING. On examination of such a weathered surface, it too will be found to be composed of layers, this time a very large number (plate 4.11). The layers may be adhering to one another and may penetrate the entire material or they may be laminating and superficial. Since these layers are highly hydrated, if the humidity in the deposit fluctuates, they may shrink and expand, leading to exfoliation. The glass core revealed when such layers are dislodged will be rough, as the flaws and bubbles once within the body are exposed. Moreover, decay is not uniform and the core is eaten away in undulating depressions.

It would appear that the glass of enamels does not laminate in this way but it may become opaque and cracked through decay. Many enamels were made originally from opaque glass which was ground up and fused *in situ* (section 5.1.2.6), such fusion not always being complete. Thus it is possible to confuse deterioration of enamels with intention or inadequacies of manufacture (plate 4.12).

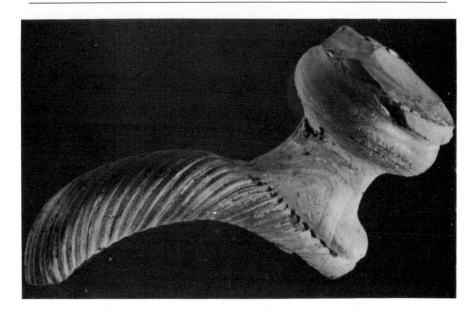

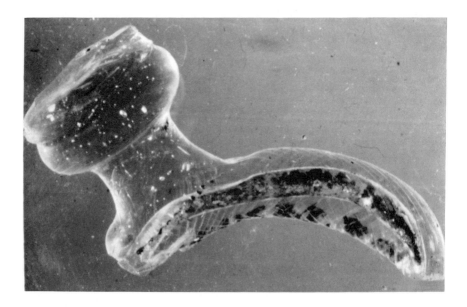

Plate 4.10 Iridescent glass. (a) Deteriorated glass showing iridescence. (b) The same glass immersed in a liquid which obliterates iridescence by displacing the air in the weathered surface

Plate 4.11 Photomicrograph of the cross-section of a piece of decayed glass to show the layering of the weathering crust: the black feathering is probably due to oxidation of iron and manganese in the glass

TOTAL LOSS OF GLASSY NATURE. Badly decayed glass may survive only as a chalky mass of silica gel and be somewhat difficult to identify as glass.

DISCOLORATION. Not only are fluxing ions leached from the glass network by water, so are any colouring metal ions present. Alternatively, the ions may change colour *in situ* by oxidation; thus from manganese ions, black manganese dioxide (MnO_2) may be deposited and the red copper/cuprite of enamels may become a green copper(II) colour. Finally, colouring ions from the environment may be taken up, a colourless crust becoming blackened with iron or manganese or stained

133

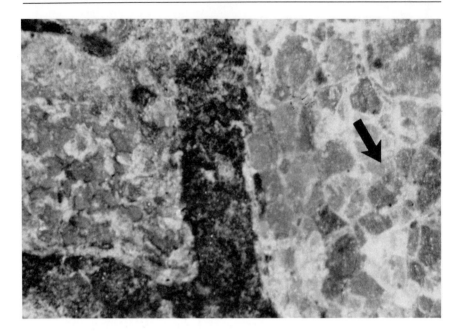

Plate 4.12 Close up of two areas of champlevé enamel to show incompletely fused frit rather than deterioration

green with copper corrosion products. Lead glass can be blackened by lead sulphide in a wet anaerobic deposit. It is possible that bacteria play a role in both decomposing and blackening this and other types of glass.

ENCRUSTATION. Here the glass and weathering crusts become obscured by encrustations of insoluble salts (section 4.1.2). These may be especially prevalent where excess lime in a glass is leached out, to be deposited as a whitish deposit on the surface or within the decayed layers of the glass forming a continuous matrix.

4.4.2.2 Presence or absence of glass in a deposit

As pointed out above, the decay of glass is dependent on a number of factors. With regard to its composition, if it is a poorly made glass in a damp deposit, it could disintegrate completely within hundreds of years (decay rate = 3–5 millimetres per millennium). The main examples of such glass in western Europe are the medieval forest glass made with potash and too little silica, some seventeenth-century Ravenscroft glass, and some eighteenth-century Venetian glass, both of which contain too little stabilizer. Absence of water will preserve any glass, whereas damp, alkaline deposits and sea-water are particularly aggressive. This is because not only are fluxes leached out but the remaining silica gel itself is broken down. Thus an alkaline deposit attacks poorly made glass ten times faster than an acidic one; no glass will withstand burial in a pH greater than 9. At present, burial experiments are being carried out in an attempt to understand the decay of glass more fully.

4.4.3 Examination

Before and during cleaning it is essential to look for paint, gilding, etc. which often is more ready to adhere to soil and encrustation than to the weathering crust of glass. From visual inspection, whilst it is dangerous to speculate about the age of glass from its condition (section 4.4.2), it might be possible to suggest something of the composition of two groups of glass in different conditions from the same site. It is likewise dangerous to speculate on the ions responsible for colouring any remaining glass (section 4.4.1.1). From the shape and distribution of gas bubbles (not present in gem-stones) and from the flaw lines present in any remaining glass, it may be possible to determine whether and how a piece of glass was blown. The fire finish, mattness, or toolmarks on the surface of unweathered glass are all useful in understanding the methods of manufacture.[27] The thickness of a sherd (this of course includes the weathering crust on decayed glass) may point to which part of a vessel it comes from, or if it is from window glass, how thick were the cames. X-radiography or UV light might assist the location of painting or engraving. Simply the relative weight of lead glass sometimes gives its make-up away but non-destructive testing must be used for confirmation. The determination of refractive index, which measures the degree to which light is slowed down when it passes through glass, and of hardness may help distinguish small pieces of glass from gems and even identify their composition. Numerous other specialist methods have been employed in the analysis of glass for technological and provenance studies.[28]

4.4.4 Cleaning

In the case of glass it is important to understand that cleaning means the removal of soil or encrustations but *not* the removal of any weathering crust; this is destruction, for it is removing some of the original artefact. Its removal means that the 'original surface' of the glass is destroyed and the thickness of the piece, an important parameter technologically and for reconstruction, is altered. Removal will reveal a core of glass *only* where this remains and whilst it will be the original colour it will have an unsightly surface (section 4.4.2.1). Cleaning of soil is carried out mechanically whilst the glass is still damp. Encrustations are extremely difficult to deal with; if chemicals are used, they will attack any remaining glass, whilst mechanical methods must be used with great skill. It is easy to detach the weathering crust where the encrustation is continuous with it.

Nothing can be done to return the *colour* of a weathered layer of glass to the original (section 4.4.2.1); thus discoloured green copper(II) crusts on enamels or blackened manganese surfaces must remain this colour. A discussion point arises where the blackening is due to infiltration from the deposit rather than to oxidized colouring agents, for little work has as yet been done to distinguish between them. Until the cause of blackening can be identified, it should be left in place even though it does make paint, for example, very difficult to see. In enamels, where it has been known that solid glass lay beneath a discoloured crust, on occasion the crust has been removed and the uneven surface filled with transparent resin, but this is not always appropriate.[29]

4.4.5 Deterioration upon excavation

DEVELOPMENT OF WEATHERING CRUST ON GLASS IN APPARENTLY GOOD CONDITION, EXFOLIATION, LAMINATION, FLAKING, OR CRUMBLING (plate 4.13). These are all aspects of the dehydration of weathered glass. Water

Plate 4.13 Sherd of deteriorated medieval glass showing flaking of dirt-covered weathered surface layer on drying out after excavation

may be masking the decay (section 4.4.2.1), keeping a decayed crust expanded, or by surface tension holding a laminated and fissured crust together. Green bottle glass from certain marine sites has been found to demonstrate this phenomenon in the extreme. The worse the decay and the greater degree of dehydration, the worse the deterioration upon excavation will be. In all probability the exfoliation and lamination is exacerbated by the crystallization of soluble salts (section 4.1.2) present in the porous crust. It is certainly aggravated by the contraction of any soil left on the surface of the decayed glass.

WEEPING GLASS.[30] Glass which contains far too little stabilizer can deteriorate even under museum conditions. Where RH > 42 per cent, the unstabilized flux can migrate to the surface, forming tears of alkali which then cause great damage to the glass. If unstable glass had been buried in constantly *very dry* conditions, it is just possible it might have survived to weep on excavation.

4.4.6 Stabilization

4.4.6.1 Passive

Much deterioration of excavated glass can be avoided temporarily if it is kept damp. This is especially important if the glass comes from a marine site, where special precautions must be taken to ensure that no part of the glass dries out even for a moment.

Wet storage will be deleterious in the longer term when the pH of the solution gradually begins to rise and any remaining glass is leached. Buffers may be suggested to keep the pH down and possibly bacteriocides to prevent damage from bacteria. Research in this area is particularly important if the problem of marine glass is to be solved.

Weeping glass can be stabilized simply by keeping it in a RH of about 40 per cent.

4.4.6.2 Active

There are several aims involved in the active stabilization of weathered glass. First, water must be removed without the crust shrinking/exfoliating/crumbling; second, the crust must be consolidated; third, it must be reaffixed to any glass core remaining; and fourth, where possible, transparency must be reintroduced. This last aim needs qualifying; where glass shows slight iridescence, this type of crust is said to be a patina giving beauty to the object. However, these iridescent layers will flake off unless consolidated, but the wrong choice of consolidant will extinguish the iridescence altogether, as does water (section 4.4.2.1). If the weathering crust is thicker, it no longer appears 'beautiful' but simply

Plate 4.14 Treatment of deteriorated medieval glass. (a) Part of a weathered glass vessel in damp soil. (b) The same sherds after treatment: lifting, consolidation, joining, and mounting

obstructs the view of any glass beneath. Thus attempts are made to fill the crust so completely with consolidant that it will behave as water, rendering the crust transparent. An even thicker crust or a more decayed one can never be rendered transparent especially when it is discoloured and so consolidation without total bulking is needed. As yet there are no really suitable consolidation systems compatible with damp glass capable of achieving all of these aims in all cases (plate 4.14). Discussion and thought must be a feature of choice of consolidant for every piece,[31] even so, consolidation of disintegrating marine glass has not always met with success.

There is as yet no means of stabilizing 'weeping' glass other than by passive means (section 4.4.6.1).

4.4.7   Reconstruction

The joining of unweathered or lightly weathered glass is difficult because, being dense, the solvent from adhesive applied to the joins cannot escape through the glass. Also the faces of the breaks are very smooth, not allowing any keying of the adhesive, and furthermore there is no room for imprecise joins. The situation has been eased by the development of thermosetting resins (section 3.4.2.2) which can be used on glass in good condition, being removable as they do not penetrate the fabric. If a resin with a refractive index similar to the glass being treated is chosen, the join will be invisible.

Weathered glass cannot be joined until it has been consolidated and then the adhesive must be compatible with the consolidant and the delicate crust. Gap filling, like joining, of water-white glass requires a non-yellowing translucent material and this, if at all, is not widely available. While for many early glasses this problem is not so acute, another difficulty arises: here the glass may be too thin to support gap-filling materials. A recent approach has been to attach the fragments to a transparent core so circumventing the difficulty. Good results in joining and gap filling can be achieved only with considerable skill and use of the correct materials (plate 4.15).[32]

4.4.8   Summary

When removing any glass from a deposit, a layer of soil or sediment is allowed to remain attached to the surface to prevent loss of detail. Before a spread of glass from a window is lifted, it should be thoroughly photographed and planned, keeping it damp all the while by spraying or covering with polyethylene or foam sheets. Sherds should be lifted individually and numbered according to the plan. No dirt or encrustations must be removed on site and all glass should be treated as if damp and

Plate 4.15 Glass vessels may be reconstructed first by strips of pressure-sensitive tape which is removed after an adhesive run into the joins has set

stored accordingly (section 3.4.1.1). Marking of glass is best avoided and individual sherds should be placed in small labelled polyethylene bags and laid *flat* so that any dislodged flakes remain *in situ*. It goes without saying that no pressure should be put on glass by packaging.

Glass vessels may contain hairline cracks and should be lifted extremely carefully, as suggested in section 3.1.1.1, with a sample of surrounding soil taken for comparison with the contents. At marine sites when a vessel is lifted out of the sea, it may fall apart because of the weight of absorbed water and contents. Thus it must be packed carefully in marine sediment or seaweed before it is lifted (plate 3.6). As with sherds, vessels must not be cleaned on site, must be stored damp (section 3.4.1.1), and packaged extremely well to prevent breakage.

Badly decayed glass can never be restored to translucency but it may be possible to consolidate it. Discussions should take place prior to laboratory treatment to determine what is required from the artefacts. In the long term, glass in good condition should be kept in relative humidities which are not extreme nor in cool conditions where dew may form. All glass must be protected from dirt and dust and handled very carefully.

4.5   Ceramics

4.5.1   Nature of materials[33]

4.5.1.1   Ceramic bodies

Ceramics are made of fired clay; their precise composition will depend upon the initial mineral content and the conditions and duration of firing. The predominant initial clay mineral is kaolinite ($Al_2O_3.2SiO_2.2H_2O$), but montmorillonite ($Al_2O_3.4SiO_2nH_2O$) and illites of various compositions are also found. Water penetrates between the submicroscopic plate-like crystals ($\simeq$ 0.01–2 micrometres in diameter), rendering them plastic when wet and thus suitable for manipulation into three-dimensional masses (figure 4.5).

(a)   (b)

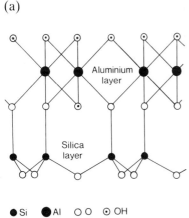
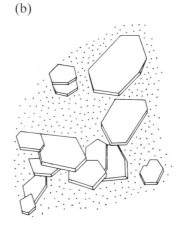

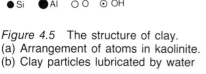

Figure 4.5   The structure of clay.
(a) Arrangement of atoms in kaolinite.
(b) Clay particles lubricated by water

Raw clays also contain a variable quantity of other minerals, namely quartz (SiO_2), feldspars (alkali metal alumino-silicates), calcite ($CaCO_3$), iron compounds (e.g. $Fe_2O_3.nH_2O$, limonite), and carbonaceous matter deriving from much altered plant and animal remains. In addition, sand (quartz) or small fragments of calcite, shell ($CaCO_3$), calcined flint (SiO_2), crushed pottery, or straw, for example, may be added deliberately as a temper (or filler) to facilitate shaping and firing of earthenwares.

When air-dried, clay bodies lose their lubricating water and become leather hard. If the temperature is in the region 100–150°C and the humidity low, water from pores and capillaries is also lost, rendering the fabric usable as unbaked clay or mudbrick. This latter material may take up to two years to dry but if kept free from saturation by water will retain its strength for a considerable length of time.

Clays are complex materials and when heated tend to melt at lower temperatures than the individual components. Thus some clay minerals such as montmorillonite begin to melt at their extremities at temperatures as low as 450°C. At such a temperature kaolinite begins to decompose, giving *meta*-kaolin ($Al_2O_3.2SiO_2$) and water. If cooling follows now, the resulting ware will be ceramic-like to some extent but prolonged soaking in water will rehydrate the *meta*-kaolin to kaolin. Alternatively, if the temperature is raised towards 700°C, the strength of the fired product is increased by further formation of *meta*-kaolin as well as by glass, which is formed by the naturally occurring fluxes of sodium and potassium (section 4.4.1.1) occurring in clays, and the silica. At temperatures above 700°C, *meta*-kaolin decomposes to give crystalline spinel ($2Al_2O_3.3SiO_2$) and finely divided silica which readily combines with modifiers (CaO and FeO especially) to form glass. If cooled, the clay has now irreversibly become a ceramic, being composed of spinel or mullite ($3Al_2O_3.2SiO_2$) crystals formed at high temperatures, held together by glass. At temperatures above 1000°C some mullite may give way to yet more glass which, being extremely fluid at these temperatures, runs into pores surrounding remaining particles which are predominantly quartz now converted to cristobalite. Above such temperatures the remaining components may become too molten and the whole body will collapse (table 4.2).

Heat will affect other materials present within a clay body. The products may either act as fluxes in the ceramic-forming process or contribute to some other property of the resulting fired body. Calcium carbonate decomposes to give carbon dioxide and quicklime (CaO) but can reform on cooling in moist air (section 4.3.1.1); if present in large lumps the hydration of CaO to $Ca(OH)_2$ involving a large volume expansion may result in disruption of the body – 'clay popping'. At higher temperatures, the CaO may form a glass or complex crystalline silicates instead. Carbonaceous material is burnt out but if insufficient oxygen is present, carbon is produced which can become trapped in the core of the

Table 4.2 Effect of temperature on ceramic-forming materials

Temperature (°C)	Effect	Reversibility
> 100	water of plasticity lost	✓
100–150	capillary water lost	✓
> 450	clay minerals begin to soften at edges	×
< 600	kaolin → *meta*-kaolin + H_2O	(✓)
> 700	*meta*-kaolin → spinel and later mullite + SiO_2	×
	crude glass formed (Na_2O, K_2O + SiO_2)	×
> 1000	massive mullite formation	×
	massive glass formation (CaO, FeO + SiO_2)	×
	quartz → cristobalite	×

body by early glass formation. Black magnetite in the presence of oxygen is oxidized to red haematite (Fe_2O_3), whilst in a reducing atmosphere haematite is reduced to black magnetite (Fe_3O_4) or wüstite (FeO) at high temperatures. The final colour of the ceramic body is dependent mainly upon the three inclusions mentioned above and is itself a document of the content and the firing regime of the raw material (table 4.3).

The porosity of a fired ceramic is dependent partly on how completely the clay minerals fuse together, partly on whether the pores have been filled with glass, partly on the original size of the particles in the body (large particles giving a coarser more porous end product), and partly on size and content of original organic matter, for when it burns out, voids will be formed.

The above is an oversimplified picture of a very complex system, the temperatures mentioned being the *minima* at which the events described could be expected to occur in the firing of any clay body. The

Table 4.3 Effect of temperature on other materials in clay bodies

Temperature (°C)	Effect
> 200	carbonaceous material oxidized $\overset{O_2}{\rightarrow}$ $CO_2 \uparrow$ or $CO \uparrow$
> 400	$Fe_3O_4 \overset{O_2}{\rightarrow} Fe_2O_3$ black red
> 650	$CaCO_3 \rightarrow CaO + CO_2 \uparrow$
800	all carbon burnt off
825	$Fe_2O_3 \overset{no\ O_2}{\rightarrow} Fe_3O_4$ or FeO red black
898	all $CaCO_3$ decomposed (CaO may → glass or complex silicates)

Table 4.4 Maturing temperatures and characteristics of ceramic bodies

Temperature (°C)	Ware	Possible constituents	Characteristics
500 ⎫ ⎬ 900 ⎭	Underfired earthenware	adhering clay minerals/ *meta*-kaolin, later mullite, crude glass, quartz, feldspars, CaCO$_3$	extremely porous (>15%) soft
1050 ⎫ 1150 ⎭	earthenware	mullite, glass, quartz	porous (6–8%) hard
1200 ⎫ 1300 ⎭	stoneware	mullite, glass, cristobalite	non-porous (<3%) very hard
1300 ⎫ ⎬ 1450 ⎭	porcelain	mullite, glass	non-porous (<1%) hard → very hard as % glass falls, translucent

temperatures at which they *do* occur will depend on a number of factors, including the clay minerals and fluxes present, the rate and duration of firing, and the atmosphere in the kiln. The temperature of the production of the most satisfactory ceramic from a given clay body in a given kiln atmosphere is known as the maturing temperature. Ceramic bodies can broadly be categorized by this temperature which will reflect the make-up of the original clay body and the constituents of the ceramic (table 4.4).

4.5.1.2 Surface finishes

The clay particles on the surface of a vessel can be aligned with it and compacted down mechanically by burnishing when leather hard to give a lustrous finish and increased impermeability after firing. Colour may be added to this layer in the form of graphite, haematite, or mica powder to give a black, black/red, or golden finish respectively.

A thin coat of diluted fluid clay, a slip, can be applied to the surface of a shaped ware for decorative purposes. By the use of a particular clay, usually based on iron-rich illites, a red or black gloss (*not* a glaze) which is highly lustrous is produced. Modelled terracottas may have a paler fine-textured 'fire skin' resulting from a slip formed when wet modelling was in progress.

A glaze applied for decoration or to increase the impermeability of a ceramic is a glass which 'fits' a fired clay body. It requires the same constituents of former, modifiers, and colourants as glass (section 4.4.1.1) but the clay body itself may provide one or more of these components. Glazes are categorized by their main modifier into alkaline (including salt) glazes and lead glazes. The first group, with sodium and/or potassium together with some calcium as modifiers, tends to mature at a high temperature and thus is commonly used on stonewares. If lead is substituted for the alkali metals, a lower maturing temperature as well as a more brilliant effect is achieved; since lead will volatilize at 1130°C, the presence of a lead glaze indicates the maximum temperature used to fire the glaze. A lustre may be given to a glaze by deposition of silver and/or copper held in the glass. There are innumerable other effects obtainable in a glaze for decorative purposes and these must not be confused with failure of the glaze in firing. Some important failures are crazing, peeling, or flaking due to poor fit or excessively fast cooling, and mattness, produced by underfiring or by crystallization resulting from excessively slow cooling preventing glass formation. The degree of bonding between the glass of the glaze and the clay minerals, quartz, or glass of the body is extremely variable.

Paint may be fixed to unglazed wares by application of pigments such as naturally occurring iron ores that also contain silica or clay minerals which partially bind the colour to the body during firing. Alternatively coloured slips might be used, but incompatibility in firing temperatures between these and the body may cause the 'paint' to be underfired. After firing, porous ceramics may be coloured with vegetable dyes or even covered with lime-plaster or gesso and painted or gilded. The pigment on glazed wares is usually applied before a firing and so is covered by/bonded into the glass.

4.5.1.3 Associated materials

To increase impermeability resins, fats, or oils may be applied to porous wares after firing. Repairs in antiquity could be carried out with plaster or bitumen to fill cracks, resins to make joins, and metal clamps, often lead, to secure them. Naturally the purposes to which ceramic vessels have been put are endless and may or may not leave a trace; likewise such traces may or may not survive burial. Constant boiling of hard water in a pot will leave a thick white deposit of calcium carbonate whilst use as a chamber pot leaves a similar rime. Ceramics may become glazed from use in or proximity to many industrial processes, or may more simply acquire a 'glassy' surface formed by heating in association with fuel-ash slag (section 4.4.1.3).

4.5.2 Nature of deteriorated ceramics

SOFT OR CRUMBLING. In a damp soil, underfired earthenware will gradually rehydrate to clay, becoming softened and liable to crumble, especially where the fabric is coarse and extremely porous; earthenwares, stonewares, and porcelain remain robust. Crumbling may be exacerbated in acidic or soft ground-water by loss of calcite filler or dispersed calcium carbonate (section 4.1.2).

It is possible that well-fired ceramics could become softened in alkaline deposits by the dissolution of the glass phase (section 4.4.2.1) but this has not been noticed in marine conditions.

FLAKING SURFACE, GLAZE, OR PAINT. If a ceramic in which the coefficient of expansion of the slip, glaze, or paint is dissimilar from that of the body underneath, is subjected to changes in temperature, crazing and then spalling of these layers may occur. Since burnished or glossed surfaces and fine skins on terracottas (section 4.5.1.2) are under tension, such surfaces are particularly prone to flaking. As with all porous materials, earthenwares are liable to deterioration by frost or soluble salts (section 4.1.2); in changing humidities the latter will readily dislodge a poorly fitting glaze or paint from an earthenware body. Non-porous bodies are not vulnerable.

GREY/WHITE ENCRUSTATIONS. Deposits of insoluble salts (section 4.1.2) readily form on pottery, particularly in marine environments where the encrusting layers consist mainly of calcium carbonate from the exoskeletons of fouling organisms such as barnacles and bryozoans (plate 4.2). These can obscure the whole surface including the broken edges of sherds and may bond onto a decaying glaze as they do to glass (section 4.4.2.1). A thin grey/white layer may be found on a ceramic body and be simply the decayed remains of a glaze (section 4.4.2.1); this may be distinguished from a deposit of salts by only appearing in areas where the glaze would have been applied, that is, not on the broken edges of sherds.

DISCOLORATION. Porous pottery is particularly prone to staining from materials within a deposit and of course this is most noticeable on pale unglazed wares. Iron oxide may in fact deposit within a porous body as iron pan does in the soil, being the result of a local high pH caused by the presence of calcium carbonate within the body. Iron oxides are also found frequently on marine ceramics either as thin powdery deposits or as thick concretions cemented to the ceramic surface. Moreover, one of the components of the ceramic itself may become discoloured during burial. Thus burning of the surroundings during deposition or subsequently may accidently change the overall tone of an iron-bearing sherd; it may turn from red to black[34] or more likely black to red in this second 'firing', depending on the presence or absence of oxygen. Occasionally lead glaze appears with a grey metallic lustre; this discoloration in a reducing deposit may be due to the reduction of the modifying lead oxide in the glass to lustrous lead sulphide (section 2.2.1.4) or, if accidentally burnt, even to metallic lead.[35] Iridescence in a glaze may be caused by the slight dissolution of the modifier as for glass itself (section 4.4.2.1).

Lead- and tin-glazed wares from marine deposits are often found to have been stained black by sulphides released by anaerobic sulphate-reducing bacteria (section 2.2.1.9). This blackening may occur only in patches on the surface of the ceramic but in some cases all of the glaze may be affected, making it impossible to see its true colour and design.

DISTORTION. The weight of overburden can readily distort softened sherds or pots. Since clay bodies shrink when they are fired, the matured ceramic of hollow vessels is under considerable tension. When a vessel breaks, the constricting force in the shape of the vessel is released and the separate sherds may flatten away from their previously enforced concavity; such a phenomenon is known as springing.

4.5.3 Examination

Even for ceramics, however easy and automatic this is to carry out, examination to decide on methods of cleaning and stabilization is necessary. Visual examination will reveal the type of body, the nature of the filler (section 4.5.1.1), and the presence of surface finishes (section 4.5.1.2) together with the strength and coherence of the ceramic, the presence of associated material (section 4.5.1.3), and the distinction between decayed glaze and an insoluble salt deposit (section 4.5.2) amongst other things. The identification of the first three aspects mentioned above will, without doubt, be facilitated and strengthened by a knowledge and understanding of the ceramic types under study; the literature in this field is of course widespread and of long standing. A conservator will also note features of the ceramic such as impressions of burnt-out organic materials or textiles; whilst these do not affect cleaning and stabilization directly, they are included to record the exact condition of the material before treatment. Detailed description of construction and decoration rests with a ceramics specialist. X-radiography may help to reveal embossed or incised decorations, graffiti, or stamps underneath a thick salt encrustation or even the direction in which inclusions/voids are aligned within a sherd, making an understanding of its fabrication clearer. X-radiography is also useful on complete urns containing unexcavated material to reveal burials, stone, ceramic, and metallic artefacts, or hidden cracks in the fabric. It should be remembered that use of x-rays on a ceramic renders it more difficult to date by thermoluminescence; records of any exposure are essential. Ultraviolet light may reveal areas of ceramic from which paint has been dislodged, areas of modern restoration, traces of plaster or gesso, whilst infrared photography may detect traces of paint or ink.

Simple wet chemical analysis will determine the presence of calcite filler or lime in a body as well as the nature of an insoluble salt deposit, but the nature of an adhering deposit within a vessel is more problematic. Most revealing are deposits containing three-dimensional bodies such as seeds which would be visible microscopically for chemical analysis but which may be extremely difficult to interpret. However, chemical micro-analyses of such deposits and even of the ceramic itself are beginning to reveal more information concerning the use of ceramic vessels which will be enhanced as reference collections of traces of decayed food etc. are built up.[36] Consolidation treatments could adversely affect such traces.

The presence of soluble salts within wet or damp ceramics can be inferred from the type of deposit from whence they come (section 2.2.1.5); when from drier soils, the salt crystals are easily visible under a microscope.

Specialist methods of analysis of ceramics for further information to aid conservation, the understanding of technology, the date of manufacture, or its provenance are numerous and much described; the reader is directed to other texts for a discussion of this topic.[37]

4.5.4 Cleaning[38]

There is a great danger in overcleaning ceramics; excessive use of mechanical methods leads to abrasion (plate 4.16) and excessive use of chemicals may weaken and alter the fabric and extract traces of decayed food etc. Therefore, water with *gentle* brushing is normally the best cleaning method and is used before adhering soil begins to harden and shrink. In the case of poorly fired ceramics and painted or poorly glazed surfaces, damp swabbing or even swabbing with alcohol (section 3.3.2.1) is preferable. For some robust ceramics, prolonged soaking in water may cause sulphate encrustations to fall off, whilst heavy carbonate crusts on marine ceramics are mechanically removed before they are allowed to dry out. Where these crusts are harder than the underlying ceramic, it is not possible to remove them completely by these methods. Resort to chemical removal of carbonate and sulphate crusts has to be made: caution is needed for the reagents necessary also dissolve any calcium carbonate in the artefact as well as attacking any iron present and any lead or tin glaze; furthermore they may dislodge a glaze by the evolution of carbon dioxide underneath it as carbonates are dissolved. The choice of chemical thus may fall on sequestering agents (section 3.3.2.1). It must be remembered that by sequestering or dissolving 'insoluble' salts, soluble salts are formed and unless these are well washed out, damage by crystal formation may follow (section 4.1.2).

The removal of stains from archaeological ceramics is usually unnecessary and may destroy information. After due consideration (section 4.4.4), it may be essential for ceramics from marine conditions where the glaze has been totally blackened. On light-coloured hard ceramics where glazes are intact, blackening and iron stains can both be removed by hydrogen peroxide which decomposes without residue. It

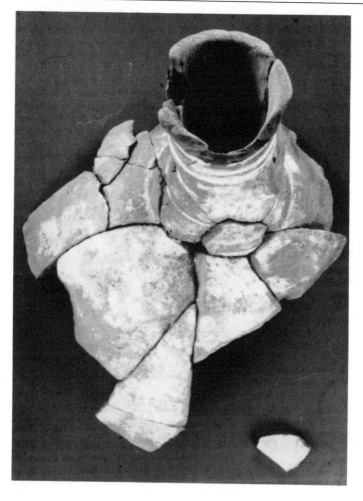

Plate 4.16 Reconstructed sherds of a Roman vessel showing excessive cleaning which has partially removed the white slip, untouched on the sherd which escaped 'cleaning'

is used in preference to chlorine bleaches which cause considerable discoloration and even damage. Heavy staining by iron rusts on marine ceramics have to be removed by local applications of stronger reagents followed by thorough washing of the cleaned area to remove salts generated by the chemicals. Such treatments cannot be used to remove iron stains from ceramics, like terracotta, which themselves contain iron oxide within the clay fabric or glaze.

4.5.5 *Deterioration upon excavation*

HARDENING OF DIRT OR SALT ENCRUSTATIONS. This will happen when sherds from wet or damp deposits are dried out. At the same time, these deposits may shrink, causing a delicate paint or glaze to be lifted off, or bond with a glaze or body in such a way that cleaning later is made much more difficult. However, drying out of some ceramic bodies may also harden the fabric which of course can be extremely useful (but see CRUMBLING, below). Dehydration of a wet deposit from inside a vessel may make it less suitable for identification if structural organic debris such as seeds shrink and crumble; these deposits are treated as are soil samples for botanical study.

WHITE EFFLORESCENCE WITH OR WITHOUT A FLAKING SURFACE OR POWDERING BODY. As a salt-laden damp ceramic dries out, or if a dry salt-ridden one is subjected to alternating dry and wet conditions, soluble salts will crystallize out causing the damage described in section 4.1.2.

CRUMBLING. Whilst certain ceramic bodies become more robust on drying out (see HARDENING, above), others, particularly very coarse underfired earthenware, may in fact become more liable to crumble. This is because the surface tension of the contained water is holding the crumbs together (plate 4.17).

BREAKAGE AND ABRASION. Perhaps the most obvious deterioration of ceramics during and after excavation is breakage, abrasion, and loss of paint or glaze as a result of the mishandling of artefacts.

4.5.6 *Stabilization*

4.5.6.1 Passive

After soil has been cleaned off, most ceramics from land sites benefit from being allowed to dry out; only the small group which crumble on drying must be treated otherwise. Ceramics from salty sites are of two types. The first are those which are visibly held together by salt crystals and must be kept dry to prevent the crystals dissolving and the material failing apart. The second are those from wet, salt-laden soils or from the sea, where water must be retained to prevent the salts from crystallizing until they can be washed out.

4.5.6.2 Active

If, after cleaning and air-drying, soft bodies do not regain adequate strength or, worse still, fall apart, active steps of consolidation must be

Plate 4.17 Underfired earthenware showing fragmentation on drying out after excavation

taken. Normally it is not difficult to consolidate porous ceramics with resoluble materials (section 3.4.2.2) but with some fabrics, notably the dry poorly fired clay of Bronze Age date, soaking in a solution of consolidant is enough to make them crumble. Here consolidant has to be brushed or dripped on. In other cases, the use of partial vacuum to enhance the penetration of the consolidant is not possible, as when a weak fabric contains air bubbles, as for example certain terracotta sculptures.[39] Wherever possible, ceramics are consolidated in a dry state but where drying leads to crumbling (section 4.5.5) it may be necessary to use a water-miscible consolidant; emulsions are useful but have inherent drawbacks (section 3.4.2.2).

To achieve stabilization of salt-laden ceramics, reduction in the level of soluble salts is required (section 4.1.3). Soaking in several changes of water (section 3.4.2.1) is usually sufficient but for marine ceramics a more rigorous regime is required. In the early stages, soaking in distilled or deionized water is not necessary and may, in fact, be harmful by producing high osmotic pressures between the salt-laden ceramic and the surrounding water. Sometimes even tap-water has had this effect and so initial soaking in sea-water diluted with tap-water has been recommended.[38] Prolonged periods of soaking are necessary to reduce salt levels sufficiently. When removing soluble salts problems arise with flaking surfaces, paint, or glaze, or with a powdering or crumbling body where soaking is destructive. As for stone (section 4.2.6.2), a search is being made for suitable consolidants which will not seal in soluble salts and will not discolour or become irreversible upon prolonged soaking in water, so that these ceramics may be consolidated before wetting.[40] More drastic steps have been taken in the case of unbaked clay artefacts where soaking is impossible and consolidation prior to soaking unsuccessful. On rare occasions, the decision has been taken to fire the clay to produce a ceramic which can be soaked.[41] Of course such treatment is only justifiable after considerable discussion and where records are well made and maintained.

The reintroduction of translucency into a decayed glaze carries with it the same problems and limitations as attempting this for decayed glass (section 4.4.6.2).

4.5.7 Reconstruction

Before sherds are rejoined with adhesives, some thought should be given as to why it is being carried out. Reconstruction is undertaken to obtain an accurate profile of a vessel or design on a tile, to enable an artefact to be displayed, to keep contiguous sherds together or to avoid further abrasion during storage. However, it does make packing of a vessel more problematic and storage more bulky. Furthermore, the adhesive is likely to discolour and may fail, especially if soaking for salts is later required (section 4.5.6.2), and much damage can be incurred and time wasted if the mending is wrongly carried out.

This damage can occur in several ways. First, if the fabric of the ceramic is powdering or crumbling, joining of sherds is inevitably harmful. The adhesive simply sticks to the crumbling surface of the broken edge which becomes detached from the rest of the sherd, causing the join to fall apart at once or in the long term (plate 4.18); an accurate reconstruction is then impossible, the detail and dimensions of the broken edges being lost. The situation is not mastered simply by painting the area around the broken edges first with a dilute adhesive to harden them, for the detachment of the weak fabric will simply occur deeper into the sherd than otherwise. The same type of damage is seen in tough earthenwares where much too strong an adhesive such as an epoxy has been used. In this case, if any stress or shock is applied, it is effective within the fabric and not at the tough adhesive line. Again, similar damage results if the chosen adhesive shrinks on setting or in the long term, and where this contraction is greater than the strength of the fabric (figure 4.6). Not only are thermosetting resins too strong for most earthenwares, they are also impossible to remove because they penetrate the porous fabric (section 3.4.2.4), a problem which does not occur with well-fired non-porous

Plate 4.18 A join fails in a reconstructed ceramic as a result of the body powdering. A detached skin of adhesive and ceramic is visible

stonewares and porcelains. This criterion of reversibility in ceramic reconstruction is not only ethical, it is also essential in practice since errors are impossible to ensure against.

Different fabrics will call for different adhesive systems, not only for the reasons given above but also to ensure adherence and setting. Many thermoplastic resins in standard solvents will set in and adhere to porous rough-surfaced earthenwares (section 3.4.2.4). However, since stonewares and more especially porcelains are dense and glassy, such systems are not useful. Thus resins setting by chemical reaction rather than loss of solvent, and ones with similar polarity to the fabric, must be used to

153

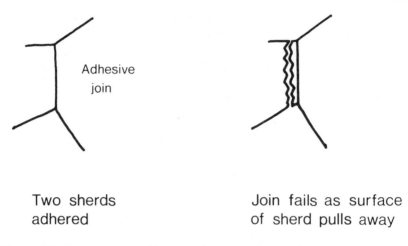

Two sherds   Join fails as surface
adhered   of sherd pulls away

Figure 4.6 Damage caused by use of wrong adhesive for joining sherds

obtain setting and adherence in this second group of fabrics. Improvements in thermosetting adhesives have now made the use of metal dowels in ceramic reconstruction obsolete. There are of course further criteria involved in the choice of adhesives in general and these are discussed in section 3.4.2.4.

Accurate reconstruction[42] can only be achieved if the broken edges are *completely* free from soil or salt encrustations and if the exposed surfaces are brought into as close a contact as possible. This means it is essential that excess adhesive is not used and that sufficient but not *excessive* physical force is used to bring about this contact; a feel for the balance of pressure required is achieved only through practice. Good contact between sherds must of course be maintained whilst the adhesive sets, by using adhesive tapes, but these *must* be removed as soon as possible after the setting of the adhesive. Tapes must never be used to join sherds for a long period of time, because their adhesives both stain the fabrics and become insoluble (plate 4.19). Tapes cannot be used at all where there is a flaking surface, glaze, or paint and so the sherds must be balanced in a sand tray (figure 4.7) whilst the adhesive sets.

If sherds are missing from an object it may be impossible or damaging to reconstruct it without filling in some of the gaps – damaging because of the asymmetrical stress put on the edges of sherds or the physical instability of the conjoined sherds. Occasionally, gap filling is required either to make an object readable in display or for aesthetic reasons. It is done either with plastic materials which are modelled into shape, or with more fluid ones which are cast in, this being the more difficult operation. The criteria for choice of material for gap filling are much as those for adhesives, lack of shrinkage being essential to prevent the adjoining sherd

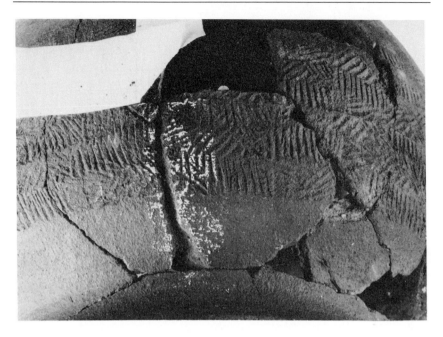

Plate 4.19 White stain resulting from allowing masking tape to remain on reconstructed ceramic

edges being ripped off (plate 3.17) or the made-up piece from falling out. Texture of the piece is important for aesthetic reasons and there is much debate concerning how completely it should be colour matched. Gap filling is a specialist job for it is difficult to achieve a visually satisfactory result without considerable practice, and for porous ceramics it is easy to cause discoloration (whitening or staining) of the neighbouring sherds. Plaster of Paris is used for casting missing pieces of earthenware and stoneware but modified commercial products based on calcium sulphate, such as Polyfilla or Hydrocal, are used for modelling in pieces. They are useful since they can be made into a putty, do not shrink as much for they usually contain a filler, and have a longer working time. Being based on gypsum, they soften in water for removal. An alternative material, BJK or Fibrenyl dough which softens in solvents and has a texture more sympathetic to coarse pottery, has been used in the past.[43] BJK dough is based on kaolin, jute fibre (now replaced by paper dust which is not nearly so suitable), and a consolidant. Unfortunately it shrinks, and unless used slowly and with great care, can damage the edges of the sherds as it contracts over a period of weeks.

4.5.8 Summary

Since in many cases ceramics form the largest quantity of artefactual material recovered from a site, and since the material, being well preserved, can be treated on site, some space is given here to its conservation in the field. This includes the joining of sherds.

4.5.8.1 Treatment on land sites

Where paint, gilding, or flaking glaze is suspected, soil must be allowed to remain adhering to a ceramic when it is lifted. If a pot is whole, it is not cleaned out but lifted full (section 3.1.1.1). It will be heavier than expected and will need considerable support. A soil sample of the surrounding deposit should be taken to compare with the contents. If the pot is broken or cracked and is of a robust fabric it may be simpler to dismantle it *in situ*, retaining the contents, unless there is reason to believe it contains a burial, coins, etc. Where ceramics are too frail to survive straightforward removal from the ground, they must be lifted using supports (section 3.1.1.1); consolidants must only be used as a last resort. A tiled pavement is best recorded, photographed, and planned and then lifted piece by piece, each being numbered separately (section 4.3.7).

Vessels lifted with their contents must be kept damp (section 3.1.1) or else shrinkage of the soil could damage the fabric and the contents. Where paint, gilding, or flaking glaze is suspected, ceramics should be kept damp until cleaned in a laboratory. Those with thick encrustations of salt also should be kept damp until treated, as should poorly fired material which crumbles on drying, and ceramics from very salty wet deposits. It is also much easier to clean most other material in the field if it too has not dried out first. After cleaning, ceramics can be air-dried, which may in fact cause them to harden. Fragile ceramics visibly held together by salt crystals must be kept dry.

Unpainted well-fired earthenwares, with or without well-fitting glazes, undecayed stonewares and porcelains may be cleaned on site. They should be washed by constant sluicing in clear water and brushing with soft brushes, all the while looking for decoration, associated material, and soft fabric which may be dislodged or scratched by such treatment. It is inadvisable to leave sherds soaking: they may be less well fired than they appear. Insoluble salt deposits could be removed mechanically with a scalpel before they harden on drying but if any damage is likely, cleaning must be left to a laboratory.

Washed sherds may be air-dried, out of direct sunlight or artificial heat sources. They can be marked by first painting just a small area on an inside/underside surface with diluted adhesive (section 3.4.2.4) and covering the ink with a second layer of adhesive; this makes the mark easier to take off at a later date if required.

No other material, whether soft-bodied fabrics, painted/gilded ceramics, ceramics with flaking surfaces/glazes, those held together by salt crystals, etc., should be cleaned on site.

Hard well-fired ceramics from very salty soils could be desalinated on site as for marine ceramics (section 4.5.8.2), so beginning the process of stabilization.

Packing for storage and transport must incorporate adequate padding to prevent abrasion, caused by sherds rubbing against each other, and crushing.

4.5.8.2   Treatment at marine sites

Ceramics from marine sites should be placed in sea-water diluted with fresh water to start the process of desalination. The water is renewed daily, gradually reducing the quantity of sea-water added. Only after prolonged periods of soaking will it be possible to dry sherds with a minimum risk of damage from salt crystallization. Drying should not take place until salt levels have been tested and are known to be low.

Insoluble marine encrustations should be removed mechanically, for example with a sharp scalpel, while they are still wet and before they harden by contact with the atmosphere. However, mechanical removal of encrustations should only be attempted where the fabric of the ceramic is completely sound. Chemical treatments are best left until the condition of the ceramic can be fully assessed in a conservation laboratory.

4.5.8.3   Joining sherds

If reconstruction is desired, in order to avoid error and damage, it must be done correctly. The following points discussed in detail in earlier sections must be considered before it is undertaken: Is it essential? Is the fabric strong enough to take an adhesive? Is it porcelain, dense stoneware, or painted, gilded, or with a flaking glaze? (None of these types is easily reconstructed.) If it is decided to go ahead, a second set of questions is posed: Are the breaks clean from soil and salt encrustations? Has the fabric been consolidated? (If so, pressure-sensitive tapes must be avoided as they may well damage the surface when pulled off.) Is there paint or glaze likely to lift? (If so, all adhesive tapes must be avoided.) Has desalting been carried out if necessary?

Before reconstruction takes place, the following *must* be made available: a workbench, a good light source, adequate ventilation, cotton wool buds, pressure-sensitive tape (drafting or cellulose) or water-wetting paper tape (for consolidated ceramics), a sand tray at least 5 centimetres deep (avoid builders' sand which contains lime, and sea-sand which contains salt), a suitable resoluble adhesive in a handy tube (section

3.4.2.4), and a small jar of solvent. When bonding ceramics, it is essential to have a small quantity of solvent to hand (not more than 100 millilitres and kept in a sealed jar) in order to take down poor joins or mop-up drips. Amyl acetate is the best choice for cellulose nitrate but acetone can be used both for this and polyvinyl acetate. Ensure that a thorough search has been made to collect every available sherd from the ceramic to be reconstructed (this saves time and temper).

Method
1. Lay out sherds and determine their positions. Temporary reconstruction using adhesive tape may assist in this.
2. Decide on a programme of joins. With a vessel, start at the base to ensure curvature is as accurate as possible. Where this is missing, start with the rim. Note if there are any pieces which can be 'locked out'; when their neighbours are set in place, are the angles now such that the piece cannot be fitted in? If so it must be put in place before one of its neighbours (figure 4.7).
3. Cut pieces of tape 5 centimetres long and touch ends to bench edge.
4. For each join: squeeze a thin trail of adhesive along centre of break of one sherd. Push the two parts of the join together and joggle into place. Run a finger over join without looking. If a 'step' exists, continue joggling until it disappears. Now press the two parts together as hard as is possible. Check for a step. Stretch a piece of tape and without moving join, place it across join at right angles. Stand in sand tray so that join is held out of the sand but parallel to the bench top with gravity helping to hold the sherd in place. Leave for at least ten minutes.
5. Only try and build up from one core per vessel; if you start from

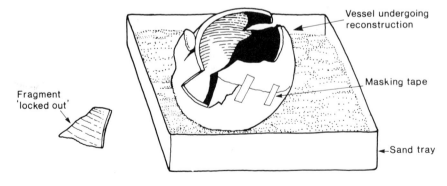

Figure 4.7 Reconstructing a ceramic vessel; a fragment has been 'locked out'

two places at once the halves will, without doubt, not fit when you attempt to join them together.

6. *Never* leave tape affixed to pottery for more than a few days. Remove excess adhesive with a swab of solvent.

7. Errors can be rectified by dissolving the join with swabs of solvent. However, if this is repeated too often, two dangers arise. One is that a white bloom appears which may be dispersed only in a different solvent which may need to be advised by a specialist. Another is that a pale porous body will become stained and can then be treated only by lengthy conservation methods.

8. Record the make of adhesive used in the artefact-recording system.

4.5.8.4   Storage and display

Once treated, most ceramics are the least problematic material to store and display. A wide range of RH and temperature is tolerated but oscillating temperatures could cause surfaces to spall. Reconstructed and consolidated material is subject to restrictions regarding the synthetics used (section 3.4.2).

The most damaging environmental hazard is poor handling, and it is essential that soiling, especially of pale fabrics, is prevented for dirt may become difficult to remove. Likewise, fungal/bacterial growth, especially on packing, must be prevented by control of RH to under 65 per cent.

Chapter Five

Metals

5.1 General[1]

5.1.1 Structure and properties[2]

Metals are made of crystals known as grains. The physical properties of metals are affected partly by the size and shape of the grains. For example, by hammering bronze, the grains are flattened, thereby giving a stronger but more brittle material. Subsequent heating, known as annealing, may produce smaller equiaxial grains which contain a degree of the increased strength and a loss of some of the brittleness. This change occurs at the recrystallization temperature which for bronze is in the region of 600°C, whilst for lead it is as low as normal room temperature.

Apart from the shape of the grains, the physical properties of metals are affected by the material comprising them. In pure metals this is simple but in alloys, which are mixtures of metals and of other elements, the grains can be made of either a pure element, or a chemical compound made from the alloying elements, or a mixture of these. Each composition which occurs is known as a phase. Different phases have different physical properties and each will lend some of these characteristics to the resultant metal; thus the presence of a brittle compound phase will make the overall metal to some degree brittle. Which phases are present in an alloy will depend on the concentration of the alloying elements, the temperatures to which these have been subjected, and the rate at which they have been cooled down. For example, a bronze containing about 5 per cent tin will be made of grains all of one type of phase, a soft mixture of copper and tin. However, if the concentration of tin is raised, not only is the melting point of the metal lowered but also a new, hard, brittle compound of tin and copper is formed, affecting the properties of the resulting bronze. If the metal has been cooled very rapidly, excessive amounts of this brittle compound form, but to some extent it can be dispersed by gentle reheating. In certain cases, this phase alteration can

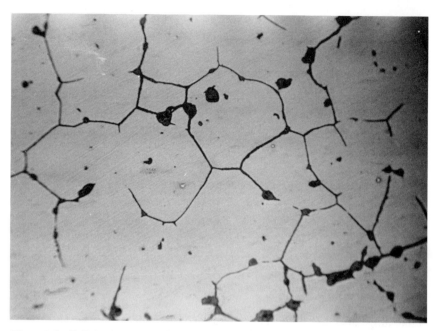

Plate 5.1 Polished section of a corroded copper alloy showing grains formed during casting

occur at normal temperatures, but usually only over a very extended time-span.

Metals usually contain other materials in small quantities as impurities, but a substance sometimes included in larger amounts is slag. Slag is a type of glass which may contain some crystalline material; it is formed during smelting (section 5.2.1) from the siliceous material present in most ores. It is found either within the grains or at the grain boundaries, affecting the properties of the metal and becoming elongated in the direction in which the metal is worked. By studying the structure and constitution of the grains and phases of metals, an understanding not only of the properties of a particular metal but also of the history of its manufacture may result. This study, metallography, is carried out using a polarizing microscope to view a polished surface of the metal in question (plate 5.1). Normally, therefore, a small sample of an artefact about 50 cubic millimetres in size is removed; this is then mounted in plastic and polished smooth. It must be noted, however, that if the metal artefact has been reheated or deformed since manufacture, an eventuality which could occur after excavation, then some of this information may be lost. The critical recrystallization temperatures vary for each metal and alloy, but a guide to them is given in the following sections.

5.1.2 Associated materials

5.1.2.1 Joins[3]

Metals can be joined either mechanically, by folding or riveting, or else structurally. Some metals, most notably iron, exhibit the extremely useful property that, when two exposed surfaces are brought into intimate contact (by heat and/or hammering), they adhere to one another by welding. However, there are other methods of joining metals and these require the addition of a variety of materials.

Soldering involves the formation of an alloy between the solder and the surface of the metal(s) being joined. Thus to function effectively a solder must be able to alloy with the metal, and must be able to come into close contact with the metal without interference from an oxide film. To obtain this intimate contact, the metal is first cleaned and then the solder applied molten, which means that it must have a lower melting point than the metal. In order further to ensure this contact, a material known as a flux is used to remove any oxide or prevent its formation during soldering, and to aid the flow of the solder over the metal. If the two edges of the metal to be joined are first covered in solder independently and then joined by localized heating, the joining is called sweating on.

Hard solders are metal alloys with high melting points which often are not far below that of the melting point of the metal being joined. This means that alloying between the solder and metal will be extensive and the join strong. It is exemplified by the use of silver solder on silver or brazing spelter on brass. In antiquity the fluxes for hard solders might have included salt plus natron, or winestone (the crystals appearing in old wine).

Soft solders have lower melting points and if these are much below that of the metal, little alloying occurs and the joint, made simply by keying, is weak. Lead/tin alloys are the commonest soft solders, used with fluxes such as beeswax and resin; whilst these fluxes do not remove oxides, they prevent film formation and then burn off.

Adhesives are used to join non-metallic materials such as glass, coral, or gems to metals. They may be organic glues or inorganic cements (section 4.3.1).

5.1.2.2 Differential metallic surfacings[4]

It is common to find that the metallic colour of the surface of a metal is different from that of the body. This may be the deliberate result of techniques used to decorate or make the metal object appear more valuable than it is, or to protect it against corrosion. Surfacings may be formed by the application of a thin layer of a different metal which is affixed by mechanical keying, adhesives, or fusion. In this latter case the problems of discontinuity caused by oxide films are parallel to those encountered during soldering joins (section 5.1.2.1), and thus surface preparation and use of fluxes are necessary preliminaries.

Alternatively, these surfacings may be obtained by the removal of one or more constituent metals from the surface of an alloy. Later (section 5.1.3.2) it is shown that this phenomenon, known as surface enrichment, may occur naturally during corrosion processes, but when it is produced artificially on silver or gold alloys it is known as blanching or depletion gilding. Here, the base metals in the surface layer of the alloys are altered by heating, the oxides produced being removed by soaking in natural acids. If the base metal is heated in brick dust, the corrosive salts present in the powder enhance the depletion.

The 'silvery' colour found on some metal artefacts can be produced by a variety of metals; until these have been identified it is more judicious to refer to them as 'white metal' rather than to prejudge the issue by assuming the surface to be one of the types described below.

A *silver* surface sometimes applied over copper alloys can appear bright even when it contains up to 70 per cent tin, when it should be more accurately termed 'tinning'. It is possible to hammer a silver sheet thin enough to weld onto an object but the fit is never very satisfactory. It is more usual to produce a silver coating by first applying silver solder (section 5.1.2.1) over the object and then blanching out the base metal. There would appear to be numerous other methods of silvering, one important method being the use of silver amalgam. Here a paste of silver and mercury is applied to a surface which is then heated, driving off the mercury and fusing the silver. Traces of mercury may be found where an amalgam has been used. Alternatively, a silver surface commonly is formed by the blanching of base silver objects (section 5.6.1).

Tinning, which can be exceedingly thin, usually appears duller than silvering owing to a covering layer of tin oxide (section 5.4.2). It is often impure, being alloyed with lead, copper, or even brass. Crude lead alone could give a similar effect. Since these alloys are relatively cheap and have low melting points, they usually are applied by dipping the object in a bath of molten alloy, but there are numerous other possibilities.[5] High-tin bronzes may have a white tin-rich layer at their surface formed by the segregation of tin during casting; this is known as 'tin sweat'.

Arsenic has been found to give a white lustrous surface to copper alloys. This can occur either from the segregation of arsenic out of a copper alloy during casting or from the application of an arsenic ore to the surface followed by reduction in charcoal.

Since *gold* can be hammered into very thin flexible sheets, it can be glued onto a metal surface with an adhesive such as size. More usually,[6] gold on a silver or copper alloy is contiguous with surface metal, this being achieved by depletion gilding of either a solid base gold alloy object or a copper alloy which has been washed with a gold/copper alloy; in this latter case it may be called wash or fusion gilding. A very thin layer of gilding can be applied by 'fire gilding' using a gold amalgam which, as in the case of silver, may leave traces of mercury at the interface. Yet another bonding technique is the welding of very thin sheets of gold onto the surface of an artefact.

It is possible that *brass* or *bronze* could be applied to iron objects, giving a yellowish surface, and it may be that such a surface would be tinned first. It should be noted that a dull golden surface deposit can be produced on a copper or a lead alloy by a corrosion phenomenon during burial (sections 5.3.2.1 & 5.5.2.1).

5.1.2.3 Patinas

Patinas will be shown to be normally a result of natural corrosion, but since it is possible to alter the colour of a metal surface deliberately as well, it is sometimes difficult to determine whether patination was intended or not. The colours obtainable by artificial means will be described within the sections on specific metals.

5.1.2.4 Lacquers and paints

To keep metals bright, it is possible to exclude a certain degree of air, moisture, and salt by the application of lacquers, waxes, and greases. These actually have been found on ancient copper alloy objects (section 5.5.4) but they may well have been used on other metals as well. Paints such as red lead have also been detected on metal surfaces.

5.1.2.5 Niello

Niello is a black lustrous material used as an inlay mainly on silver or gold. It is either a mixture of the sulphides of copper and silver or, more simply, silver sulphide;[7] it is fused to the metal substrate.

5.1.2.6 Enamels

Enamels are made by covering copper alloys, silver, gold, and even iron with glass. Usually glass powder is placed on the metal and heated so that it fuses within itself and to the metal, the temperature required depending on the composition of the glass (section 4.4.1.1) and the metal. A glass must be chosen which will fuse below the melting point of the metal, run over the metal as it liquefies, fuse to the metal, and contract at the same rate and to the same degree as the metal, preventing the glass cracking and falling off. If, instead of powder, blocks of glass are used, these will have to be held in place mechanically or with adhesives. Glass blocks made by slicing up multicoloured rods known as millefiori (figure 5.1a) cannot be applied as a powder and it seems as though they were often attached by a matrix of more fusible red glass (figure 5.1b).[8] The deterioration and treatment of enamels is discussed in chapter 4.

(a) Formation of a millefiori element.

1. Square sectioned glass rod formed

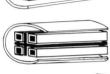
2. Rod encased in sheet of glass of another colour

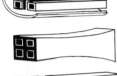
3. Several similar rods placed together and encased in another glass sheet.

4. Whole heated up and drawn out to form thinner and longer rod.

5. Rod cut into elements

(b) Formation of a champlevé enamel

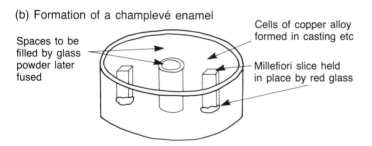

Cells of copper alloy formed in casting etc

Spaces to be filled by glass powder later fused

Millefiori slice held in place by red glass

Figure 5.1 Manufacture of an enamel.

5.1.2.7 Metallic inlays

Metals can be set in recesses in other metals either by simple mechanical keying or else by a bonding similar to that described for solders. In this case, the choice and application of inlay will mirror those used to join materials (section 5.1.2.1).

5.1.3 Deterioration

By far the most important type of deterioration in metals results in chemical rather than physical damage. Chemicals derived from both inorganic sources and the activity of biological organisms are ever-present in the environment and usually bring about a chemical change in the metals, known as corrosion. Except for gold, the metals used in antiquity are not particularly stable and in most natural environments they tend to react with other components to form more stable compounds. This should not be surprising since the raw material for these metals is ore, that is, stable chemical compounds of the metals which can only be extracted by the process of smelting, the reverse of corrosion. There are two types of corrosion a metal can undergo: 'dry' corrosion, usually taking the form of thin surface patination or tarnishing; and 'aqueous' corrosion, where the metal is attacked more vigorously because of the presence of moisture.

5.1.3.1 Dry corrosion

Since virtually every natural environment contains some moisture, this type of corrosion in relation to archaeological artefacts is less significant than corrosion involving water. When a metal is polished to a bright fresh surface and left exposed to a dry atmosphere, it becomes dull and tarnished. This is because the oxygen and/or pollutants such as hydrogen sulphide in the atmosphere attack the surface:

$$
\text{metal} +
\begin{cases}
\text{oxygen} \longrightarrow \text{metal oxide} \\
\text{hydrogen sulphide} \longrightarrow \text{metal sulphide}
\end{cases}
$$

The resulting oxide or sulphide film may have a very similar crystal structure to the underlying parent metal, fitting it well and preventing the access of further gases. Such films are said to be protective as they only allow superficial corrosion to occur. However, some films fail to mimic the metal crystal structure, do not adhere well, and so fail to prevent further corrosion. These reactions occur more readily in the presence of moisture, as described below.

5.1.3.2 Aqueous corrosion[9]

Much more common than dry corrosion is that where moisture is involved. Moisture is present in most natural environments and, unless it is locked up as ice, can cause considerable corrosion damage. In normal atmospheric conditions moisture is present as water vapour, but it may condense onto a cold metal surface, or be attracted by hygroscopic compounds soiling a metal surface. Where moisture is present, corrosion processes are no longer simple chemical combinations, but involve electrochemistry.

ELECTROCHEMICAL CORROSION. Electrons, negatively charged particles, are released when a metal atom forms an ion, in this case a positively charged particle called a cation. This whole process is termed *oxidation* and is essentially the removal of electrons; oxygen itself need not be involved, nor an oxide necessarily formed. Thus when n electrons are lost:

$$
\underset{\text{metal atom}}{M} \xrightarrow{\text{oxidation}} \underset{\text{metal ion}}{M^{n+}} + \underset{\text{electrons}}{ne^-}
$$

Anode (oxidation)   Cathode (reduction)

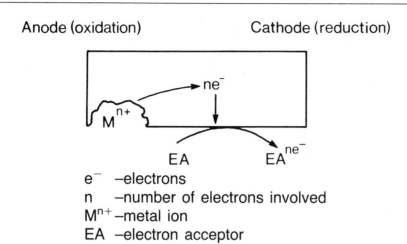

e⁻ –electrons
n –number of electrons involved
M^{n+} –metal ion
EA –electron acceptor

Figure 5.2 Aqueous corrosion of a metal

This reaction takes place at a site known as the anode and results in the destruction of the metal. The electrons which are released as the metal corrodes must be consumed in a complementary reaction called *reduction*, which takes place at a site known as the cathode. This new site may be an adjacent area of the metal surface, or the outermost layers of an existing corrosion deposit, but it depends on an electron acceptor being present; the rate of replenishment of this electron acceptor at the cathode will determine the rate of corrosion of the metal (figure 5.2). Since this system results in an electron flow and thus a current, it is called a corrosion cell.

In aqueous environments, where oxygen is freely available, the electron acceptor at the cathode is oxygen itself: oxygen and water combine accepting electrons to form hydroxyl ions in the oxygen absorption reaction:

$$O_2 \quad + 2H_2O + \quad 4e^- \quad \rightarrow \quad 4(OH)^-$$
oxygen   water   electrons   hydroxyl ions

Where oxygen levels are low, hydrogen ions act as electron acceptors instead, being reduced to hydrogen atoms:

$$2H^+ \quad + \quad 2e^- \quad \rightarrow \quad H + H \quad \rightarrow \quad H_2$$
hydrogen ion   electron   absorbed hydrogen   hydrogen molecule

This reaction, however, is sluggish unless hydrogen ions are in great excess, that is at around pH 4. There are other factors which affect corrosion in oxygen-free conditions and these are discussed later.

ACTIVE CORROSION, PASSIVATION, AND IMMUNITY. The metal cations released at the anode now have two options. First, they may enter the environment as aqueous ions and precipitate away from the metal which continues to corrode. This usually occurs in very acid or extreme alkaline environments when all trace of the metal is lost, apart from perhaps a stain in the surrounding soil. Alternatively they may react immediately with anions in the environment and form corrosion products (carbonates, oxides, hydroxides, sulphates, etc.) which adhere to the surface of the metal. Such solid products, especially the carbonates found in alkaline soils together with certain oxide films, tend to stifle corrosion cells, preventing further corrosion. This preserves the bulk of the metal of the artefact and is termed 'passivation'.

Thus, in general, one of two situations develops: (a) active corrosion – the metal forms soluble products which move away from the metal into the surrounding environment; (b) passivation – the metal forms solid corrosion products which adhere to its surface and prevent or restrict further attack.

Metals are sometimes found to corrode in environments where it would be supposed that passive films would develop to prevent attack. This can be due to the presence of certain aggressive ions, chlorides being the prime example. Unlike other ions, these migrate through protective films and cause the metal beneath to corrode.

Although, as is shown above, whether a metal corrodes away or is passified depends on the stability of the corrosion products which in turn depends on the pH of the environment, this is not the whole picture. Since corrosion is a reaction involving oxidation and reduction, it is also dependent on the energy of the system; this is described by the redox potential (E_H). The more energy there is in a system, the more oxidizing it is and the more likely it is that the metal will corrode. Where the E_H is very low, as in a reducing environment, no corrosion can occur and the metal is said to be immune. The combined effect of these two variables of pH and E_H acting together on a metal can be shown on a diagram (figure 5.3). This device was first exploited by Marcel Pourbaix and thus the display may be referred to as a 'Pourbaix diagram'.[10] Conditions of low redox potential resulting in immunity rarely occur in normal soils, because percolating rain-water is continuously replenishing the soil with oxygen which raises the redox potential. However, such conditions often prevail in stagnant environments (estuarine, foreshore and compacted urban deposits and some peat bogs) and allow certain metals such as copper to be immune to corrosion. Other more reactive metals, for example iron, which need relatively little energy for corrosion, would require abnormally low redox potentials to achieve immunity. However, in environments where oxygen availability is restricted there is yet another contributor to the corrosion environment, namely the micro-organism.

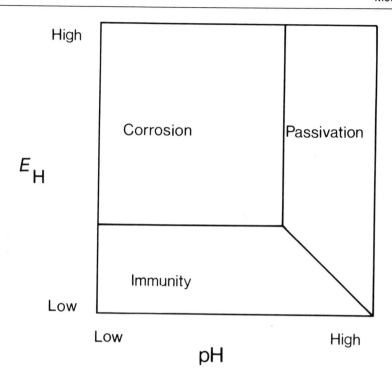

Figure 5.3 Simplified 'Pourbaix diagram' for the activity of copper in water

ANAEROBIC MICROBIAL CORROSION. It was not long before corrosion scientists realized that the above was not the complete picture since freshly buried iron was corroding even in conditions of very low redox potential. It was realized that anaerobic sulphate-reducing bacteria (section 2.1.1.2) facilitate corrosion, probably by the production of sulphide ions which at once combine with metal ions at the anode thereby allowing more metal to oxidize. The metabolism of the bacteria is summarized as

$$SO_4^{2-} + 8H \rightarrow [S^{2-}] + 4H_2O$$
sulphate hydrogen   sulphide

These bacteria only function in particular deposits when the redox potential is −150 to +110 millivolts and the pH is 5.5 to 8, such as are found in dense terrestrial or marine muds. Copper alloys are exempt from this enhanced corrosion since copper is toxic to bacteria.

DIFFERENTIAL AERATION AND GALVANIC CELLS. In order that a corrosion cell may be set up, one area of the material must become a cathode and another an anode. This differentiation can be brought about in several ways. If oxygen is more concentrated at one point of the surface than it is at another, this area will assume the role of the cathode whilst the low oxygen area will corrode. This is called a differential aeration cell, and can be seen when an area of metal under a rivet corrodes at the expense of the surrounding metal. High-energy areas are inclined to lose electrons more readily than low-energy areas; since there is high energy where one crystal lattice meets another, grain boundaries within a metal will become anodic to the enclosed grain and will corrode preferentially. Anodes and cathodes can be set up therefore either on a large scale or at a microscopic level.

A further cause of the production of anodes and cathodes is found where, within an artefact, two dissimilar metals or phases, both of which lose electrons with different degrees of readiness, are in contact. The ease with which electrons are lost is measured by the electrode potential of the material, and for metals this can be ordered by susceptibility as in the 'galvanic series' for example (see below). The metals most likely to lose electrons are called electronegative, and can be seen to be the base metals which therefore will corrode more rapidly than those least likely to lose electrons, the electropositive or noble, non-corroding metals.

Galvanic series

	wrought	cast								
Zn	Fe	Fe	pewter (50:50)	Pb	Sn	brass	Cu	bronze	Ag	Au
Base										Noble
electronegative (vice versa in USA)			electropositive (vice versa in USA)							

In theory, where two dissimilar metals or phases are in contact, such as copper and iron, the 'noble' metal, in this case copper, will corrode less than usual, acting as a cathode. It thus becomes what is termed cathodically protected. The base metal, in this case iron, would corrode more than usual. Cathodic protection would continue until all the iron had been converted into corrosion products. With alloys the picture is complex: it may be that the base component is present in such small quantities that its loss is not noticeable, and thus the alloy appears more resistant to corrosion than the more noble metal alone. Alternatively, intermetallic phases may occur which act as sacrificial anodes or as corrosion-resistant cathodically protected areas.

In practice, galvanic corrosion is influenced by factors in addition to the ones described. Thus the relative areas of the metals, the properties of the local environment, and the resistivity of surface films may all affect the predicted behaviour.

This introduction to corrosion is inevitably incomplete; for comprehensive explanations, the reader is referred to the numerous specialized texts on the subject (see note 9).

SUMMARY OF AQUEOUS CORROSION. Whilst most metals tend to tarnish in dry air, they will corrode much faster in the presence of water. The metal reacts with chemicals in the environment such as oxygen, carbon dioxide, salts, etc. and forms corrosion products such as oxides, carbonates, and sulphates. If these products are soluble, as is usual in acidic environments, the metal will continue to corrode to nothing, or at most a stain in the soil. However, if the products are insoluble, they will slow down or even prevent further corrosion of the remaining metal. This process, known as passivation, unfortunately can be disrupted by certain pollutants such as chlorides, a constituent of common salt.

Corrosion is also controlled by the level of oxygen in the environment. Its absence normally results in the prevention of corrosion but in the case of iron, the activity of sulphate-reducing bacteria (section 2.1.1.2) complicates the picture.

Some metals known as base metals are much more likely to corrode than the noble metals gold and silver. The common metals of antiquity can be graded in reactivity from highly corrodable (base) to unreactive (noble):

Zinc Iron Tin Lead Copper Silver Gold
Most base   Most noble

Where two metals are in contact, a particular type of corrosion occurs so that the more base metal corrodes faster than usual whilst the more noble corrodes more slowly. This is galvanic corrosion where the more noble metal is protected from attack.

Since corrosion processes are so complex, it is difficult to generalize on the probable state of artefacts from particular deposits. However, because rates of corrosion, except of gold, are relatively fast when considered in relation to the time archaeological material has been buried, it is unlikely that uncorroded metal will be found on excavation except where corrosion has been prevented altogether.

5.1.3.3 Corrosion products

The chemical constituents of corrosion products will depend on the reactants present in the environment. The products may be laid down as amorphous powders but it is more usual that crystals will be formed. Since many of these crystals are similar to those of the naturally occurring minerals, corrosion products are often described by their mineral name. When crystals are formed slowly they tend to grow large and so appear translucent, whilst those formed rapidly are small and appear paler and opaque. Corrosion crusts are seldom composed of a single pure corrosion product; normally they comprise a number of products, the crystals of which may be intertwined and may incorporate impurities from the surrounding deposit.[11]

5.1.3.4 Pseudomorphs and original surfaces

It may be that the base metal iron, but sometimes the nobler metals of lead, copper, and even silver, when buried for more than a few hundred years, do not survive. Where a deposit has a very high or low pH, the corrosion products are soluble and no artefacts remain to be excavated. It is possible that their presence could be detected from a stain in the deposit or by some more subtle chemical test. In many other deposits where corrosion products neither dissolve nor protect particular metals from attack, buried metal artefacts are only retrieved on excavation as pseudomorphs. That is, the original shapes of the artefacts are retained but they are now composed of different materials, in this case corrosion products such as oxides and carbonates: little or no metal remains. The phrase 'original surface' in relation to these pseudomorphs is used to designate the level and topography of the surfaces of the artefacts before they decayed. In certain cases, an original surface may be readily seen, being maintained by a dense, compact, corrosion product or by the noble part of an alloy, the base part having dissolved out. On other occasions, the original surface is not immediately visible, being obscured by bulky corrosion products. However, it will be shown in the following sections that normally the level and topography of the original surface of an artefact is retained within its pseudomorph and, by careful conservation, can be exposed. The reliability of this 'original surface' is less certain for some metals than others but it is a concept of utmost importance in the investigative cleaning of artefacts.

Another result of corrosion, which requires great care in investigative cleaning, is that of pseudomorphic replacement of organic materials. Here it is not just the metal artefact which is retained by corrosion products, but also any organic material associated with it.[12] Thus, in neutral to alkaline oxygenated environments in which organic materials normally decay and metals produce insoluble corrosion products, small traces of wood, leather, bone, etc. may be found within corrosion crusts.

5.1.4 *Investigative cleaning*

Like all artefacts, metal objects must be recorded before they receive any treatment. As will be shown in the following sections, radiography (3.3.1.3), is particularly important. Also crucial in investigative cleaning, is an understanding of the phenomena of 'original surface' and of 'replaced organic material' (section 5.1.3.4). A problem can arise when it comes to visible corrosion products, for, as pointed out earlier (section

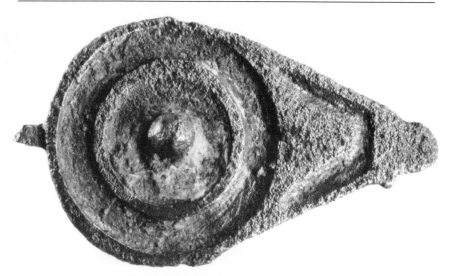

Plate 5.2 Copper alloy seal-box lid which has been stripped; any trace of enamel has been removed and the metal revealed is badly pitted

5.1.3.3), the colour of such products can be extremely varied and somewhat misleading. Thus when recording metal artefacts, it is usual to identify corrosion products by colour and texture only, appending a mineral name where this has been demonstrated by analysis. Analysis will also be needed to identify any metal or surfacing revealed.

Until recently, metallic artefacts were generally cleaned with chemicals or by electrolysis. This involved stripping the objects, that is the total removal of all corrosion products to reveal the metal below. However, it has now become clear that such methods in almost all circumstances are neither satisfactory nor ethical. If corrosion products are stripped off, evidence within them, such as original surfaces, replaced organic materials, metallic coatings, traces of ancient lacquer or other surface treatments, decayed enamels, insecure inlays, etc., are all lost. Second, stripping does not reveal original surfaces except on the rare occasions when these are maintained by dense metal. Any metallic surface revealed is usually pockmarked as corrosion pits are scoured out (plate 5.2), and will often be of a colour not representative of the original alloy since base metal has been leached out over the years to form the corrosion crust. Also these stripping methods attack the metal once it has been exposed, leaching material still further, rendering both analytical studies yet more misleading and smooth surfaces etched. Furthermore, metals and compounds dissolved in solution may plate out irreversibly over the surface of the artefact in a matter of minutes. Finally, the chemicals introduced or formed during dissolution of the corrosion crust must be removed after treatment to prevent further deterioration in the future.

This is not easy and may be impossible where the chemicals have become bonded onto the surface of the corrosion products.

For these reasons, stripping methods have largely been abandoned for iron and copper alloys. However, for lead and silver alloys, the case is not so clear cut. Both these materials are relatively soft and, especially silver, may retain the original metallic surface of an artefact. Mechanical cleaning could possibly damage this surface and so chemicals or electrolysis might be preferred.

5.1.4.1 Mechanical methods

The mechanical methods used have been described in section 3.3.2.1 and will be discussed in more detail, together with the chemicals used to assist, if any, under the sections for particular metals.

5.1.4.2 Stripping methods

Electrolytic cleaning involves a current flow almost the reverse of that occurring during electrochemical corrosion (section 5.1.3.2). Here the voltage is supplied by an external source such as a battery or transformer rectifier, but a similar effect can be achieved by mixing chemicals, when the process is known as electrochemical cleaning.

In electrolytic cleaning,[13] the metal to be cleaned is connected to the negative terminal of a low-voltage DC source whilst an inert metal such as stainless steel is connected to the positive terminal. Both are immersed in an electrolyte. When the current is turned on, the inert metal becomes the anode whilst that to be cleaned is the cathode being fed with electrons (figure 5.4).

The main reduction reaction at the cathode is the formation of hydrogen gas which, forming as bubbles on the metal surface below the corrosion crust, tends to force this layer off into the bath, thereby

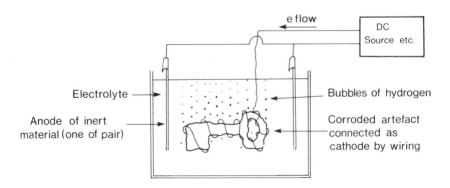

Figure 5.4 Electrolytic cleaning of a corroded metal key

cleaning the metal 'mechanically'. Secondary reduction reactions of the corrosion crust to form either more easily removed corrosion products or even powdery metal, which is then brushed off, may occur. Apart from electrolysis, hydrogen for these reduction reactions can be produced by the reaction of an amphoteric metal such as zinc or aluminium with sodium hydroxide. This method is called electrochemical or galvanic cleaning; some enhanced reduction/protection by the formation of a current-producing cell (section 5.1.3.2) with the metal object as the cathode also occurs.

Electrolytic methods can be carried out without immersion in order to clean local areas of a metallic artefact. Here, the object again is made the cathode, but the circuit is made through a damp swab of electrolyte which is wrapped around a probe attached to the anode. This is touched onto the unwanted corrosion product which is then stripped off as above.

Bearing in mind the drawbacks to stripping methods discussed above, they are on occasion used where it is known that an original surface is maintained by dense metal and that this metal is soft and could possibly be damaged by mechanical cleaning. Where stripping is used in preference to mechanical methods because it is 'cheaper', being less labour intensive, the cost to the artefact itself must be taken into account.

5.1.5 Stabilization

On the removal of a metal object from an environment in which the metal and the corrosion products are in equilibrium after centuries of burial, attempts must be made to stabilize it. Earlier, the greatest effort was put into treating bright metal, but more recently attention has been paid to preserving the corrosion crusts as well, since these have been shown to contain considerable information. As these crusts vary so widely from metal to metal, their stabilization is considered in the sections following.

It is possible, however, to make some generalizations concerning the prevention of further corrosion. This can be achieved almost completely by the removal of water from the object and the environment, thus prohibiting aqueous corrosion. Once dried out, barriers such as waxes or lacquers may be applied to prevent the re-entry of water, but since these are never totally successful, their use is limited. Again, if oxygen is removed from the atmosphere, oxidation and more especially the oxygen absorption reaction is checked. Where present, attempts have been made to remove corrosion stimulators such as chloride ions, aggressive species which destroy passivation. After their removal a transparent lacquer or wax is sometimes added to prevent recontamination and to protect a delicate surface. Care needs to be taken here to prevent a glare (section 3.4.3) or a build-up of coating which hinders study and photography. In a different approach, it is possible to add chemicals to the system to prevent continued corrosion. These chemicals, known as inhibitors,[14] may be in the form of deposits or films which form over the metal, passivating it and so preventing further corrosion. Inhibitors may also work as vapours by bombarding the metal with molecules and here are known as vapour phase inhibitors (VPIs); inhibition ceases if the vapour is dispersed. It should be noted that in high concentration these vapours are toxic.

Composite objects (section 3.5) of metals with organic materials are often difficult to stabilize, since these components require such different treatments and are usually inseparable. In the short term, passive stabilization must favour the organic part since this is the most likely to decay. Where the composite is wet, then wet storage which excludes oxygen (section 3.4.1.3) is the best device.

5.2 Iron and its alloys

5.2.1 Nature of artefacts[15]

Iron is seldom pure and minor levels of other constituents can introduce very different properties into the resultant alloy. Phosphorus usefully hardens and strengthens iron but makes it brittle when cold worked; sulphur detrimentally introduces brittleness alone. The alloying element of greatest interest, however, is carbon, which in concentrations ranging from 0 to 5 per cent greatly affects the properties of the different alloys formed. The most common phases found are soft ferrite (pure iron), hard brittle cementite (the compound iron carbide), pearlite (laminations of ferrite and cementite), and graphite (pure carbon). An outline of the properties of alloys containing different amounts of carbon, the phases present, and their nomenclature, is given in table 5.1.

Iron formed by primitive smelting is a spongy mass or 'bloom' which can be consolidated into a solid lump by forging. When the bloom is heated in a reducing atmosphere in contact with carbon, as may happen during smelting, the iron on the surface becomes alloyed with carbon. When the lump is worked, the alloy areas become distributed throughout the object, resulting in a metal with an extremely heterogeneous composition, but with an average of 0.1 per cent carbon. To raise deliberately the carbon content of an entire bloom by heating in this manner, called *carburization*, is an extremely slow and expensive process requiring large amounts of charcoal. Thus in antiquity a tool or knife may have been fashioned from wrought iron and then only the working edges hardened by raising their content of carbon to about 0.3 per cent through carburization, producing a zone of steel.

Other methods of economically raising the carbon content of iron

Table 5.1 Carbon alloys of iron

Carbon content %	Modern name		Archaeological name	Phases present	Properties
0–0.008	wrought		wrought iron	ferrite mixed with carbon	very malleable
0.008–0.07	iron				
0.07–0.15	dead mild	low carbon steel	'wrought iron'	ferrite + pearlite	+ slag in 'wrought iron'
0.15–0.25	mild				
0.25–0.55	medium carbon steel		carburized iron (steel)		
0.55–0.85	high carbon steel			pearlite	
0.85					
0.85–0.9					
0.9–1.6	tool steel			cementite + pearlite	
2.5–5	cast iron: white grey		cast iron: white grey	graphite + ferrite + pearlite	very brittle: cannot be worked

increase in strength ⟶

increase in hardness on quenching due to martensite ⟶

increase in hardness ⟶

respond well to hardening by quenching

involve welding. Strips of carburized iron (steel) may be welded onto the cutting edge of a tool or weapon made from wrought iron. To obtain a more even distribution of steel throughout the artefact, it may be made from sheets or bars of carburized iron which are welded together and repeatedly forged to distribute the carbon compounds throughout the object. This process is termed piling. A more complicated method of increasing the mechanical strength of tools and weapons, is the process of pattern welding; here, rods of iron are twisted into barleycorns, flattened and welded together. Grinding and polishing the surface of the resultant bars will produce a decorative pattern; this pattern and the increased strength may result, however, simply from the incorporation of slag into the metal during forging.[15]

Depending on their carbon content, iron alloys may be hardened still further by hammering. Steel owes its great usefulness to the enormous hardening derived when the alloy is rapidly cooled or quenched from 720°C, as a new very hard phase called martensite is formed.

Iron made from primitive solid state smelting will contain much slag from the iron ore trapped within its pores. This, a mixture of glassy and crystalline fayalite $2FeO.SiO_2$, is squeezed out to some degree by hammering. However, a certain percentage always remains in wrought iron and steel, drawn out in stringers along the line of working (plate 1.3).

Much cast iron, if made from liquid state smelting, is 'grey' as it contains flakes of black graphite; it also contains high levels of phosphorus and silicon as impurities. 'White' cast iron contains similarly high levels of carbon but here it combines with iron to form cementite (FeC_3); its silicon level is lower than in 'grey' cast iron. They are both extremely brittle and thus not workable, but they have much higher compressive strengths than does wrought iron.

Recently the temperatures to which it is safe to heat ancient iron without destroying metallurgical information have been undergoing investigation. These would seem to be in the region of 380 to 400°C; prolonged heating at 100°C during treatment does not appear to bias archaeometallurgical studies.[16]

Because iron can be readily hot welded, it was used widely in antiquity; during welding the oxide is mechanically removed or fluxed off. This allows the joining not only of parts of an object but also of pieces of iron with differing carbon contents, allowing control over the properties of different areas within an object.[17] Iron may also be joined by hard brazing spelter (section 5.5.1). It may be tinned[18] for decorative or protective purposes, but tinning for the latter reason is only successful where the coating is perfect, or where the tin and iron are in very specific pH/E_H conditions (e.g. in fruit acid inside a tin can); otherwise the iron where exposed, being more base than the tin, will corrode very rapidly by galvanic corrosion. Before solders or metal coatings are applied to iron, the surface must be well prepared and fluxes employed to counteract the marked tendency of iron to corrode and form obstructing oxide films.

5.2.2 *Nature of deteriorated material*

5.2.2.1 From land sites

PATINA OR THIN RED/BROWN CRUST. Whilst blue, black, or brown oxide patinas can be made deliberately by controlled heating of iron, brown patinas may form naturally in relatively dry air containing no pollution. However, humidity and the presence of corrosion stimulators will normally cause such a patina to develop into a thicker crust of minerals as noted below.

BULKY RED/BROWN MASS (plate 5.3). This condition is the typical appearance of iron excavated from damp aerated sites. The shape of the mass is often no longer recognizable as a particular object, and sand/stones may have become incorporated into it. The mass is composed of iron oxides and carbonates. In the main these are iron(III) oxyhydroxides (FeO.OH), the bulk being in the form of red/brown/yellow goethite (αFeO.OH) with some orange lepidocrocite (γFeO.OH), but there can also be considerable quantities of amorphous limonite

Plate 5.3 Typical bulky red/brown mass of ironwork from aerated sites

Plate 5.4 Totally corroded ironwork where exposed slag stringers lying in a void appear fibrous like wood

(FeO.OH). Siderite ($FeCO_3$) and calcium carbonate also may be found on iron from calcareous soils. Pale buff/yellow powdery jarosite, a basic iron(III) sulphate ($NaFe_3(OH)_6(SO_4)_2$), has also been identified.

Where slag stringers (section 5.2.1) become exposed they give the corroded mass a fibrous look as of wood (plate 5.4). This must be differentiated from the 'replacement' (section 5.2.2.3) of wood by corrosion products. Where replaced organic material is not immediately identifiable, it sometimes appears as areas of orange-yellow powdery corrosion products.

BRICK-RED COMPACT SURFACE OR LAYER. If iron is heated to above 200°C a bright-red layer of haematite (αFe_2O_3) will form. This is an extremely protective layer and may prevent further corrosion for a considerable time. Alternatively, such a bright-red layer may be found within a corrosion crust when the protection of the haematite has been broken down. Haematite could indicate the burning of material surrounding the iron before it was buried.

BLACK COLORATION. Iron objects from wet oxygen-free deposits often appear black because of iron(II) sulphide formed by sulphate-reducing bacteria (section 5.1.3.2). The layer can be hard and shiny or sludge-like with much of the metal, if not all, corroded away in large depressions.

BRIGHT-BLUE TO BLUE-BLACK COLORATION. Such a range of colours can be due to deposits of vivianite (iron phosphate); immediately upon excavation the material may even appear white. It is in the form of iron(II) phosphate ($Fe_3(PO_4)_2.8H_2O$). Vivianite can form an exceedingly protective coating over iron, protecting it from any further corrosion for a considerable period. Complete protective coverings of vivianite are found in objects from wet organic layers, but it can be found in small patches on iron from many other types of deposit where there is a source of phosphate.

It may be that oxygenated organic deposits can form other blue-black coatings comprised of phenolic iron complexes, for example, which are similarly protective. These protective coatings may well incorporate black sulphides (plate 2.2).

5.2.2.2 From marine sites

AMORPHOUS MASSES OF FERROUS CONCRETION. Ferrous concretions of iron corrosion products, calcium carbonate and debris, usually form around a piece of corroding iron, either wrought or cast. These concretions can spread across the site, embedding any other material in their way until the whole deposit is sealed by a concrete-hard layer. This benefits the preservation of the embedded non-ferrous metals and organic material, although in extreme cases underwater explosives may be needed to extract them.

The surface of these concretions is occasionally covered by a thin, white or pale brown crust, but more often it is coated with a loose deposit of rusty corrosion products which also stain any encrusting barnacles. These outer layers contain a high proportion of calcium and magnesium carbonate and hydroxide which precipitate from the surrounding sea-water, and also siderite ($FeCO_3$), but inside they consist almost entirely of the oxides and hydrated oxides of iron, as in section 5.2.2.1. Silica (SiO_2) and black iron sulphide (FeS) may also occur. Concretions found within a marine sediment, where oxygen is relatively scarce, contain higher proportions of lepidocrocite ($\gamma FeO.OH$), black magnetite (Fe_3O_4), and the magnetic sulphide, pyrrhotite. Other compounds which are unstable in atmospheric conditions, and thus difficult to identify, may also be present.

Marine wrought iron, like that from land sites, tends to corrode along the lines of the slag stringers it contains so that the corroded metal, where exposed, often has a fibrous surface which resembles wood.

BLACK COLORATION. Iron from marine sludges may appear as in section 5.2.2.1; whilst cast iron is likely to retain its shape under such conditions, wrought iron may well disappear completely for the reason described below.

GREEN COLORATION. Green rust, a mixture of iron(II) and iron(III) hydrated oxides, is found occasionally on marine cast and wrought iron but it has also been seen within the corrosion crusts of wrought iron from land sites.

5.2.2.3 Corrosion of iron and its implications

In a moist oxygenated environment, wrought iron tends to corrode by loss of metal from the surface of the object; corrosion then proceeds in a front which moves down into the metal more or less parallel to the surfaces (figure 5.5). This is in contrast to copper which tends to corrode

(a) Cross-sections of a wrought iron blade.

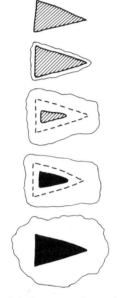

1. Well preserved: covered by tarnish

2. Original surface still preserved by metal: covered in layer of corrosion products

3. Original surface retained within thick layer of corrosion products: little or no metal remaining

4. Original surface retained within thick layer of corrosion products: centre now a void: no metal remaining

5. Original surface retained by internal surface of thick overlying concretion: centre a complete void: no metal remaining [normally found in aerated seawater]

(b) Cross-sections of a cast iron cannon ball

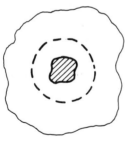

1. Original surface retained by graphitized zone: covered in very thick overlying concretion: some metal remains [found in aerated seawater]

2. As (1) but with no overlying concretion [found in anaerobic deposits]

Figure 5.5 Common conditions of ironwork found on excavation.

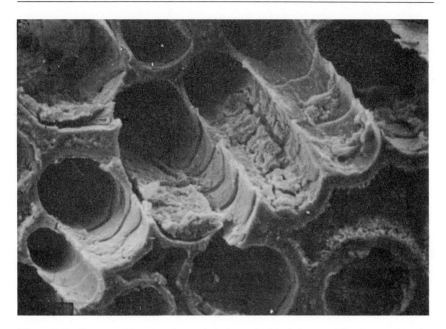

Plate 5.5 Outer surfaces of wool hairs moulded by mobile iron corrosion products

intergranularly, that is internally (section 5.5.2.2). The dissolved iron ions, being mobile, move away from the metal and either disperse or, in alkaline/neutral soils, are deposited as iron oxides and carbonates. The volume of these products is considerably larger than that of the metal dissolved.

The consequences of these mechanisms of corrosion can be distinguished in excavated artefacts. First, if iron suffers only minor attack, the metallic surface underneath the rust layer will be pitted by shallow depressions where the corrosion has been most severe. Second, iron artefacts may appear as misshapen lumps of oxides incorporating on the outer layers sand, stones, etc. from the deposit. One positive aspect here is the replacement of organic materials by corrosion products and their incorporation into the bulky masses.[19] If wood is in association with iron as decay sets in, the mobile corrosion products appear to move into the deteriorating wood and deposit inside the cells.[20] Thus, after the wood has long since decayed, a record of its structure and at least some degree of the shape of the fragment will be retained by the iron corrosion products. Using the scanning electron microscope it is possible to identify wood types from this information, in some instances. Likewise seeds, horn, antler, and bone may be preserved and identified. For wool, it would seem that the corrosion deposits are on the outside of the fibre (plate 5.5) but, even so, identification may be possible. If a fibre is part of

Plate 5.6 Bulky orange-yellow corrosion products on an iron knife perhaps indicating remains of a leather scabbard preserved by replacement

a textile, information regarding the weave may be retrieved. Decaying leather gives a less easily interpreted record (plate 5.6). Within these masses of oxides, distorting blisters with convoluted inner surfaces may occur.

Below the outer rust-coloured oxides, the black oxide magnetite (Fe_3O_4) which forms in regions of low oxygen is often found. Where corrosion is complete, the metal is replaced entirely by black, dense, lustrous magnetite underlying a greater or lesser zone of brown oxides. There is considerable argument as to whether the original surface level and topography exists within these corrosion masses. Some authorities[21] feel that it is not possible to locate them for there is no apparent physico-chemical mechanism by which they could be retained within a crust. However, it will be shown (section 5.2.3) that an original surface can in practice often be detected by careful investigative cleaning; the original surface can be seen as a denser zone of corrosion which, unlike the overlying bulk, does not incorporate grains of sand, etc. (plate 1.2).

An important feature of iron corrosion products in relation to conservation is the material which cannot be seen; that is the chemicals contained within the crust which lead to deterioration after excavation (section 5.2.5). Since these are not visible in freshly excavated ironwork, they will be discussed in this later section.

In certain moist oxygenated deposits, which occur both in the sea and on the land, it is found that all the oxidized iron of an object has migrated into the surrounding environment. This means that, beneath the ferrous concretion or bulky oxide mass, there is a hollow where the object was. This phenomenon is found frequently in the sea where small wrought iron objects may disperse completely within a hundred years. However, in such cases, the cavities formed invariably accurately represent the size and shape of the original objects and casts using the concretions as moulds can be made (section 5.2.4.2) (plate 5.7).

Unlike wrought iron, cast iron from the sea always remains solid, even though totally corroded and encased within a crust of ferrous concretion. Under this crust, the surface of the corroded object is very soft and often consists of a matrix of rusty corrosion products with small lustrous inclusions. These are the flakes of graphite of grey cast iron which survive, having been the cathodic (noble) part of an iron/carbon galvanic corrosion cell, whilst the base iron corrodes preferentially. The iron oxides and carbonates formed are held *in situ* between the graphite flakes, and so the shape of the artefact, albeit in a mineralized state, is preserved. Cast iron in this condition is said to be 'graphitized' (plate 5.8).

Plate 5.7 Nodule of iron concretion. (a) As retrieved from the sea.

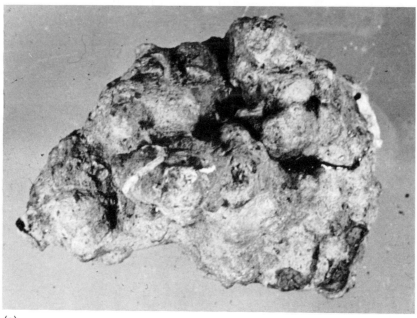

(a)

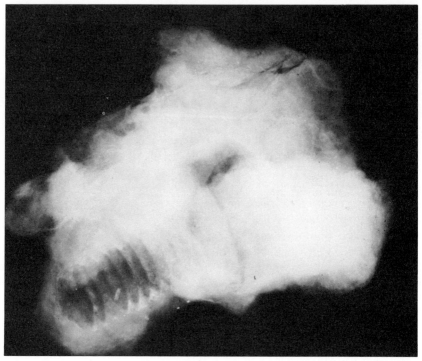

(b)

(c)

(b) Radiograph to show hollow void retaining the shape of a bolt. (c) Void cast in silicone rubber and concretion cut open

Plate 5.8 Part of a cannon retrieved from the sea where a fragment of the outer graphitized zone has broken away from the remaining cast iron core

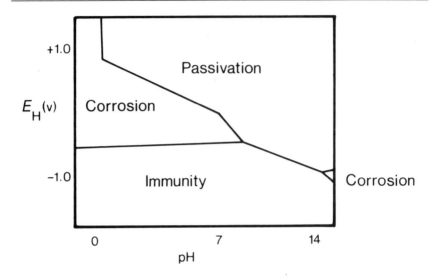

Figure 5.6 Sketch of 'Pourbaix diagram' for iron in water at 25°C

In white cast iron, similar internal galvanic corrosion cells form between the metal and the more noble areas of cementite, and again the original shape of the artefact is preserved.

PRESERVATION OF IRON. Turning now to consider the conditions from which true metal might be retrieved, it can be said that since iron is so base, this will occur only where for some reason it has been passified, for example by a phosphate layer, or where oxygen is absent.

'Pourbaix diagrams' (section 5.1.3.2) such as the one above (figure 5.6) are useful in understanding the conditions required for preservation. Here it can be seen that iron may be preserved either by passivation in deposits of high redox potential and pH due to stifling by oxide/carbonate crusts or by immunity in deposits of low redox potential, that is where oxygen is low. However, this in no way represents the whole complex picture; thus preservation can be prevented by the activity of sulphate-reducing bacteria, the presence of chloride ions, or enhanced by phosphates in deposits of low redox potential. Ironwork from marine sites, in particular, never seems to be found truly well preserved.[22] This topic is an extremely complex one, and before further conclusions can be drawn, much research must be carried out.

5.2.3 *Examination*

The visual examination of a corrosion crust is all-important to identify any organic pseudomorphs; if they are identified, it must be determined whether the organic material was an artefact (either part of the iron object or simply associated with it) or whether it is more relevant to environmental studies.

X-radiography (section 3.3.1.3) cannot be recommended too strongly for ironwork, since the normal heavy corrosion and overburden of crusts obscure the shape and associated features of the original object (plates 5.3 and 5.9). It is normal practice to scan much if not all ironwork from excavations; sorting can be carried out using radiographs *and* they act as records if no further work is carried out on the artefacts. Ironwork can be sorted into artefacts requiring investigative cleaning, those not meriting

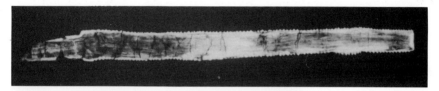

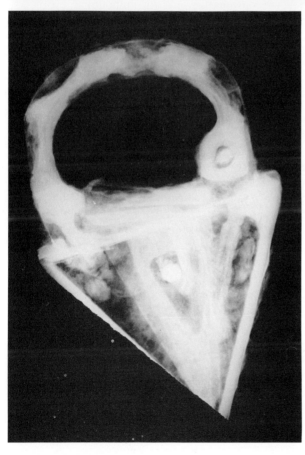

Plate 5.9 Radiographs of ironwork to reveal features not visible prior to investigative cleaning. (a) A strap of iron is shown to be a file. (b) Plating on a padlock and its internal workings are revealed.

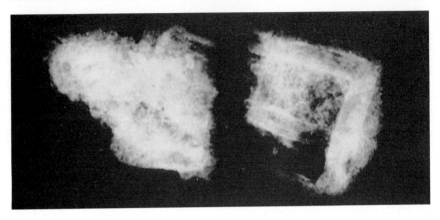

Plate 5.10 Radiograph of a lump of iron corrosion products reveals the shape of a buckle, much of which is hollow

cleaning, and slag. Those requiring cleaning are unidentifiable objects, those required for display, and artefacts which might reveal substantially more information on cleaning. Into this latter category comes artefacts which might have been tinned or brazed, objects such as keys, spurs and jointed pieces, files containing residues of material abraded,[23] etc., for these features do not always show up on radiographs and must be sought by investigative cleaning. Likewise, replaced organic material is not always visible. It is not always easy to interpret radiographs, for they are two-dimensional. Both blades and straps, for example, appear similar on them, and investigative cleaning is required to reveal their cross-sections. However, where the original surface is retained beneath obscuring crusts, the plan of the object is recorded as the x-rays distinguish between compact and dense corrosion. Moreover, considerable technological information may be elucidated. Pattern welding even of highly corroded material can be seen, as can joining welds and the more usual features of rivet holes and internal structures of solid artefacts such as locks. It is possible to determine the condition of artefacts from radiographs, whether they have corroded to hollowness, whether the original surface is distorted by blisters, and whether any metal at all remains (plate 5.10). Further discussion of radiography of ironwork may be found in Corfield.[24]

The original surface of ironwork was discussed in section 5.2.2.3. For cast iron it may be well preserved in soft graphite. For wrought iron, just occasionally it is possible that the original surface remains as metal, but in this case it will be badly pitted. For ironwork corroded to bulky masses, it is less clear but often the original surface can be found within the mass. Lying on it will be found inlays and platings if present, possibly slightly distorted by underlying blisters (plate 1.2).

Metallographic studies are curtailed where corrosion has been extensive, but tiny islands of metal as well as 'relic' structures have been recognized within badly corroded objects.[25]

5.2.4 Cleaning

5.2.4.1 Iron from land sites

The two features which make the cleaning of heavily corroded ironwork a specialized and time-consuming job have been described above; these are the constant examination required for evidence retained in the corrosion products, and the lack of chemical distinction between superficial corrosion and that maintaining an original surface (section 5.2.2.3). Chemicals and electrolytic techniques are not applicable, and so manual mechanical methods using small tools or, more commonly, air abrasion with continuous visual examination alone can be used, making cleaning extremely labour intensive (plate 5.11). This means that for identification for publication, only limited areas of a corroded object may be cleaned, areas which reveal cross-sections or samples of coatings (plate 1.2). This partial cleaning inevitably introduces a degree of risk, with features being misinterpreted or undiscovered, but it is more reliable than using x-radiographs alone (section 5.2.3). Such partially cleaned objects may be unacceptable for display, further work being essential, but it must be remembered that badly corroded ironwork cleaned to whatever level can never have the same 'look' as the original material. Where corrosion is so severe that the artefact is partly hollow, cleaning to reveal the thin skin maintaining its surface is extremely difficult, if not impossible (plate 5.4).

Ironwork with only a thin layer of corrosion products overlying metal is rare in archaeology but common in historic and ethnographic material. It would be possible to 'strip' (section 5.1.4) such objects by dissolving the iron oxides. This could be achieved with acids, but since iron is a base metal (section 5.1.3.2), it too will dissolve in many acids and so become etched. Commercial rust removers are usually based on mild inhibited organic acids or phosphoric acids, but they often leave a layer of visible 'protective' deposit over the metal. Electrolytic cleaning (section 5.1.4) does not have these drawbacks since the iron is cathodically protected by the electric current from etching and no deposits form. However, all these methods ruthlessly expose existing pits in the metal surface, which is unsightly, and cause platings and inlays to react or become displaced (plate 1.3). Today, because of these dangers, archaeological iron even of this type is never stripped. Abrasive mechanical methods are preferred.

A variety of methods of cleaning by causing the corrosion products to spall by heating/cooling have been suggested for archaeological wrought

Plate 5.11 Careful mechanical investigative cleaning of ironwork reveals plating and original surface (cf. plate 1.3)

iron, but like all cleaning and stabilization methods involving stripping and excessive heat, they are to be deplored (section 5.2.1).

5.2.4.2 Iron from marine sites

It can be assumed, until shown by radiography or a *strong* pull on a magnet to be otherwise, that concretions covering small wrought iron 'objects' are hollow; when this is the case, cleaning is replaced by casting (section 5.2.2.3). In the past, plaster of Paris or polyester resins were

Plate 5.12 Cleaning the concretion off marine ironwork using a hammer and chisel

used, but now flexible rubbers such as silicone or polysulphide rubbers are preferred.[26]

Where the concretion is solid, as is generally the case with larger artefacts, concretion crusts are removed from the artefact before storage otherwise stabilization is difficult to achieve (section 5.2.6.2). Since it is often found that concretions fracture at the original surface of the artefact, whether this was of wrought or cast iron. Tools such as chisels and hammers, when in the hands of experts, can effect this removal (plate 5.12). Unfortunately, the problem of whether or not to clean iron objects which are not to be removed from the site is much greater. As a rule these should never be cleaned of concretion, for then the soft corroded surface of the object would lose its only source of protection against the marine environment. This often puts the excavator in a dilemma, because there may be much important information about a wreck and its naval history which could only be obtained if such ironwork were cleaned. Selective cleaning may thus seem to be necessary, although such action would bring about the ultimate destruction of the cleaned artefacts.

5.2.5   Deterioration after excavation

5.2.5.1   Breaking up of corroded artefacts

On some occasions it is found that heavily corroded iron objects are stable after excavation, but it is more usual to find that after some weeks or years, artefacts, whether still as misshapen lumps or as cleaned iron corrosion product pseudomorphs, begin to disintegrate (plate 5.13). The artefact splits up, in the case of wrought iron, along the direction of working, to reveal damp, dark-orange-brown spots. In some cases it is impossible to fit the fragments back together as they have changed shape. It has been noted that artefacts which still retain metallic iron, even though this is only vestigial, are those which are most likely to break up; the totally corroded or hollow artefacts often appear stable.[27]

RESEARCH.   The cause of this breaking up is one of the major concerns of conservation research at the present time but some progress has already been made. Turgoose[28] suggests that as a corrosion crust laden with iron(II) ions and chloride ions dries out, oxygen penetrates and, in the damp environment, oxidizes this to dark-orange β-iron(III) oxy-hydroxide (akaganeite). The formation of this mineral deep within the corrosion layers causes them to split apart. Where no metallic iron remains, it is unlikely that sufficient quantities of iron(II) ions will exist for much akaganeite to be found and thus break-up does not occur.

Plate 5.13   Post-excavation corrosion causing break-up of wrought ironwork

However, where metallic iron does remain, there can be a continuous source of iron(II) ions from the corrosion of the metal, which is discussed below. Iron from marine environments will contain the highest levels of chloride ions and so will be the most susceptible to this decay. However, material from terrestrial sites often contains sufficient levels to suffer deterioration also. It is still unclear as to what form these chloride ions take;[29] it would appear that they may be in solution in the water distributed throughout the crust, but they are also adsorbed onto the iron oxides and even trapped within their crystalline structure, as in the case of akaganeite. This product is not stable, and after a lapse of time will convert to αFeO.OH (goethite), releasing the trapped chloride ions which can then be involved in further metal corrosion. Another suggestion[30] is that disintegration is aggravated by the shrinkage of corrosion products caused by their drying out and by the spalling of corrosion layers from fluctuating temperatures, both encountered after excavation. Yet again,[31] the crystallization of soluble salts on drying out could break up porous corrosion crusts, in much the same way as they damage pottery or stone (section 4.1.2).

SUMMARY OF RESEARCH. Research into why ironwork breaks up is still inconclusive; a likely cause is the continued corrosion of vestigial iron due to the presence of chlorides, water, and oxygen, but dehydration could also cause damage. Further work in this area continues.

5.2.5.2 Corrosion of metallic iron

If *much* metal remains within excavated artefacts, orange 'tears' or 'sweat' may appear on the surface. This weeping/sweating is a sign of continued corrosion due to the presence of water, oxygen, and chlorides (section 5.1.3.2). These tears are iron(II) and (III) chloride which hydrolyse to brown oxyhydroxides. These release chloride ions which then reactivate corrosion, and the cycle continues until all metal is converted to oxyhydroxides.

Iron which is excavated with a passivating layer such as iron phosphate may begin to corrode after excavation; this is a result of the cracking of the protective film, probably as a result of fluctuating temperatures encountered in post-excavation environments. Likewise iron which has been actively stabilized (section 5.2.6.2), cannot be subjected to extreme environmental conditions without the risk of corrosion. Exposed metal will corrode if the ambient RH is greater than 80 per cent, but this figure is lowered considerably where gaseous pollutants such as sulphur dioxide are present. The presence of chloride ions either from burial, pollution, contamination by handling, or from poor conservation will allow corrosion at a much lower RH,[32] perhaps in the region of 20 per cent, whilst localized corrosion can occur in relatively dry air if hygroscopic salts/dust are in contact with the metal surface.

5.2.6 Stabilization

Until shown to be otherwise, it must be assumed that all excavated ironwork is unstable, and attempts must be made to prevent the deterioration described above which can set in immediately on exposure by excavation. In the first instance this is carried out using passive techniques (section 3.4.1), that is by controlling the environment, but the question of what variable should be controlled, and at what levels, is perhaps the most disputed topic in archaeological conservation today. Moreover, the most intractable problem in conservation falls in this area too, namely the development of reliable techniques for *active* stabilization of iron. But overall, passive stabilization is to be preferred to as yet untried and, in some cases, unethical active techniques.

5.2.6.1 Passive

IRON FROM LAND SITES. As yet, it is not possible to describe one system of stabilization which is agreed upon universally but this could well be simply a reflection of the enormous variety in the condition of excavated ironwork and in its response to a variety of post-excavation environments.

Desiccation has been the dominant approach in Britain; it attempts to remove water to prevent further corrosion and the break-up of corrosion crusts (section 5.2.5). Below an RH of 20 per cent corrosion is unlikely to take place and akaganeite is not produced. On-site, such an RH is most easily created by the use of silica gel, but in store or on display dehumidifiers could be used to dry out large spaces (section 3.4.1.1). Unfortunately, the blue indicator incorporated, in most self-indicating silica gels is not particularly helpful here since it only becomes pink at an RH of about 40 per cent, that is, when the air is already too damp. Thus, until a gel containing a different indicator becomes available, small paper strips which indicate a range of humidities reading as low as 20 per cent will have to be incorporated within the sealed containers (plate 5.14). Failures which have been experienced with this technique may well be due to its incorrect execution; the guidelines laid down in section 3.4.1.1 must be followed rigorously. Desiccation is an extreme technique, in no way mimicking the burial environment. Furthermore, it could lead to shrinkage of the corrosion crusts and it may impede later washing techniques. Future research may show it is not the best method to adopt.

Desiccation by use of solvents has been preferred in Scandinavia but it carries with it the danger of using these chemicals on site and during transportation. Deep freezing to achieve desiccation could provide an

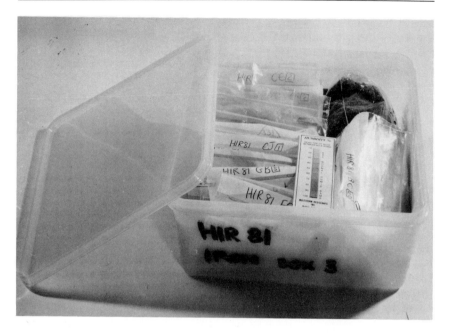

Plate 5.14 Suggestion for the post-excavation storage of ironwork – desiccation with silica gel in a sealed polyethylene box incorporating a humidity strip

alternative approach, but the dangers caused by the expansion of water on freezing require investigation.

Paradoxically, the other method of passive stabilization of ironwork from damp sites is to keep it wet. This helps to keep oxygen levels within the corrosion crust down, whilst avoiding the problems related to desiccation. For very short periods ironwork can be kept damp simply by sealing it in containers; the rate of any chemical reaction which could now occur is reduced by keeping the containers at reduced temperatures in a refrigerator or by adding sachets of vapour phase inhibitor. For longer periods repacking in soil or an artificial medium which mimics the burial environment within sealed containers is a possibility.[30] Recent research[32] lends weight to the argument for wet anoxic storage. It has been suggested[33] that iron could be stored in sodium sulphite solutions which prevent oxidation reactions; alkaline sulphite may even commence long-term stabilization (section 5.2.6.2), but this solution is a very strong reagent and appears destructive to some ironwork. Oxygen can be removed from the environment totally by displacement with an inert gas; storage in nitrogen has on occasion been used for ironwork which cannot be desiccated.[34]

The use of alkaline corrosion inhibitors (section 5.1.5) in solutions has also been suggested for storage of iron. Sodium sesquicarbonate

($Na_2CO_3.NaHCO_3$) does not give a sufficiently alkaline pH and should be substituted by sodium hydroxide (NaOH) but it is still unclear how satisfactory such methods of preventing corrosion are for heavily corroded ironwork.[35]

IRON FROM MARINE SITES. Since levels of chloride in this material will be high, it is very likely that destructive reactions involving chloride ions (section 5.2.5) will occur after excavation. Thus it is essential to stabilize marine iron *immediately* upon removal from the sea; even incrustations assumed to be hollow should be treated as though they contain metal until it is known to be otherwise. Concretions on large solid objects, however, have to be removed from the objects before storage because they form a partial barrier to desalination.

The most usual approach to stabilization is by wet storage, but because of the high chloride levels, more extreme steps to prevent corrosion than those used on land iron are required. It may seem paradoxical, but a strongly oxidizing solution will inhibit iron corrosion (section 5.1.5) since a resistant oxide film forms which passifies the metal. A solution of alkaline potassium dichromate has been used successfully in this context, although this method is inadvisable since it has several disadvantages, not least that the toxicity of the chromate ion presents a serious health hazard. An easier and less hazardous method of stabilization is the use of highly alkaline inhibiting solutions of pH 10–13 described above.[36] Even if the chloride ion concentration is high, providing that the solution contains dissolved oxygen, it is probable that a sufficiently protective oxide film will form. However, the effectiveness of these solutions has been called into question recently.[35] If ironwork is to be treated by the alkaline sulphite method (section 5.2.6.2), rather than immediately immersing objects in this strong reagent, it might be possible to store marine iron in a reducing solution of neutral sodium sulphite to prevent corrosion prior to treatment.

Because of the high salt levels, stabilization by desiccation is only suitable where it can be guaranteed, since even slight dampness will allow chlorides to continue their damaging reactions (section 5.2.5). Thus, it can be used only for small wrought iron artefacts which do not have concretions, or which can easily be freed from them, and which will then fit into sealed containers. Graphitized cast iron and large wrought iron objects cannot be dried out reliably. Desiccation can be used for hollow concretions too since they contain no metal but, like the small wrought iron objects, they are first soaked in fresh water to avoid damage from the crystallization of salts (section 4.1.2).

5.2.6.2 Active

Most techniques of stabilization in the past have aimed at the removal of chlorides, but none has been particularly successful. To understand the reasons behind this failure, work currently is being undertaken by conservation researchers to identify the nature of chlorides within excavated ironwork.[37] It is becoming apparent that whilst chlorides may be present in the crust of freshly excavated iron only as ions dissolved in water, they are actually held there by the neutralizing positive charges produced by the continuing corrosion of the remaining metal.[32] Thus whilst the common but largely unpublished technique of simply washing out chlorides in hot water may remove them where no metal remains, where this is not the case, no amount of washing will flush the held chlorides out: the charges will simply increase as corrosion speeds up in this hot, wet, oxygenated environment. However, some success using washing can be gained by preventing the activity of corrosion cells, either by hot washing in an inert atmosphere of nitrogen[38] or by incorporating reducing agents or other types of corrosion inhibitors into the washing solution.[39]

Another suggestion as to why stabilization treatments fail is that the chlorides are trapped in voluminous corrosion products, and to release them the oxyhydroxides must first be reduced to compact magnetite. If, after excavation, akaganeite has been allowed to form (section 5.2.5.1), chlorides become trapped in the crystal lattice, and in order to release them the akaganeite must be reduced to magnetite. In 1975, in order to bring about this reduction, a new method of stabilization using alkaline sodium sulphite was developed for marine iron,[40] but it has had mixed results especially when used on land ironwork.[41] The success of this treatment may result from the reducing agent preventing further corrosion and thus allowing chloride ions to be released, rather than the reduction of oxyhydroxides to magnetite as first proposed. It certainly is not successful where akaganeite has been allowed to form, and thus artefacts to be treated with this reagent must be stored wet from the moment of excavation.

The use of applied electric fields in attempts to reduce chloride levels has been widespread and varied. If very low currents are used, an input of electrons into an artefact, rather than resulting in stripping (section 5.2.4.1), could prevent continued corrosion during washing, a technique known as cathodic desalting.[42] A slightly higher current will reduce oxyhydroxides to magnetite which might result in the release of chlorides.[43] Another method aimed at preventing corrosion during chloride removal is the use of a non-aqueous solution to dissolve the salts[44] but this appears not to be a very efficient technique.[45]

Finally, chlorides in iron can be driven off as gases at high temperatures. This approach has proved successful for the stabilization of marine cast iron, where the temperature required can be reduced to 850 or 600°C by heating in a reducing atmosphere of hydrogen, or even 400°C by heating for long periods of time.[46] The cast iron is not only stripped of chloride ions, it is also strengthened and made to appear more like the original material by the reduction of iron oxide in the graphitized zone (section 5.2.2.3) to metallic iron and magnetite. There is, however, some alteration in the metallurgical structure of any original iron at these high temperatures. It may be considered that this loss of information is permissible in return for the success in the stabilization of marine cast iron, which is extremely difficult to achieve by any other method. Controversy[47] has arisen when this treatment has been applied to ancient steel and wrought iron which, as shown in section 5.2.1, in all likelihood will also contain carbon. A great deal of metallurgical detail will be lost if these materials are heated over 380°C. Moreover, if reduction takes place at these lower temperatures, it is unlikely that all the chloride will be driven off. Compared with other methods of chloride removal, hydrogen reduction is relatively quick, but this alone cannot outweigh the drawbacks in its use on low-carbon alloys.

Thus at present there are no wholly satisfactory methods for the reduction in chloride levels in excavated ironwork available, and in most cases passive stabilization techniques for chloride-laden iron are to be preferred until reliable methods of active stabilization have been developed and tested.

Having reduced the chloride levels, it is essential to remove as much water as possible from ironwork; this is best achieved using displacement by solvents rather than heat (see above). It is then usual to put a film over the surface of the object to prevent recontamination by chlorides, dust pick-up, and wear and tear during handling. The incorporation of pigments or graphite into the wax or lacquer applied is neither useful nor, since it obscures the surface, in the interests of future examination. On the rare occasions in archaeological material where the surface of the object is of metallic iron, a protective chemical coating in the form of tannins or phosphates (section 5.2.2.1), or even paint, could be applied where the object unavoidably is to be exposed to harsh climatic conditions. However, since these alter the colour of the iron and mask details, and are not enduring nor reliable, it is more advisable to remove the object to an environment which can be controlled.

After chemical stabilization, consolidation of fragile artefacts using synthetic materials (section 3.4.2.2) may be necessary, but resort to embedding in a transparent block of resin, as has been suggested, should be avoided for obvious reasons.

5.2.6.3 Long-term environmental control

To consider this, ironwork must be divided into two types, namely that which is found to be stable or has been actively stabilized and that which is only stable by means of passive control of the environment. If ironwork falls into this latter category, then long-term stabilization simply consists of an indefinite continuation of the techniques described in section 5.2.6.1. It is known that at least some iron excavated from land sites will withstand up to ten years' storage in desiccated environments, but lengthy wet storage is likely to prove less satisfactory.

Alternatively, if ironwork falls into the first category, whilst less stringent conditions of RH control are required, it has to be treated as a sensitive material. This means that neither temperature nor RH can be allowed to fluctuate greatly. To prevent the advent of corrosion of any remaining metal, the RH is kept below 65 per cent, metallic surfaces are handled only with gloves, and dust is prevented from settling on the objects. As for all other artefacts, gross pollution is destructive; in extreme cases of atmospheric pollution by sulphur dioxide or salt spray, corrosion can be prevented only by maintaining a very low RH. Vapour phase inhibitors (section 5.1.5) might be used in an enclosed container but some of these suitable for iron actually cause copper to corrode and so must be used advisedly.

5.2.7 Summary

Ironwork, especially wrought iron and artefacts from the sea, is perhaps the most problematic, in terms of both investigative cleaning and stabilization, of all material excavated. Research being carried out will, it is hoped, point to means of developing more satisfactory conservation techniques than are available at present.

On site, the only treatment given to iron should be that of careful handling and passive stabilization, and this should begin as soon as possible after exposure. Since the technique of stabilizing ironwork from land sites varies between conservation laboratories, it is essential that liaison with the laboratory which is to treat the iron is established before excavation, to determine the method of passive stabilization required. Where there has been a failure to liaise with a laboratory before excavation, an indefinite delay in the treatment of the material is likely; in this case it is suggested that the ironwork be desiccated (section 3.4.1.1), a process which should begin within forty-eight hours of exposure. The opposite is correct for marine ironwork: it must be kept wet (section 5.2.6.1) from the moment of removal from the sea. Again, advice is essential.

Adequate publication of ironwork cannot take place without radiography; without this, much evidence is missed or misinterpreted. Investigative cleaning, likewise, is essential for competent assessment of a site and cannot be performed without the use of radiographs. Illustration of ironwork should be carried out with reference both to the artefact and to its radiograph: if the artefact is used alone, corrosion crusts may be misinterpreted; and if radiographs are used alone, distortion occurs and a third dimension of morphology is lost. It cannot be said too often that for publication and display of ironwork liaison between excavator, conservator, and curator is essential.

In the absence of satisfactory methods of active stabilization of iron, control of the storage and display environment is indispensable. As ironwork is a sensitive material, its condition has to be monitored regularly and indefinitely.

5.3 Lead and its alloys

5.3.1 Nature of artefacts

Pure lead has a low melting point of 327°C and since its recrystallization temperature (section 5.1.1) is below normal, ambient, room temperature it does not respond to work hardening. Soft lead is not suitable for thin-walled hollow vessels etc., and for these and other cast objects, harder and stronger alloys are used. Such an alloy is pewter but, being in the main tin, it is dealt with in section 5.4. Silver is often present in lead objects in small percentages since the metals have a common ore type; both this and cold working increase the corrosion resistance of a lead artefact. Also common in low-grade lead may be impurities such as chlorides and sulphur. Joins in leaden objects can be made either by cold welding or by soft soldering (section 5.1.2.1) and the relative softness of the metal and even of pewter means that it can be readily inscribed or stamped.

5.3.2 Nature of deteriorated material

5.3.2.1 Appearance

DULLED OR SHINY BROWN SURFACE. In the atmosphere, a thin layer of lead oxide (PbO) will form a protective layer over the metal; sometimes this layer may contain darker lead sulphides as well.

THIN WHITE/DISCOLOURED LAYER (plate 5.15a). This is normally cerussite, lead carbonate ($PbCO_3$) and/or hydrocerussite, basic lead carbonate ($2PbCO_3.Pb(OH)_2$), which, having been formed slowly in the presence of air and water, have protective structures made of compact adhering

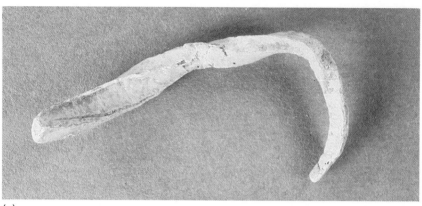

(a)

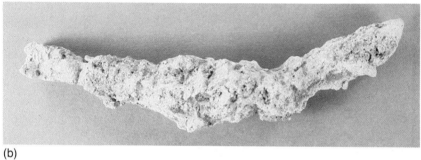

(b)

(c)

Plate 5.15 Corroded lead: (a) thin white layer of lead carbonate; (b) thick, bulky lead carbonate layer lying both over and under the original surface; (c) protective layer of black lead sulphide from an anaerobic deposit

crystals. They are found on lead from damp, calcareous soils and also on lead from the sea and in both cases protect the metal from greater corrosion. This layer may include the white lead sulphates, anglesite, and leadhillite and be contaminated with phosgenite ($PbCl_2.PbCO_3$) and other chlorides in the sea.

WHITE OR DISCOLOURED CRUST (plate 5.15b). Again this crust is mainly cerussite or hydrocerussite but it can be discoloured by oxides; pink/red/brown litharge (αPbO), yellow massicot (βPbO) or brown plattnerite (PbO_2). It may be tinged grey, by black galena (PbS), and become fissured horizontally and vertically, the crevices becoming filled by soil and roots. Corrosion forming these crusts occurs only in alkaline soils since the carbonates dissolve in acidic pH. In alkaline soils where carbonates are sparse, lead appears to corrode to reddish brown oxides with little if any carbonate; specks of lead metal may remain in this crazed and fissured crust.

BLACK OR DULL GOLD COLOUR LEAD (plate 5.15c). From anaerobic environments, whether marine or terrestrial, containing active sulphate-reducing bacteria (section 2.1.1.2), lead is blackened with lead sulphide, galena (PbS). This may be an adhering protective coat or just a sludge with no lead remaining. Occasionally lead from such deposits may appear dull gold in colour: this may result from deposition of copper and iron sulphides.[48]

OVERLYING ENCRUSTATIONS. In conditions where lead is well preserved (section 5.3.2.2), overlying concretions of calcium carbonate (calcite and aragonite) are found; in sea-water these are accompanied by barnacles.

5.3.2.2 Implications of corrosion

In the presence of air, water, *and* organic acids, lead corrodes extremely quickly since the primary corrosion products of organic salts, such as acetates and formates, are all soluble (figure 5.7). Similar rapid corrosion occurs in soft, acidic waters when no protective carbonate layers form.[49] If such conditions prevailed in a deposit, it is unlikely that lead would survive more than half a century of burial. At the other extreme, lead is extremely resistant to corrosion by sea-water and chalky soils. Topographical details of the original surface are often maintained by the outer surface of a corrosion film or crust. However, sometimes the crust is distorted and the only detail remains in an underlying metal core where this does survive. Such remaining metal will be much pitted and only retain diminished details. It would seem that, unlike iron, there is no level of an 'original' surface to be found within a distorted lead corrosion

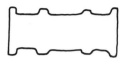

1. Well preserved covered by thin film of corrosion products

2. Original surface retained by metal surface which is slightly eroded: covered in layer of corrosion products or concretions of varying thickness

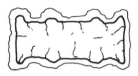

3. Original surface retained by exposed surface of corrosion products: remaining metal (if any) bisected by cracks.

Figure 5.7 Common conditions of lead found on excavations; cross-section of a token

crust. Corrosion can penetrate deep into lead, down grain boundaries, and thus it is much more brittle than it appears.

5.3.3 Examination

Some notion of the amount of lead in an alloy can be estimated simply by weight, but where bright metal is exposed it is found that lead will mark paper but tin and fine pewter will not. Since topographical details such as incised markings or stamps or an original surface are often maintained by the surface of a corrosion layer or crust, maximum information about a lead object can often be gained without having to remove corrosion products. Corroded lead can be very brittle since corrosion may have penetrated deep into it; care is taken to distinguish between corrosion products and earth/rootlets within the crevices of a crust. If much lead metal remains, x-radiography is of little help since this material absorbs x-rays, preventing exposure of the underlying film. In exceptional cases, neutron radiography (section 3.3.1.3) would be used.

5.3.4 Cleaning

5.3.4.1 Cleaning of lead from land sites

Investigative cleaning of this material usually consists of careful manual removal of overlying soil and concretions without dislodging the corrosion crusts or material within the crevices holding it together.

Plate 5.16 Stripping corroded lead. (a) A medieval badge as excavated showing obscuring concretions overlying a well preserved lead surface. (b) The badge after stripping reveals details of the original surface retained in the metal which is pitted by corrosion

Where the crust is distorted *and* examination shows that a good core of metal remains, for examination and display it may be necessary to strip the object (plate 5.16). This type of cleaning is normally carried out electrolytically[50] (section 5.1.4.2), for several reasons. First, since most of the corrosion products of lead are very insoluble, any reagent which will dissolve the crust tends to attack the lead too. This problem extends to the use of the sequestering agent (section 3.3.2.1) disodium EDTA,[51] for if traces of this are left behind after treatment long-term deterioration due to organic acids (section 5.3.2.2) may occur. Second, mechanical cleaning may smear or scratch the very soft metal underlying a lead corrosion crust. Third, there is no 'original' surface to locate within the crust mechanically. Furthermore, since lead and its corrosion products are poisonous, the dust produced by mechanical cleaning is toxic. On occasions, objects require this 'stripping' treatment only in discrete areas; here local electrolysis (section 5.1.4.2) using a pencil as an anode is used.

5.3.4.2 Cleaning of marine lead

It is not usually necessary to clean marine lead because surface encrustations are rarely obscuring. Occasionally, however, lead ingots or the stocks of Roman anchors may have identification marks which are disfigured by corrosion crusts. In this case, mechanical removal to reveal the blurred metal may be undertaken with wooden tools which minimize the risk of damaging the lead. Such cleaning is kept to a minimum and only carried out when the information possibly to be gained is essential to the dating or identification of the wreck or artefact, for it may result in damage without the benefit of information revealed. The mechanical removal of small patches of tightly adherent carbonate deposits from lead which is otherwise uncorroded can cause damage, but so also will almost any chemical used to dissolve the carbonate. Oddly, dilute sulphuric acid, subsequently neutralized, is the least damaging as it reacts to form an insoluble but often visible layer of lead sulphate on the surface of the etched metal, preventing further attack.

5.3.5 *Deterioration of lead alloys after excavation*

Lead alloys and their corrosion crusts after excavation are normally chemically stable, unless they become contaminated by organic acids either from injudicious conservation treatments or injudicious storage. Sources of these acids are certain waxes, lacquers, cleaning chemicals, papers, cardboard, cotton wool, woods (especially oak), paints, fabric finishes, and adhesives. With only slight moisture, these acids cause the corrosion described in section 5.3.2.2. Since the organic lead salts are not washed away, they react further turning the lead within a matter of months into soft white carbonate which crumbles on touching (plate

5.17a). Lead containing chloride and sulphur impurities may react with oxygen and moisture disrupting an already decayed object.[52]

Normally lead corrosion crusts containing details of an original surface (section 5.3.3) are not physically robust and can be destroyed by mishandling. Furthermore, if corrosion crusts are held together by soil in crevices, drying out after excavation may lead to crumbling. Even a relatively low level of heat, such as that from a light, can cause leaden artefacts to sag and become distorted.

5.3.6 Stabilization

5.3.6.1 Passive

Stabilization of lead is mainly confined to the avoidance of heat, mishandling, and contamination by organic acids. This latter condition is achieved by storing the artefacts, once dry, in sealed polypropylene boxes which do *not* contain materials which give off organic acid vapours; to be avoided are crude papers, cardboards, and cotton wool etc. Alternatively, objects can be placed inside acid-free paper envelopes which have been impregnated with calcium carbonate to absorb any such vapour. When on display, again lead must not be allowed to become contaminated; in these situations sources of organic acid include oak cabinets, paint, and cloth. Testing materials suspected of giving off organic vapours has been mentioned earlier (section 3.4.1.5).

Where it is found that lead has been contaminated or contains chloride and sulphur impurities, decay may be slowed down by desiccating it to an extremely low RH with silica gel; long-term stabilization is achieved only by an active technique described below.

5.3.6.2 Active

Crumbling carbonate crusts may be consolidated only with resins which do not contain nor break down to form organic acids; many waxes, PVAC, etc., are thus excluded. A technique called 'consolidative reduction' has been devised to reduce lead carbonate to lead making a much corroded object stronger and more visually attractive.[50] Unlike when reducing corroded iron (section 5.2.6.2) or lead ore, heat and a reducing atmosphere are not used; instead a very low electric current is applied whose direction is the exact opposite of the corrosion current (section 5.1.3.2). Electrons are taken up by the lead ions, reducing them to lead. It is a tricky procedure and carries with it ethical considerations (section 3.4.2.3). But since this technique alone also removes organic acids from a crumbling contaminated crust, it has to be employed to stabilize this type of material (plate 5.17b).

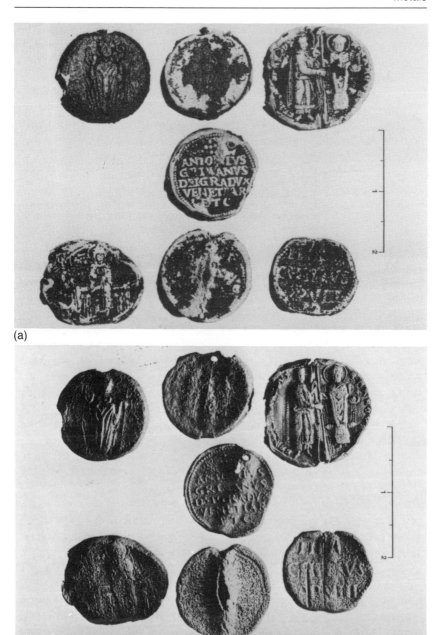

(a)

(b)

Plate 5.17 (a) Lead seals, corroded in store to soft, white lead carbonate, have survived only because the powder is held together by an old blackened wax coating. (b) Same seals after the lead carbonate has been electrolytically reduced back to lead

It is usual to prevent surface contamination and corrosion of clean lead by the application of a coat of synthetic resin, but as with consolidants the choice is restricted to those which are free from organic acids.[50]

5.3.7 Reshaping

Although lead can be worked without the need for annealing, reshaping is a specialist technique. Lead which appears sound may have corrosion penetrating deep into it (section 5.3.3), introducing brittleness into the material and thus precluding reshaping without the danger of cracking. Moreover, any corrosion crust containing surface detail such as lettering could crumble or become abraded in the process.

5.3.8 Summary

Objects made of lead or its alloys cannot be cleaned or reshaped without damage except under laboratory conditions. On the whole, excavated material does not require extensive environmental control, careful handling and avoidance of heat perhaps being most essential. Where the lead is thought or feared to be low grade, it should be desiccated (section 3.4.1.1). In the longer term, however, the role of organic acids as corrosion stimulators becomes important and thus care has to be taken to avoid excavated material becoming contaminated by organic acid vapours or solutions. Once contaminated, there exists only the one rather drastic recourse of consolidative reduction for stabilization. Cleaning of lead likewise does not usually entail extensive work; virtually all detail that can be seen on excavation is all that there is preserved.

5.4 Tin and its alloys

5.4.1 Nature of artefacts

Tin has a very low melting point (232°C) and good wetting power, and so is often used for casting or as a coating. However, cast tin objects are soft and so it is usually alloyed for strength as well as economy, giving pewter.[53] This term covers a wide range of mainly casting alloys from 25–50 per cent lead (Roman), to less than 25 per cent lead ('lay' medieval), to tin with a small amount of copper, bismuth, or antimony ('fine' medieval and modern). An alloy with more than 25 per cent lead must be considered poisonous. Coatings of tin alloys are generally referred to as 'tinning', and whilst they could be of almost pure tin, they are more likely to be low-melting-point tin alloys; the alloying material is lead, but antimony, copper, and zinc are also possible. Since tin/lead and lead/tin alloys have such low melting points, that of 63 per cent tin being 183°C, they are used frequently as soft solders (section 5.1.2.1).

5.4.2 Nature of deteriorated material

BRIGHT TIN OR PATINATED PEWTER. Though a base metal, tin and tinning often present a bright surface even after many years, as a result of the formation of a thin film of protective tin(IV) oxide (SnO_2) which is resistant even to acid attack. This oxide layer helps preserve tin even when it should be forming the anode in a galvanic cell (section 5.1.3.2), as it is when being used to coat copper alloys. When combined with lead oxide and possibly sulphide, tin oxide gives pewter, especially from the sea, a fine grey patina.

BLACK SPOTS, PITS, OR WARTS. If a damp environment contains corrosion stimulators such as chlorides or sulphates, localized roughening of the surface appearing as black spots occurs.[54] If corrosion continues, pits are formed. Alternatively, cassiterite (SnO_2) is found and appears as hard warts.

GREY/WHITE/BROWN CRUST. Continued corrosion caused by stimulators can produce a crust usually of SnO_2 with some tin(II) oxide. Black romarchite (SnO) and white hydroromarchite ($5SnO.2H_2O$) have been identified on tin from fresh water.[55] These crusts may be discoloured by other metals present, copper for example, turning them green, or they may be dissected by crevices. Crusts on alloys with lead, will also contain lead corrosion products (section 5.3.2.1); pewter from marine sites may appear with a soft grey surface sprinkled with warts as above. That pewter sometimes appears disfigured and sometimes with a preserving patina, seems to depend more on the proportion of lead in the alloy than on any recognizable feature of the environment. In extreme conditions, crusts may crack, curl up, and spall off.

GREY/WHITE/BROWN POWDER OR PASTE. Corrosion may continue right through an object or solder, reducing them to powder which normally crumbles away. On occasion it may be held together fortuitously by other salts, such as silicates, from the soil, in which case it may be difficult to recognize the object as having been originally metallic.

There are few examples of tin from marine environments, probably because here its main corrosion product, tin oxide (SnO_2) forms white paste-like deposits. These usually only survive when they are protected by marine sediment or concretion. Romarchite (SnO) and yellow varlamoffite $((Sn.Fe)(O.OH)_2)$ also form in marine environments, but so far have only been recorded in association with corroded bronze and brass. Hydrated chlorides have also been found.

ISOLATED PITS CONTAINING GREY POWDER. This type of decay is seen only rarely and should not be confused with those described above. It can occur only where the temperature is less than 13°C, when the crystal structure of the tin is altered in discrete areas, turning the bright metal to a grey powder called 'tin pest'. The reason for this alteration is still unclear, but the possibility that much buried tin has been lost through long exposure to temperatures below 13°C is not credited by some metallurgists.[56]

5.4.3   Examination

If an object of tin or pewter just has a thin oxide film, the original surface topography and dimensions will be well maintained. If the film's crust and corrosion is extreme, neither any remaining metal core nor any corrosion layer within the crust retains details of the original surface; the outside surface of the corrosion products must be used as a guide to the original. Fortunately, the volume expansion of the corrosion crust is not normally excessive.

On objects made of metals other than tin, any 'tinning' present may not be visible; being less base than iron and being protected by its oxide film (section 5.3.2.1), tinning can become covered by iron or copper corrosion products. X-radiography assists in this search, but it often fails to detect thin coatings. Solder also should be looked for, but, being rich in lead, it is often corroded to powder when in contact with copper alloys.

5.4.4   Cleaning[57]

As with lead alloys (section 5.3.4), little cleaning, apart from dirt removal, is carried out. Warts of tin oxide are not removed, as corrosion of the exposed metal is liable to occur very quickly. If, for some reason, removal of cassiterite is required, it would be extremely difficult to carry out chemically since this is so insoluble. Patinas on pewter are prized and should always be retained.

5.4.5   Deterioration after excavation and stabilization

After excavation, tin alloys usually are found to be chemically stable, either because they are preserved by a layer of oxide, or because no metal remains. Occurrences of tin pest (section 5.4.2) have been found on historic tin, but the extent of this type of decay is not known. At present, tin alloys are stabilized only passively, by maintaining the temperature above 13°C, whilst bearing in mind the low melting point of tin. Pewter, like lead (section 5.3.6.1), must be protected from organic acids.

5.4.6 Summary

As for lead (section 5.3.8).

5.5 Copper and its alloys

5.5.1 Nature of artefacts[58]

The melting point of pinkish copper (1084°C) is reduced by small quantities of natural impurities such as arsenic, antimony, tin, lead, or iron. Arsenical copper is more easily work hardened than pure copper, but if present in concentrations greater than 2.5 per cent, the arsenic may cause embrittlement and if greater than 15 per cent, it may rise to the surface of the alloy when cast, giving it a 'silver' skin. Where tin is present in concentrations greater than 2 per cent, it may be considered deliberate alloying to produce bronze, which is harder than pure copper, even without working. A common alloy mixture of 10 per cent tin is a reddish yellow and is readily cold worked; at 14 per cent, a brittle phase makes the now golden bronze harder but more difficult to work; at over 20 per cent, the virtually unworkable bell-metal bronze looks paler; at above 30 per cent, tin may separate out in casting to give a white surface layer or form the brittle high-tin bronze, speculum, used for mirrors etc. To improve casting properties, lead is added to bronze. Alternatively a ternary alloy composed of copper, tin, and zinc (the latter resulting in a paler metal) has increased malleability. This alloy is nearer in character to the modern alloy 'gun metal' than to bronze. Copper alloyed with zinc on its own at about 20 per cent gives golden brasses, whilst higher concentrations give whiter alloys. Since it is impossible to gauge the exact make-up of copper alloys without analysis, in the absence of this it is essential that the alloys are referred to by the generic name of 'copper alloy' rather than by a specific, unproven, prejudicial term such as 'bronze'.

Copper alloys can be joined (section 5.1.2.1) by hard solders, this being known as brazing. The solder itself is frequently a copper alloy; thus a high-tin bronze can be used to braze a low-tin bronze. Brazing solders (or spelters) of copper alloys, especially brass, are used to braze iron as well. Alternatively, weaker joins in a copper alloy artefact can be made with soft solders.

Parts of copper alloy objects can be joined together other than mechanically or with solders, by burning or running on, that is the casting of part of an object directly onto a previously formed piece. However, because of the adhesion of oxide films, copper alloys cannot be welded together. Within hollow cast objects there may be remains of baked clay cores and, embedded in the metal of such objects, the ends of chaplets used to hold the cores in position whilst the casting was taking place. Chaplets usually are made of a similar but slightly less readily fused alloy than that of the casting metal, but if of a more base metal, they may corrode out. In some cases, large gas holes found in the metal during casting are filled by running on more metal.

The surface of copper alloy objects (sections 5.1.2.2–6) are often gilded, silvered, or even tinned[59] to preserve or enhance them. It is known that lacquers were used in antiquity to alter surface colour, turpentine and pitch enhancing with a golden colour, others giving a red-brown tint, and others producing a dark colour to conceal repairs. It is possible that, in antiquity, patinas similar to those described in section 5.5.2.1, were made deliberately, and that surface colour was altered by blanching, but the extent of such practices is as yet unknown.[60]

5.5.2 Nature of decayed material[61]

5.5.2.1 Appearance

DARKENING AND TARNISHING (plate 5.18a). If pitch has been used as a lacquer, this darkens over time, but the usual cause of darkening of copper alloys in the air is the development of a thin protective tarnish of red/brown copper(I) oxide, cuprite (Cu_2O), possibly with some black copper(II) oxide (CuO), copper sulphide, and the oxides of the alloying metals. However, the exact nature of tarnish has yet to be confirmed analytically.

BRIGHT METAL (plate 5.18b). From certain wet sites such as urban, marine, estuarine, and foreshore deposits, where oxygen is scarce, copper and its alloys often appear bright and virtually uncorroded. Some pitting of the surface from localized corrosion may have occurred. On occasion, in environments of low redox potential, objects may appear coated in copper; this is a result of the redeposition of the metal following previous dissolution from the alloy during corrosion. These appearances of bright metal should not be confused with a dull golden surface deposit of copper/iron sulphides, which can be found on copper alloys from similar environments.[62] Sometimes patches of white metal may be seen beneath corrosion patinas/crusts and misinterpreted as tinning. Whilst indeed the white metal may be tin, it can be deposited during the corrosion of a high-tin bronze described in section 5.5.2.2.

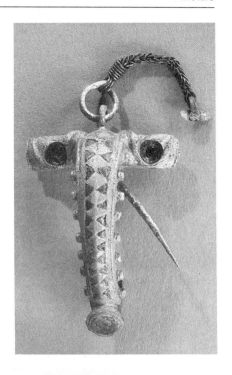

Plate 5.18 Corroded copper alloys. (a) Protective tarnish on an artefact only buried for a relatively short period. (b) Enamelled Roman brooch as excavated from a waterlogged deposit in Carlisle, showing no build up of corrosion products; the brooch parts are made from different coloured copper alloys. (c) Copper alloy annular brooch showing smooth green patina disrupted on one side by warts of corrosion products

BLACKENING. If metal is not found bright from deposits of low oxygen/redox potential (section 5.1.3.2), it may be black or blue-black from the presence of copper sulphides, for example covellite (CuS) and chalcocite (Cu_2S); reliable identification of these products is often difficult. These sulphides can form solid protective layers or bubbly crusts, but they may slough off into the deposit, leaving the metal to waste away. Any surface platings containing silver or lead often appear black from sulphides after burial in such deposits.

PATINAS (plate 5.18c). Coloured patinas form on copper alloys by very slow controlled corrosion either in the presence of moisture, carbon dioxide, and oxygen, or in sea-water. The colour depends on the corrosion products formed, which depend partly on the environment and partly on the alloy. A basic green coloration is given by emerald/dark-green malachite, basic copper(II) carbonate ($CuCO_3.Cu(OH)_2$), whilst, less commonly in drier environments, a blue colour develops from another basic copper(II) carbonate, azurite ($2CuCO_3.Cu(OH)_2$). The tone of green is darkened by the presence of sulphides of copper and lead, dulled by arsenical corrosion products, and lightened by lead carbonate, but more especially by cassiterite, tin oxide (SnO_2). On some high-tin bronzes, white to grey to turquoise patinas called 'water' patinas are found, and consist mainly of tin oxide. Surprisingly, on similar bronzes, black patinas are also found; at present this blackening is undergoing study to determine what it is and whether it was formed artificially or naturally. The hue of a patina can be reddened by an underlying layer of copper(I) oxide, cuprite, which may be exposed on some surfaces. Sometimes a patina is disrupted by hard warts of corrosion products; these are caused by isolated areas of the type of corrosion described below. Yellow-green patinas found on copper alloys exposed to the atmosphere are different chemically; these are mainly basic copper(II) sulphate, brochantite ($CuSO_4.3Cu(OH)_2$). Even before industrialization there was enough hydrogen sulphide and sulphur dioxide in the air to cause its formation.

GREEN/BLUISH CRUSTS. These crusts, common on excavated objects, often contain the same minerals as the patinas above, but, being formed under different conditions, they create rough uneven encrustations instead of smooth surfaces. Thus, for example, the green coloration of many of the crusts found on copper alloys would seem to be due mainly to malachite. As well as the minerals mentioned above, crusts may contain chloride minerals, such as basic copper(II) chloride ($CuCl_2.3Cu(OH)_2$) forming large dark-green crystals of paratacamite or atacamite. Tin oxides and lead corrosion products are also found on alloys, as well as a range of more exotic copper corrosion products which form as a result of particular micro-environments.

MARINE ARTEFACTS WITH ENCRUSTATIONS.[63] Copper in solution is toxic to most forms of marine life, so the presence of encrusting marine creatures on the surface of copper, bronze, or brass is a good indication that the metal is stable and free from active corrosion. However, concretions which are composed almost entirely of calcium carbonate and copper(II) oxychlorides (paratacamite etc.) mixed with tin oxides, are sometimes found. These may become quite thick and so embed the shells and skeletons of marine creatures and other kinds of marine deposit. Thin crusts of calcium carbonate may also form. Yet another type of encrustation forms if iron has corroded near copper and its alloys, for these usually become firmly embedded within a ferrous concretion shell. This protects them completely and reduces corrosion to negligible levels.

5.5.2.2 Corrosion and its implications

Even though copper is approaching the stability of a truly noble metal, both it and base alloying metals are likely to corrode in many archaeological environments. Recently, new research in this area has shown the corrosion of artefacts to be very variable and in some cases extremely complex. However, many excavated objects do exhibit similarities in their corrosion product structure and this will be described first.

In an uncomplicated but unfortunately not universal situation,[64] copper may be considered to corrode along the edges of the grains of the metal, that is the grain boundaries, which, because they have higher energy, become anodic to the centre of the grains (section 5.1.3.2).

When a metal artefact first falls into a deposit, corrosive attack is delayed by the almost inevitable layer of oxide it will have gained during its useful lifetime. In a damp oxygenated deposit, however, corrosion will slowly commence. As copper dissolves along the grain boundaries it forms compact primary cuprite (Cu_2O) which fills these corroded areas. As corrosion continues, the dissolved copper is forced to migrate out past the surface of the object to deposit over it as secondary cuprite. The outer zone of this cuprite is subject to reaction with other chemicals in the environment, and so a layer of basic carbonates and possibly basic chlorides forms. As more copper is dissolved from the diminished metal core, it either deposits internally as cuprite or migrates out to deposit in the growing corrosion crust (figure 5.8).

There are three features here which differ from the corrosion of iron: in the first instance, the volume of corrosion products is similar to that of the metal and so the corrosion crust is never very bulky; second, corrosion is intergranular and thus some corrosion products can be

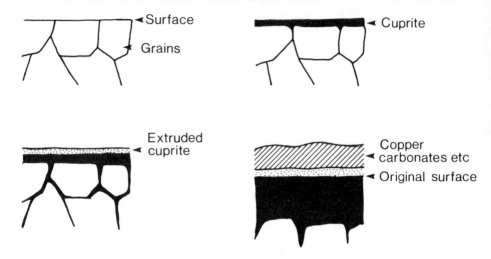

Figure 5.8 Sections to show corrosion of a copper alloy

deposited within the metal; and, third, distinct layers develop.

Where extrusion of dissolved copper occurs slowly, a compact patina develops, but where this is more rapid, a crust forms. Sometimes certain areas of the surface corrode faster than others producing warts of corrosion products overlying pits in the metal (figure 5.9). Usually this leads to a loss in original surface within the wart.

More complicated corrosion patterns than this have been known for some time to occur in bronzes. It would appear that corrosion crusts may be composed of a large number of very thin lamellae, both within the cuprite zones and where cuprite alternates with other corrosion products, often disrupting the original surface. Mechanisms for these phenomena are the focus of current research.[65]

On high-tin bronzes, the corrosion crusts are often rich in tin oxide stained green to a lesser or greater extent by copper salts. In some cases, as previously described, the original surface actually appears tinned. Here, because of complex phase structures and the insolubility of tin oxide, tin has been preserved at the expense of the copper which is the reverse of what is expected (section 5.1.3.1).

Chloride ions are known to facilitate the corrosion of copper. They migrate through protective oxide films stimulating corrosion, and forming a layer of white, waxy, copper(I) chloride, nantokite (CuCl), on the surface of the corroding metal. In time, the nantokite slowly reacts with water to produce cuprite.

It is usual for copper or copper alloy artefacts to survive burial in oxygenated deposits, whether as metals or as corrosion products (figure 5.10). However, where chloritic corrosion is fast, the corrosion crust built

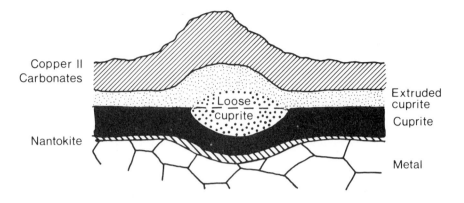

Copper II Carbonates

Extruded cuprite

Cuprite

Nantokite

Loose cuprite

Metal

Figure 5.9 Section through a wart on a corroded copper alloy (after Leidheiser)[66]

up is so porous that oxygen and water penetrate to the metal and react with the nantokite, forming paratacamite. In these cases the reaction is too fast for compact crystals to form, and instead tiny crystals of non-adhering pale-green powdery paratacamite develop. The corrosion crust is no longer coherent and the artefact may crumble away.

In extremely acidic oxygen-rich deposits, such as some through-draining gravels, soluble corrosion products may form and nothing can be detected of an artefact except perhaps a green stain.

The situation in deposits of low oxygen/redox potential is different: oxide and carbonate layers do not form. Here, even in acidic conditions, corrosion of copper is very slight but, where there are sulphides present, copper alloys are usually attacked, becoming pitted and covered in black sulphides. Surprisingly, peaty moorland waters may be benign, such a phenomenon possibly being due to the presence of natural corrosion inhibitors.[67]

On certain artefacts in the marine environment, thin crusts of calcite develop, formed as a by-product of corrosion, signifying the cathodic region of a corrosion cell (section 5.1.3.2). At the cathode, hydroxyl ions are released so that there is a slight local increase in pH. This change affects the carbonate buffer system (section 2.2.1.3) and calcium carbonate is deposited at the end of a series of reactions.

5.5.3 Examination

Since copper is toxic to living organisms, it is not uncommon to find organic debris such as seeds and fibres preserved from biodeterioration in the vicinity of corroding copper alloy objects (plate 2.3). They are frequently impregnated with copper salts staining them green, or else

1. Well preserved: covered by thin tarnish or green patina

   2. Original surface mostly retained within layer of corrosion products: covered by fine patina except where wart erupts; remaining metal is pitted

   3. Original surface retained within thick layers of corrosion products: covered by bulk green crust; little or no metal remaining

Figure 5.10   Common conditions of copper alloys found on excavations. Cross-section of a large pin

entirely replaced by corrosion products and preserved as a pseudomorph.[68]

In patinated artefacts, the visible surface, except where distorted by warts, will fairly accurately represent the original surface. But in encrusted artefacts, it will be more or less contorted by uneven corrosion and warts. During investigative cleaning of this second type, it is often found that the original surface is maintained *within* the cuprite layer, that is by the discontinuity between the internally deposited and the extruded mineral (section 5.5.2.2) (plate 5.19). Where warts and lamellae are too numerous, no coherent oxide layer remains and the original surface is lost (plate 5.20). In encrusted artefacts, any remaining metal will not retain surface detail and will be badly pitted.

Associated materials (plate 5.21), such as gilding, silvering, tinning, inlay, and enamels, on an original surface are covered by corrosion crusts. But as the metal continues to dissolve from below, they may become dislodged into these crusts or even into the surrounding soil. In the vicinity of original surfaces, black or vitreous deposits have been found which have been shown by analysis to be the remains of ancient lacquers.[69]

In copper alloys, it should be noted that the colour and composition of any remaining metal, whether found 'bright' (section 5.5.2.1) or under a patina or crust, may be misleading. This is because surface enrichment (section 5.1.2.2), that is, the leaching out of one of the alloying constituents during corrosion, will lead to a colour change. So a brass will appear more pink and deficient in zinc than the original was, distorting visual interpretation and surface analyses. Second, pure copper may have

(a)

(b)

Plate 5.19 Original surface of a copper alloy buckle retained in the cuprite layer. (a) Buckle before investigative cleaning showing overlying green crust. (b) Original surface revealed by mechanical cleaning

Plate 5.20 Totally corroded copper alloy coin; corrosion layers are so distorted that no detail of the original surface can be retrieved

(a)

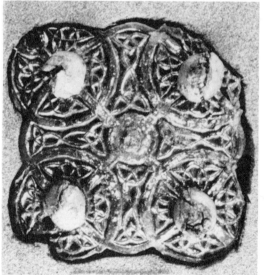

(b)

Plate 5.21 Associated materials on copper alloys. (a) Traces of silver (appearing white) on a corroded coin, the last remnants of a silvered surface. (b) Traces of gilding (appearing white) on the surface of an early medieval bookplate (this is shown before investigative cleaning in plate 5.22)

redeposited over the surface of the object (section 5.5.2.1).

Analyses of patinas and corrosion crusts are undertaken for numerous reasons. For example, to discover if it is possible to identify fake artefacts by their artificial, as against natural, corrosion products, to deduce the type of deposit from which an unprovenanced museum artefact derives, to interpret the deposit from which artefacts are excavated, or to determine original composition even though no metal remains.

During examination, radiography helps in the identification of coins, engravings, technological features including clay cores and tool marks, and in revealing decorative effects (plate 5.22). Since copper alloy objects are usually less encrusted, radiography is less essential here than it is for ironwork. However, even on beautifully patinated objects, radiography can be useful in determining the condition of the object, revealing perhaps that, even though a surface is well preserved, no metal core remains, a situation which can arise if corrosion has been uniform and slow.

5.5.4 Cleaning

The choice of method for cleaning depends on what is required from the object (type of information, display, etc.), what it is made of, and what condition it is in. Since chemicals cannot distinguish the discontinuity of an original surface within a cuprite layer, they can destroy this information and dislodge surface components (metallic coatings, enamels, etc.) if used injudiciously. Therefore objects with corrosion crusts are cleaned mechanically using simple tools such as pins and scalpels with only the occasional use (with extreme care) of chemicals to soften overlying copper(II) minerals. Skill and practice are needed to locate the original surface and to remove overlying corrosion products without damaging it (plates 5.21b, 5.22a, and 5.19). Where there are warts, in order to retain a coherent surface rather than reveal a pit, it is necessary to leave some of the overlying cuprite slightly proud of the original surface.

Stripping, or the total removal of corrosion products by chemicals, has been widely practised in the past. However, the metal revealed, as discussed in section 5.5.2.1, will be pitted, surface enriched, diminished, etc., and thus unsatisfactory for display or study (plate 5.2). Moreover, the chemicals used to dissolve the corrosion have been shown to leach further elements from the metal core.[70]

Electrolytic cleaning (section 5.1.4) cannot be used, for the dissolved copper from the crust readily reduces to metallic copper and so tends to plate the exposed core in pink metal. Today, therefore, stripping of archaeological material is seldom practised. In particular, for a number of reasons, the cleaning of copper alloy coins must be considered carefully

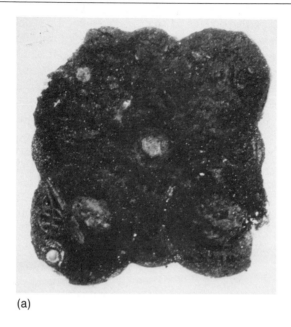

(a)

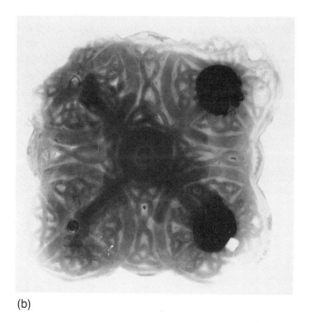

(b)

Plate 5.22 Radiography of copper alloy. (a) Early medieval bookplate before investigation. (b) Radiograph of bookplate from the Brough of Birsay, Orkney reveals intricate design but not the gilding found during investigative cleaning

before work is undertaken: to avoid excessive time being spent on trivial material; to avoid loss of perhaps unexpected information; and to avoid endangering the existence or stability of the coin. Such aims require collaboration (section 1.3); it is essential that maximum information concerning the interest of a particular coin in the fields both of numismatics and of archaeology, the expected composition and legend of the coin, and the cleaning techniques are pooled. Skilled mechanical cleaning often assisted by judicial use of chemicals under a microscope to soften hard, overlying copper(II) encrustations may reveal dislodged silvering (plate 5.21a), decayed lacquer, etc., and the original surface within a cuprite layer. Heavy-handed use of brushes, excessively strong chemicals, or lack of numismatic awareness all lead to disaster. This controversial subject is more fully discussed in the proceedings of a symposium held in 1980.[71]

5.5.5   Deterioration after excavation

Upon excavation it seems that many patinated and crusted copper/copper alloys are stable, with corrosion of any remaining metal only occurring at an RH greater than 80 per cent. This figure is lower in polluted air, especially if contaminated by chlorides. In marine artefacts, corrosion by chlorides is particularly noticeable locally where these are trapped in calcareous and ferrous concretions. However, if nantokite (CuCl) is present within any patina or crust, an extremely destructive type of decay known as 'bronze disease' can occur at RH as low as 35–50 per cent.[72] Nantokite is stable so long as both oxygen and water are absent and thus it can exist sealed beneath layers of compact corrosion without causing any damage. If water is present, it slowly reacts to give cuprite as shown in section 5.5.2.2. But if there is plentiful oxygen as well as water present, it reacts extremely quickly to give, amongst other products, the basic copper(II) chloride, paratacamite. This appears as small, bulky, loose-fitting, pale-green crystals which are a component of 'bronze disease' (plate 2.6):

$$4CuCl + 4H_2O + O_2 \rightarrow CuCl_2.3Cu(OH)_2 + 2HCl$$
$$\text{nantokite} \qquad\qquad\qquad \text{paratacamite}$$

Since nantokite is the deepest of all the corrosion layers, when it forms paratacamite in this fashion, the layers above are physically disrupted as the pressure from the growing bulk of crystals forces them apart. Finally it erupts on the surface. If any metal remains, the released chloride from the above reaction causes renewed corrosion. 'Bronze disease' thus causes, not only disruption of patinas and informative cuprite layers, but also continued corrosion of remaining metal (figure 5.11).

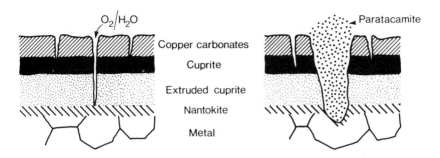

Figure 5.11 Deterioration of a copper alloy caused by 'bronze disease'

Freshly excavated material may develop 'bronze disease' in a matter of hours, as a result of the drying out of a wet or damp crust. As the water recedes and/or the crust shrinks, air, and thus oxygen, enters, and when it penetrates to the nantokite, deterioration ensues. However, even if nantokite is present, a crust, and more especially a compact patina, may remain stable for many years after excavation, since the entry of oxygen and water is blocked by the denseness of the overlying minerals. But if for some reason the crust loses its seal, perhaps as a result of being cracked by handling, cleaning, or continual temperature fluctuation, 'bronze disease' could develop if the ambient relative humidity is over 40 per cent.

Other types of post-excavation deterioration involve the formation of white deposits of lead carbonate on heavily leaded bronzes from corrosion by organic acid vapours (section 5.3.5), and the appearance of brown or black hairy crystals on copper alloys, but these are far less common than 'bronze disease'.

5.5.6 Stabilization

5.5.6.1 Passive

For objects that do not contain chloride but do contain metal, further corrosion may be prevented by maintaining the RH at less than 75 per cent and preventing contamination with chlorides and dust by air-conditioning or tight-fitting containers (section 3.4.1.4). For small objects containing nantokite, 'bronze disease' can be prevented by removing either water or oxygen from the system, and since the latter is difficult to achieve, desiccation of copper alloys is the recommended approach. This must be done within forty-eight hours of excavation, and is easily accomplished using silica gel. Resort to removal of water by solvent storage is only necessary for waterlogged enamels (section 4.4.6.1) and *preserved* textile (i.e. not simply replaced) (section 6.6.5.1); neither of these may be desiccated nor stored wet if oxygen is not excluded. Temperatures of less than $-10°C$ also could be used to prevent 'bronze disease', but there is the usual untested hazard of ice expansion. It has been suggested that, to ensure prevention of deterioration, copper alloys should be subjected to a vapour phase inhibitor (section 5.1.5). Thus tissue paper impregnated with benzotriazole (section 5.5.6.2) could be included within a sealed desiccated pack, but this is not standard practice.

Large objects from marine sites present more of a problem as the metal is very unstable. If small enough, they can be stored in baths of benzotriazole (section 5.5.6.2), but if too large for this, they are cleaned of any thick concretions, wrapped in absorbent material soaked in this inhibitor, and then sealed in polyethylene.

5.5.6.2 Active

The most common approach to the stabilization of copper alloys now in use in Britain is inhibition (section 5.1.5). This has been brought about largely by the development of the inhibitor benzotriazole (BTA)[73] (figure 5.12). In 1967, the use of this chemical for archaeological material was suggested by Madsen, even though it had already been in use commercially for seventeen years. The actual mechanism of inhibition is still undergoing study but it would appear that the benzotriazole molecules are adsorbed onto the cuprite and complexed onto the nantokite, rendering them inert and forming a water barrier protecting any remaining copper.

The inhibitor is applied by immersing the object in a dilute solution of BTA in water or alcohol. A partial vacuum is applied to ensure the solution penetrates through a patina or crust as far as the nantokite and metal core. Thus the outer corrosion layers do not have to be removed first, degreasing in a solvent being the sole requirement. This means that the inhibitor can be used before examination and cleaning. Sometimes the reaction is not completed by one immersion, and an object might have to be retreated several times before stability is achieved. Some copper alloys, notably those with high nantokite levels, have been

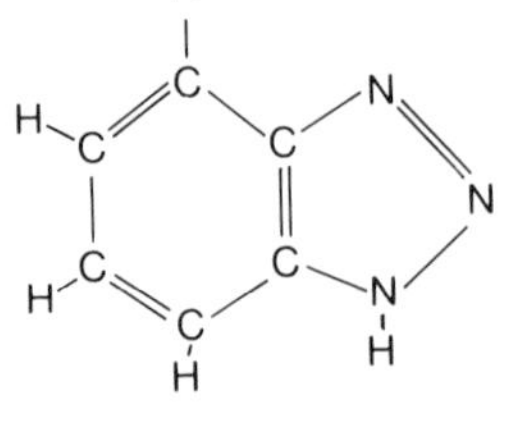

Figure 5.12 The structure of a benzotriazole molecule

notoriously difficult to stabilize with BTA. Recent work[74], however, has shown that pre-treatment with sodium carbonate to raise the pH may circumvent these problems. After treatment, the object is lacquered to prevent the physical rupture of BTA films, and contamination by dirt and sweat. BTA is destabilized by UV light; to prevent this occurring over time, a special commercially available lacquer, Incralac,[75] which contains not only a reserve of BTA, but also a UV screening agent, is used. The object can then be subjected to RH of up to approximately 70 per cent without further deterioration. Occasionally objects have to be retreated after several years and so their condition must be monitored periodically.

A word of warning must be given here: although it has not yet been demonstrated, BTA has the potential of being a carcinogen, and thus solutions should not be made up, or applied by, unskilled personnel. Gloves are worn when objects which have been treated with BTA are examined.

BTA used alone or following sodium carbonate treatment has now superseded virtually all other methods for stabilizing archaeological copper alloys. These other methods attempted to remove the nantokite from the crust, but since it is not readily soluble and lies beneath all other layers of corrosion, this is not simple. Some methods, such as that of using sodium sesquicarbonate, attempt to dissolve the nantokite out through the crust, but this takes several years and has unwanted side effects. Other methods require the upper layers to be stripped off (section 5.5.4) first before the nantokite is removed chemically or electrochemically. All these methods result in leaching of the remaining alloy.[76] For very large objects with patinas interrupted by eruptions of 'bronze disease', treatment avoiding formidable immersion in BTA is achieved by excavating the paratacamite pits and reacting the exposed nantokite at their base with silver oxide, so sealing it from the atmosphere by a layer of silver chloride.

In order to assist in the stabilization of marine copper and copper alloys, it is necessary to remove the chloride-laden calcareous and ferrous concretions. This is best done mechanically, although citric acid, with thiourea as an inhibitor to prevent acid etching or leaching of the underlying metal, has to be used on resistant patches.

5.5.7 Summary

Copper and its alloys corrode in such a way that it is highly likely that the level and topography of an original surface will be retained, either by the outermost patina or within the corrosion crust. Patinas and crusts are often more fragile than they appear, and casual cleaning, even brushing or rubbing with a thumb, can destroy important information. This is especially true of coins. Cleaning should thus be restricted to the laboratory. Here stripping techniques are avoided, mechanical methods being preferred. Deterioration of copper and its alloys can usually be achieved by desiccation (section 3.4.1.1), which should be carried out within forty-eight hours of excavation; but there are notable exceptions (section 5.5.6.1). For long-term stabilization, BTA has been found to be highly effective but even when treated thus, extremely high RH and fluctuating temperatures (especially for enamels) (section 2.4.3), have to be avoided. Bright metal, and objects treated with BTA, should be handled only in gloves.

5.6   Silver and its alloys

5.6.1   Nature of artefacts[77]

Silver (melting point 960.5°C) often contains up to 5 per cent of impurities such as copper, lead, and even iron, but it is also commonly alloyed deliberately, to harden or debase it. Sterling silver is at least 92.5 per cent silver, whilst crude silver may be only 80 per cent pure; very base alloys containing less than 50 per cent silver are termed billon. The distinctive bright white appearance of silver is evident in these alloys, with a tendency to dulling and discoloration with increasing copper content. To make base silver such as billon appear more noble than it is, it is often blanched. Amongst other applied decorative techniques, silver may be gilded or given other yellow surfacings (section 5.1.2.2) and inlaid with black niello (section 5.1.2.5). Glass does not fuse well to silver and so enamelling is rare.

When base silver is worked, the copper content oxidizes, and whilst this is usually removed from the surface by the craftsman, it can remain in the zone just below the surface as 'fire stain'. During its useful life, silverware may develop a much prized dark patina, which can be caused by the uncovering of fire stain as the overlying silver is polished away.

Pure silver can be cold welded but alloys must be soldered with either soft or hard solders (section 5.1.2.1), 'silver solder' being made by alloying silver with copper and sometimes zinc as well. 'Silvering' applied to other metals is usually an alloy of silver with tin (section 5.1.2.2).

5.6.2   Nature of deteriorated material[78]

BLACKENED SURFACE (plate 5.23a). Even in dry air, base silver is tarnished by a layer of copper oxide (section 5.5.2.1), whilst the presence of as little as 2 parts per million of sulphur in the form of hydrogen sulphide or sulphur dioxide, will cause silver itself to blacken by the formation of a protective layer of silver sulphide, argentite (Ag_2S). This sulphide is found on silver from virtually all environments, including the

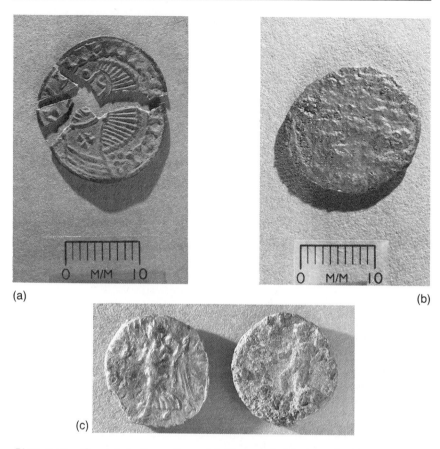

Plate 5.23. Corroded silver alloys. (a) Silver coin blackened with a protective sulphide tarnish. Fracturing shows the embrittled condition of much ancient silver. (b) Swollen crust of silver chloride on a coin. (c) Right-hand coin shows crust of copper corrosion products on base silver. A similar coin (left-hand) after investigative cleaning

sea. In extreme conditions, the protection afforded by the thin layer of sulphide may fail, and corrosion may continue until all the silver has become silver sulphide.

BLACK/GREY/PINK/LILAC/PURPLE OR BROWN SWOLLEN CRUST (plate 5.23b). Such crusts are composed of a mixture of grey waxy cerargyrite, 'horn silver', silver chloride (AgCl), and brown opaque bromyrite, silver bromide (AgBr), stained to pink hues by cuprite or darkened by silver and copper sulphides. The balance of chloride to bromide is variable, but high-bromide levels would be expected in finds from deposits rich in organic matter. Low corrosion levels lead to the formation of a protective

231

patina, but higher levels result in a thick, sometimes swollen, crust in which no metal may remain. Marine objects may be covered by such a crust which also includes copper corrosion products, iron oxides, and calcium carbonate. Beneath this may be found either a core of unconverted metal, or else a hollow mould like those found within ferrous concretions (section 5.2.2.3).

GREEN CRUSTS (plate 5.23c). Copper in a base silver alloy corrodes preferentially to the silver, and deposits typical corrosion products both on the surface and between the silver grains (section 5.5.2.1). A base silver alloy on excavation may appear indistinguishable from a copper alloy. In acidic conditions where the copper corrosion products are dissolved away, the remaining silver will probably be blackened.

EMBRITTLED (plate 5.23a). A bright or corroded silver object is often more brittle than would be imagined. There may be more than one cause of this; for example, it may be a result of phase alterations over time or of intergranular corrosion deep within the alloy.

5.6.3 Examination

Where a corrosion crust exists, it may be possible to deduce something about the composition of the original alloy from it (section 5.6.2); thus a thick green crust implies a base silver/copper alloy, whilst a pale, waxy, horn-silver one indicates a purer silver. Details of an original suface may be seen on the outside of a silver chloride crust in a somewhat blurred, swollen state, but in many cases a more accurate representation can be found within the corrosion, much as it can be for copper alloys (section 5.5.2.2).

Silver corrodes intergranularly, with some silver chloride depositing *in situ* and some being extruded; removal of the outside layer of horn silver will reveal an original surface still appearing silver. As corrosion continues, the silver is lost, but the original surface is still maintained by a discontinuity within the corrosion. In a base silver object, whilst the external surface of a copper corrosion crust is uninformative, the original surface may well be perfectly maintained beneath this by the uncorroded silver portion of the alloy; being more noble than the copper, the silver will be cathodically protected (section 5.1.3.2). The analysis of corroded silver alloys is difficult to interpret, for a surface enriched in silver may be a result of several phenomena; for example, corrosion, deliberate blanching, working, and cooling during manufacture, or even silvering a copper alloy. It is possible that this interpretation may be further confused by the redeposition of silver on the surface of a corroding alloy in certain reducing environments.

Radiography will assist in locating engraving, niello, gilding, and the original surface where this is maintained in a corrosion crust by silver.

5.6.4   Cleaning

Once it has been determined that surface blackening is neither a deliberate nor an aesthetically pleasing patina, it should still be removed only when an object is required for display. Not only is it protective, but every time it is removed a new layer forms to be later removed, thereby continually wearing away the metal. When necessary, this removal is often carried out mechanically with extremely fine, soft, abrasive pastes, but excavated artefacts are usually too brittle and cracked to withstand such treatment. For these, chemicals are used, except of course where niello, which is itself silver sulphide, is suspected.

Care is needed in the removal of silver chloride crusts for, as shown in section 5.6.3, the original surface will be maintained, either by weakened silver or by a discontinuity within the horn silver. Cleaning of such material is sometimes done mechanically when, with considerable skill, the outer layer can be picked off the original surface. Alternatively, to avoid scratching any remaining silver, chemicals are used under the microscope; cleaning is halted as soon as the discontinuity or a silver surface appears.

The removal of copper corrosion crusts is carried out chemically since they are much harder than horn silver, and scratching of the underlying metal is difficult to avoid. Moreover, the original surface is likely to be maintained by silver (section 5.6.3) which is not likely to be attacked by the chemicals required to dissolve the copper salts when these reagents are used with discretion.

That silver is a noble metal is useful in cleaning since it remains unaffected by chemicals used, but it is a problem in that dissolved silver (and even copper) is likely to be reduced and plate out as silver (or copper) on the object during cleaning. Thus sequestering agents (section 3.3.2.1), for example thiourea, which remove these metals from solution are used alongside the chemicals used to dissolve the corrosion crusts. Commercial dips containing oxidizing acids are too powerful for archaeological silver and, to break up a crust, organic acids or complexing agents such as ammonium thiosulphate $(NH_4)_2S_2O_3)$, are preferred. Another approach is to reduce overlying silver corrosion crusts to a soft powdery silver, which may then be brushed off to reveal the original surface. This may be done either electrolytically (section 5.1.4.2), or with a chemical reducing agent such as sodium dithionite $(Na_2S_2O_4)$ which has been used to treat marine silver in bulk.[79]

5.6.5 Deterioration after excavation

Both horn silver and silver bromide darken on exposure to light; they can change from white to pink, grey, or black within seconds of excavation. In the longer term, excessive UV can superficially reduce horn silver to silver, giving it a metallic sheen. Sulphur is present in the air from industrial pollution, but high localized contamination can arise from rubber, paint, casein glue, wool, cloth finishings, and certain woods. It is not surprising, therefore, that bright silver usually tarnishes, but unless it is heavily alloyed with copper, no other corrosion is likely after excavation. Brittle ancient silver is liable to shatter with poor handling.

5.6.6 Stabilization

5.6.6.1 Passive

To prevent bright cleaned silver from tarnishing, sulphur must be removed from the environment. In the first instance, all materials for display/storage should be tested for sulphur (section 3.4.1.5). Ultimately sulphur can be removed by air-conditioning, but on a less grand scale, hydrogen-sulphide-absorbing materials can be used locally, such as in plugs in vents in showcases or in tissue for wrapping objects. Alternatively, vapour phase inhibitors (section 5.1.5) can be used in sealed cases or boxes.[80] Close proximity to a source of chloride which will corrode silver must also be avoided. Silver which contains a high proportion of copper can be stabilized by dry storage as in section 5.5.6.1.

5.6.6.2 Active

In the past, in order to debrittle fragile silver, a variety of heat treatments were used, but until further research in this area is published, they should be avoided. Attempts have been made to consolidate objects which have been entirely corroded to horn silver, by reducing them back to silver. This has been done chemically (see note 79) on coins and electrolytically[81] on one famous example at the British Museum, the lyre from Ur, but neither method is as yet routine.

Silver may be treated to retard attack by hydrogen sulphide by the application of a lacquer or a polish which contains an inhibitor (see section 5.1.5 and note 80). Copper in base silver is stabilized by benzotriazole (section 5.5.6.2).

5.6.7 Reshaping

In certain instances deformed silver objects have been reshaped at high temperatures but the technique is limited and cannot be used where intergranular corrosion has occurred. It is never used until a rigorous metallographic examination has been carried out, both to check for absence of this corrosion and to record the structure which will be lost by this heating.

5.6.8 Summary

Even though silver is a noble metal, when excavated, it can be in a delicate and badly corroded state, worse even than base lead. On site it must be handled with great care and given adequate packing. An original surface may be retained within a corrosion crust, and thus cleaning is carried out only in a laboratory. Since silver is a soft but noble metal, where the metal is to be exposed, chemical cleaning is preferred over mechanical methods. Bright silver is most affected by hydrogen sulphide in the environment and, once blackened, is cleaned only when required for display; it should then be handled only with gloves.

Base silver behaves as a copper alloy, which indeed it is. It is treated in a similar manner to other copper alloys except for cleaning; the original surface of a high-silver/copper alloy is uniquely maintained by noble silver metal. Problems of treatment, interpretation, and analysis of base silver arise as a result of the phenomenon of surface enrichment.

5.7 Gold and its alloys

5.7.1 Nature of artefacts[82]

Gold in artefacts is seldom pure. One cause of this is impurities from the raw material which, since gold is extremely noble, is in the form of metal, not ore. An important naturally occurring alloy is electrum, or white gold, which has a silver content of more than 20 per cent. This level can be reduced by purification to about 1 per cent, giving a rich red-yellow-coloured metal which is even redder when contaminated with copper. However, gold is usually deliberately alloyed for strength and economy with silver or copper; in this latter case the alloy may be called tumbaga. When gold is mixed with both silver and copper, a pale-yellow base alloy called corinthian bronze[83] or green gold may be made. The surface colour of this alloy may be altered by oxidation and/or blanching for decorative effects. Depletion gilding (section 5.1.2.2) of gold alloys in general is common, in order to give the object a rich-yellow pure gold surface. Today the purity of gold is measured in carats, where one carat represents one-twenty-fourth part of the whole.

Gold (melting point 1063°C) is the most malleable of all metals used in antiquity, and without annealing it can be hammered into sheets only 0.2 micrometres thick. It is easily cast and can be joined by cold welding or gold solder, a binary alloy with 18 per cent copper or a ternary one which, because it contains silver as well, gives a better colour. Alternatively, it may be joined by a technique called colloid hard soldering, whereby the join is made temporarily with a paste consisting of a glue, a copper salt, and water; when set, the joint is heated so that the reduced metallic copper alloys with the gold, forming a bond. Applied gold decoration includes enamelling and niello (section 5.1.2.5–6).

5.7.2 Nature of deteriorated material[83-4]

The corrosion of debased gold can be extremely rapid because of the galvanic cells formed with the alloying metals.

BRIGHT GOLD. Gold, being the noblest metal, does not react with any normal environments, and so may be found unchanged on excavation. However, even debased gold, if the quantity of base metal present is slight or if the environment dissolves the corrosion products of the base metal, may be found bright. Where debased gold has been gilded by depletion, considerable corrosion products in the form of black cuprite (Cu_2O) may be formed under the gold surface layer. The metal may well be brittle for the reasons described for embrittled silver (section 5.6.2.5).

SILVER, COPPER, OR IRON CORROSION CRUSTS. Debased gold containing one or more of these metals may become completely obscured by the products of corrosion typical of them.

5.7.3 Examination

By examining corrosion products and metal colours, attempts are made to identify where surface enrichment is present and, if so, whether it has occurred intentionally or not. Likewise, the content of the whole alloy is studied but the simple resort to specific gravity which has been used in many analytical programmes cannot be used on objects with corrosion crusts or casting blow holes. The original surface of objects, although often misleading in colour, will always be represented by the remaining uncorroded gold.

5.7.4 Cleaning

Gold is never cleaned, however gently, without a microscope; the danger of abrasion of a surface-enriched layer or of scratching the soft metal is too great. Care must be taken, then, in the field, to prevent hands rubbing the surface of an object. Even in the laboratory, mechanical cleaning is kept to a minimum, whilst chemicals which remove copper and/or silver corrosion products must be used judiciously, to prevent leaching of the base metals and dissolution of internal corrosion products.

5.7.5 Deterioration after excavation and stabilization

Gold itself does not deteriorate but alloys will suffer corrosion of the base metal as described in earlier sections of this chapter; they must be stabilized accordingly. Gold can be extremely weak and brittle and must be handled with care.

5.7.6 Reshaping

Like silver, certain gold objects could be reshaped except where there is a fine surface detail or where there is internal corrosion. Again metallographic information will be lost by such treatment.

5.7.7 Summary

Gold should not be polished 'bright' on site; gentle washing alone is permissible. Packaging must ensure abrasion is prevented. Gold alloys encrusted with copper corrosion products also should have no on-site cleaning and are treated as for copper alloys (section 5.5.6).

Chapter Six

Organic materials

6.1 General

6.1.1 Structure and composition[1]

The reason why a group of materials as diverse as leather, beeswax, and alcohol can be classified together as organic, is not that they derive from living organisms, even though this is the case, but that their composition is based on carbon. Today, organic materials such as plastic and pesticides seem far removed from living things, but in antiquity organic materials were mostly derived from organisms which were living or had recently lived; these ranged from mammals to green plants but did include minerals such as bitumen formed from much altered plant debris. Not only was the range of sources wide, but the different types of material obtained were numerous. Thus, structural materials such as wood and ivory, as well as preserving materials such as tannins and adhesives such as resin, were all available from natural sources. Mankind either employed these materials virtually unaltered from their original source in, for example, wooden artefacts, or they carried out considerable work on them in order to make them more suitable for their use in, for example, leather artefacts.

Most of the organic materials found in artefacts are not composed of a mass of small molecules; instead they are made from large molecules, or polymers. These are formed by the chemical bonding of numerous identical or similar small units called monomers. These molecules may join together in a chain which aligns with others to form microfibrils which are bundled to form fibrils; thus is formed a basic structural unit for tough, solid materials.

In vivo much organic material is associated with water. This water may simply be filling voids or it can be held in small capillaries within fibrils by physical forces. Alternatively it can be adsorbed onto the organic molecule where it is held by hydrogen bonds; this water keeps fibrils extended and acts as a lubricant. In addition, water may be an actual constituent of the molecule, in which case it is only released when the

238

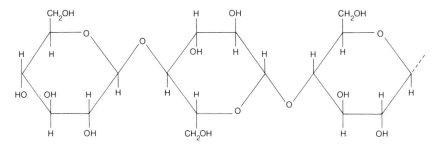

Figure 6.1 The structure of a cellulose molecule

material is chemically broken down. One aspect of human adaption of organic material for artefacts, its subsequent decay, and conservation, involves the balance of its water content with that of the environment.

6.1.1.1 Polysaccharides

As their name suggests, these compounds consist of polymers of sugar molecules which contain carbon, together with oxygen and hydrogen. They are common to both plants and animals, but since they form the skeleton of the former, for artefacts these provide the greater source.

Cellulose is the most common polysaccharide. It is a polymer of single glucose units with often as many as 3,500 units in one chain (figure 6.1). Because of the hydroxyl groups, water can be adsorbed onto the polymer by hydrogen bonding. Plant tissue is formed when cellulose molecules align into fibrils which then combine to form the fibres of cell walls, different cells having a variety of form and function. For example, skeletal tissue normally has cells with thick walls which give support to the plant.

Other polysaccharides found in artefacts are non-structural and include gums and starch derived from plants.

6.1.1.2 Proteins

Proteins are polymers of amino acids which have the generic formula

$$\begin{array}{c} NH_2 \\ | \\ R-\ C-COOH \\ | \\ H \end{array}$$

R is variable in that there are twenty different amino acids. Proteins, unlike cellulose, are built up from a selection of these basic units. Water can be adsorbed onto the polymers by hydrogen bonding but this adsorption may be much more marked at one pH than at another. This is

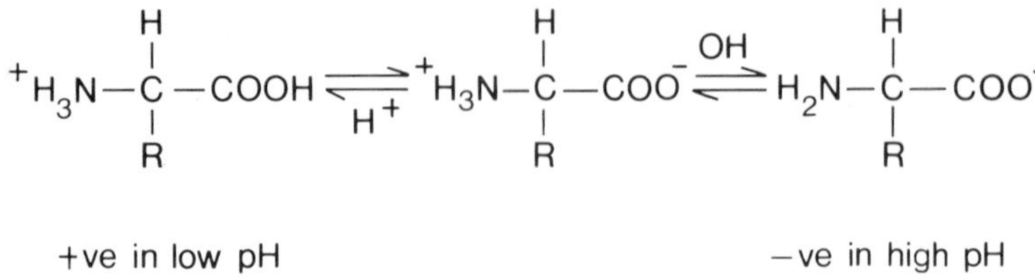

$$^{+}H_3N-\overset{\overset{\displaystyle H}{|}}{\underset{\underset{\displaystyle R}{|}}{C}}-COOH \underset{H^{+}}{\rightleftharpoons} {}^{+}H_3N-\overset{\overset{\displaystyle H}{|}}{\underset{\underset{\displaystyle R}{|}}{C}}-COO^{-} \overset{OH^{-}}{\rightleftharpoons} H_2N-\overset{\overset{\displaystyle H}{|}}{\underset{\underset{\displaystyle R}{|}}{C}}-COO^{-}$$

+ve in low pH   −ve in high pH

Figure 6.2   Charge of an amino acid

because proteins can become charged, either negatively or positively, as the pH changes (figure 6.2). Proteins too are common to both plants and animals but, in animals, they form the structural tissues useful to mankind.

6.1.1.3   Lignin and tannins

Both these chemical substances found in artefacts are basically complex polymers based on phenol. One characteristic is the presence of numerous hydroxyl groups, which means that water may readily bond with them. They are not primarily structural, in that they do not form fibrils, although a lignin is laid down in plant cell walls to give rigidity; they act as naturally occurring preservatives in plants.

6.1.1.4   Resins

These are non-water-soluble materials found in plant tissue where they protect it from decay. They are complex non-fibrous viscous liquids containing a variety of polymers of hydrocarbons which over time lose volatile portions, causing the liquids to harden.

6.1.1.5   Pigments

Organic artefacts can be coloured naturally by the inclusion of pigments; thus feathers may contain red and yellow lipochromes, and wool, black or brown melanin. Alternatively they may be deliberately coloured with dyes or with paint made from either organic or inorganic pigments. The incorporation of organic pigments in paints has been discussed briefly in section 4.3.1.2. The main group of organic pigments is the quinones, which include alizarin and juglone, but there are other types such as indigotin. These pigments can be isolated from natural dyes such as madder (alizarin) and woad (indigotin). Many of them change colour, not only with pH, but also with metal ions, as is discussed later (section 6.6.1.4).

6.1.2   Deterioration

Since the organic materials of antiquity were derived from natural sources, they are part of the natural process of decay and their carbon is recycled into the environment. For their artefacts, mankind usually chose those materials which are most resistant to this decay but, even so, the materials cannot be considered stable in the long term.

6.1.2.1 Biodeterioration

Decay caused by organisms, whether chemical or physical, is called biodeterioration. It constitutes the major type of decay of organic artefacts in two ways: not only do organisms destroy organic materials when they use them as a food source, but chemicals excreted by organisms indirectly attack artefacts. As was shown in section 2.1, not all organisms can be or are present in every environment. Many factors, such as food source, temperature, pH, salinity, and toxins are involved, but probably the major criteria are water and oxygen. Because of this complexity, it is difficult to predict what organisms will be active in a particular environment.

In this section those organisms which destroy organic material only are mentioned; general biodeterioration is covered in chapter 2.

INSECTS AND ARACHNIDS. Most insects and arachnids (spiders and mites) are terrestrial, requiring a relatively dry environment containing oxygen. They destroy artefacts by using them as a food source, but the understanding of this and of their control is complicated by the phenomenon of metamorphosis. Certain insects such as silverfish, earwigs, lice, cockroaches, and termites have a normal life cycle of eggs hatching to produce young which gradually develop into adults. On the other hand, insects such as beetles and moths exhibit metamorphosis whereby their life cycle is completed by two distinct stages. Here the eggs hatch into larvae (grubs) which grow until they pupate, emerging later as adults. In most cases, it is the growing larvae which devour artefacts, but it can be the reproductive adult. Most insects and arachnids are encouraged by warm temperatures, but inhibited by natural preservatives such as resins and tannins.

MOLLUSCS AND CRUSTACEANS. Molluscs such as snails, and crustaceans such as woodlice, contribute to the breakdown of organic material in the natural cycle of decay, but only once the material is already well rotted. In the sea, however, their marine counterparts, piddocks and shipworms (molluscs), and gribbles (crustacea), are particularly damaging to robust timbers (section 6.2.2.4); some types of marine molluscs will even attack stone.

MICRO-ORGANISMS. Biodeterioration caused by micro-organisms is of supreme importance. The description and metabolism of this form of life have been given in section 2.1.1.2, but here are noted some points related specifically to decay of organics. Anaerobic bacteria alone can flourish in environments without oxygen, but whilst some of these are cellulolytic (able to break down cellulose), they tend not to attack other structural organic materials from which artefacts are made. Thus biodeterioration in environments of low redox potential is extremely limited. Whilst some fungi and bacteria can utilize a wide range of materials as a food source, others are much more restricted. Furthermore, certain organic materials can be broken down only by a very limited number of micro-organisms which produce specific enzymes; it is these materials which mankind tends to choose to make into artefacts.

6.1.2.2 Physical and chemical decay

Since much organic material used in artefacts is associated with water (section 6.1.1), much destruction can be brought about by its removal. When water is removed, fibrils contract together causing material to shrink. If the artefact contains areas of fibrils of different thickness, density, or direction, this can lead to uneven shrinkage and thus warping. In this way, artefacts lose their shape, and adhering material, such as paint, is dislodged. If shrinkage is not excessive, the material may expand back when water is reintroduced, resulting in further disruptive forces. In excessively high humidities, organic materials may take up more than their normal quantity of water and so become swollen.

Abrasion by running water is likely for much buried material, and further damage by soluble salts (section 4.1.2) could occur in porous matter. Very commonly in waterlogged deposits, organic materials appear blackened; this may be due to iron or manganese (section 2.2.1.4), to sulphate-reducing bacteria (section 2.1.1.2), or to other unidentified causes (plate 6.1).

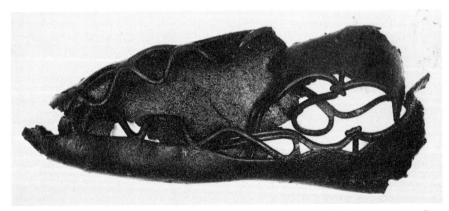

Plate 6.1 A Roman shoe from a waterlogged deposit showing overall blackening

Even though most organic materials during their life are associated with water, in damp environments they slowly hydrolyse (break down in water). Polymers are broken down into smaller units and finally into monomers, both of which suffer more rapid deterioration than the polymer itself. The rate of hydrolysis is usually increased if the pH is raised or lowered, as it is if the temperature is raised.

Organic materials are also prone to oxidation which is most apparent in the museum environment; here reactions with oxygen lead to the breakdown of polymers resulting in the embrittlement, weakening, and discoloration of leather, textiles, wood, etc., as well as in the fading of pigments. The energy for these reactions can be given by light or heat, and they are speeded up by damp environments.[2]

6.1.2.3 Preservation of material during burial

The phenomenon of preservation (section 2.2.2) is especially interesting in organic material which, being part of the natural cycle of decay, is unlikely to survive burial. Preservation is uneven and not easy to predict and thus the failure to discover organic artefacts in excavations can be misinterpreted. Ambrose,[3] studying this inconsistent survival in Australia, singles out biological activity as the most important factor, pointing out that this can vary radically at very local levels leading to great unevenness in the archaeological record. More recently, puzzling inconsistencies of preservation in relation to human bodies have been illustrated.[4]

As shown in section 2.2.2, absence of water by its fixation as ice is the most favourable condition for the preservation of organic artefacts, as can be seen in the continuously frozen Scythian tombs of the seventh to third centuries BC in the Altai mountains.[5] Here organics are attacked neither biologically, physically, nor chemically. Preservation by complete desiccation is rare, but has been found in shallow burials in sand in Egypt from predynastic times.[6] Less impressive but nevertheless important preservation has been found in dry, if not desiccated, tombs of western Europe (plate 2.1). More common in this part of the world is preservation by absence of oxygen caused by waterlogging, as is found in urban sites such as York[7] (plate 2.2) or in estuarine sites such as the one which preserved the Hasholme logboat (plate 3.13).[8] Whilst the biological and physical elements of decay are absent from these environments, chemical hydrolysis continues and so 'preservation' is only partial; artefacts will look much stronger than they are. If anaerobic conditions are caused by sealing instead of by waterlogging, hydrolysis is considerably reduced. In the pre-Hadrianic levels of the site at Vindolanda, preservation by clay sealing is enhanced by toxic tannins and polyphenols from decaying bracken.[9] It should be noted that preservation in tombs may be due to anaerobic conditions caused by sealing rather than to desiccation, for here organic material, whilst being protected from gross decay, often shows signs of attack by micro-organisms indicating conditions of high humidity.[6]

During burial, environmental conditions may change from preserving to destructive. If this has happened only very recently, as for example where fenland is being drained,[10] there is hope that some, albeit less well preserved, organic material will remain. Usually, however, the environment during at least part of the burial period has been such that all organic material is destroyed. Fortunately, where it has been associated with a corroding metal artefact, tiny traces may be preserved, traces which are difficult to recognize even under a microscope.[11] As explained in section 5.2.2.3, iron corrosion products can totally replace wood, wool, leather, etc., producing a pseudomorph which preserves the shape, but not the composition, of the organic material. Corroding copper may preserve the *actual* organic material by preventing micro-organism activity (section 2.1.1); small areas are preserved but stained green by the toxic copper salts. All these traces may be identifiable only by using the scanning electron microscope (section 3.3.2.2), but they are invaluable for the understanding of artefacts from sites where no bulk organic materials remain.

6.1.3   Conservation

Examination and cleaning of organic materials is comparatively straight-forward. It usually involves the removal of adhering silt, taking great care not to damage the soft original surface of the artefact, nor to remove any associated matter such as paint. Removal of the black coloration of many waterlogged organic materials is more problematic in that it is not often clear what is causing the discoloration (section 6.1.2.2), and harsh chemicals are needed for its removal.

When stabilization is considered, organic materials need to be divided into two groups: wet or waterlogged materials, and those which are 'dry' either because they were excavated from near-desiccated environments, or because they have been preserved by toxic salts, or because they have been treated – stabilized – to remove excess water. Whilst the first part of the adage that 'wet material should be kept wet' is useful, the second part that 'dry material should be kept dry' can be misleading.

6.1.3.1   Stabilization of wet or waterlogged material

Upon excavation these materials can be passively stabilized by preventing them from drying out. However, because they have been brought from a cool oxygen-free environment into a warmer oxygen-rich one, organisms will begin to grow, whether on the material, the adhering debris, the packaging, or even the water within a storage tank. Control of algae and some bacteria is assisted by keeping out the light, but this encourages fungal growth and so oxygen levels are kept as low as possible. Lowering the temperature is also useful, but actual freezing cannot yet be advised for all materials since the damage caused by the expansion of ice is still uncertain. Biocides have been used but it must be noted that they do 'interfere' with archaeological evidence; they may prevent future dating by ^{14}C by introducing modern carbon, and make future conservation treatments unsuccessful by blocking necessary reactions. Of course, hydrolysis of organic materials is not prevented by wet passive storage. Because of this and because study and display of the material is difficult if not impossible, further treatment is often necessary.

This treatment involves the controlled removal of water and, where necessary, active stabilization by the introduction of a synthetic material to replace the water. Whilst for some organic artefacts such stabilization is routine, for others this is not the case: it is difficult, for example, to prevent ivory cracking by using consolidants alone, and it is expensive to stabilize large timbers in this way; thus selection for active stabilization is required.

6.1.3.2 Stabilization of dry or treated material

All organic material, even that treated with synthetics, contains water. Thus when it is suggested that dry material is kept 'dry', what is really intended is that the existing level of water in the material is maintained. If the material is overdried, it will shrink and distort; if the RH is too high, it will expand; if the RH fluctuates, the material expands and contracts causing the maximum destruction. But since at RH > 65 per cent microorganism activity is likely, passive stabilization requires a fine control of RH to prevent both physical disruption and biodeterioration. Dry material can be fumigated to kill off existing organisms and since the biocide does not remain in the artefacts, there is less of a health hazard than when remnant action biocides are used (section 3.4.2.2).

In order to make dry organic material less vulnerable to changes in the ambient humidity, it can be treated with a humectant such as glycerol or sorbitol. These are hygroscopic chemicals which bond to the organic material, masking the sites in the decayed material which normally take up and lose water. If the RH falls, instead of the organic material losing water to the environment, it absorbs small quantities from the humectant and thus does not shrink and distort. However, there is a problem with the use of these chemicals in that, if the RH falls to very low levels, they take up water from the decayed material and thus are aggressive rather than protective.

6.2 Wood

6.2.1 Nature of wooden artefacts[12]

Wood is the skeletal tissue of higher green plants. Its main component is cellulose fibrils (section 6.1.1.1) but lignin (section 6.1.1.3) is present to varying degrees, reinforcing and preserving the cellulose. These fibrils are bundled together to form the walls of cells which form the structure of plants (figure 6.3).

Living cells contain cell sap made of a dilute solution of sugars, salts, and other metabolic materials, but if the cells are redundant for this purpose they may contain waste and preservative materials such as tannins (section 6.1.1.3) and resins (section 6.1.1.4): the outer sapwood of a tree is made of a tissue of living cells whilst the inner heartwood is formed of dead cells. The structural cells are elongated along the vertical axis of the trunk, giving the direction of the 'grain' of the wood.

Trees are divided into two groups, each with its own cell types: one is the hardwoods generally comprising deciduous trees, and the other is the softwoods comprising the conifers. The density, porosity, hardness, strength, and flexibility of wood differs from species to species and to a

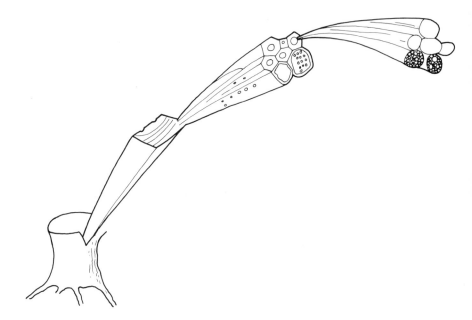

Figure 6.3 The structure of wood (exploded): fibrils bundled together as fibres to form cell walls which compose the trunk of a tree exhibiting annual rings (after Hoffman in Grattan and McCawley, 1982)

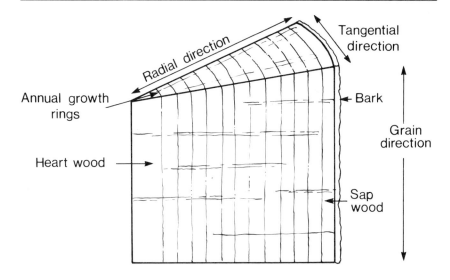

Figure 6.4 Structure of the trunk of a tree

lesser extent within species from the age and part of the tree and where it has grown. Because of this variation amongst species, it is common to find structural timbers made of oak; ships' timbers from heart oak; ships' keels, wheel hubs, mallets, etc., from elm; posts from chestnut; handles and hafts from ash; and turned vessels from birch, alder, beech, or sycamore. Woven hurdles are often made from hazel (whole or split) or willow (osier) and rigid baskets from thin osiers. Flexible basketry made from non-lignified stems of rush etc. is dealt with later in section 6.6.

Wood is anisotropic, which means that its physical characteristics in different directions are not similar. This is because the elongated cellulose fibres and cells lie along the longitudinal axis of the trunk or stem. As a result, when fibres contract or expand, the overall response of the timber in the longitudinal (or grain direction), the radial, and the tangential planes will vary (figure 6.4). After felling, the moisture content of wood equilibrates with that of the environment. In humid environments, this entails the gradual loss of cell sap, capillary water, and some adsorbed water (section 6.1.1). This natural seasoning hardens the wood and removes a ready food source for fungi and bacteria. In drier environments, deliberate seasoning or slow drying of the timber may be necessary before it can be used; here natural drying could lead to too rapid a loss of water from the outside of the timber, resulting in non-uniform contraction or even the excessive loss of water. These events result in the cracking and warping described in section 6.2.2.1.

The range of possibilities of other materials associated with wood in artefacts is too wide to be classifiable. Other materials could represent decoration such as paint, gilding, or metal studs; writing, as ink on tablets; construction, as wooden treenails or iron rivets, copper or lead sheathing applied to the hulls of seafaring craft, or simply another part of a composite artefact such as a metal blade or leather binding. Before or during use, wood may have been treated with preservatives such as pitch, or it may have been scorched to harden it. Bark may still be adhering; this is 'dead' tissue containing more lignin and tannin than wood itself.

6.2.2   Nature of deteriorated wood

6.2.2.1   Deterioration before burial[13]

SHRINKAGE, WARPING, AND CRACKING. This destruction results from the loss of bound water within the cell walls, which *in vivo* bulks out the volume of the tissue (section 6.1.1). Loss of water causes the cellulose fibrils to move together, resulting in the greater degree of shrinkage occurring at right angles to the length of the fibrils, that is across the grain (section 6.2.1). Since this plane is anisotropic, shrinkage is uneven and may lead to warping and cracking (figure 6.5). Dampening will cause the timber to move back again. Continued movement will dislodge any surface material such as gesso or paint, cause joints to fail, and finally disrupt the wood itself.

INSECT FLIGHT HOLES, FRASS, AND GENERAL WEAKENING. The larvae of many beetles (section 6.1.2.1) use wood as a food source. They grow and

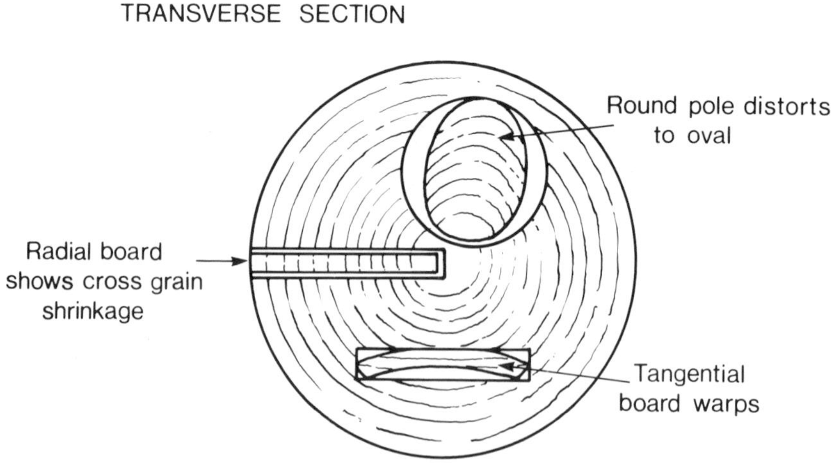

TRANSVERSE SECTION

Figure 6.5 Movement of timber on drying

pupate within the wood and the adults emerge by cutting a flight hole. These holes, and the sawdust (or frass) which falls from them, are a sign that internal insect damage has already occurred; often the entire core of an artefact can be destroyed or perforated, with little sign of the damage externally. The species of insect which has attacked wood can be determined by the size and shape of the flight holes and frass pellets. Many insects such as death-watch beetle will only attack wood which has already been weakened by fungal growth as described below.

DISCOLORATION. In light, lignin becomes oxidized and the wood darkens but, if subject to running water, the wood becomes grey as the solubilized lignin washes out. Certain fungi grow on damp wood, living on nutritious cell sap rather than cellulose. Whilst they do not cause weakening, they can stain the wood, but this is limited to the outer layers since they require oxygen to live. In these conditions, bacteria begin to penetrate wood, perforating cell walls. This allows oxygen to enter and opens up the core of the timber to more deleterious fungal decay. Metal in association with wood will stain it, copper producing green or brown tannate, and iron, a blacker tannate. Wood surrounding iron nails can be eaten away by the alkalis produced by the corrosion of the metal (section 5.1.2.3).

BLACKENING AND CUBING. This type of decay is caused by cellulotytic hyphal fungi (section 2.1.1.2), but can be mistaken for charring. Both dry and wet rot fungi produce this effect by removing cellulose and leaving behind the cellular structure composed only of lignin. This structure is frail and eventually crumbles away.

6.2.2.2 Wood from aerated soils

Wood, which might show some of the features of decay described above, will survive burial or entombment only in abnormal conditions (as described in section 6.1.2.3). Even individual pieces of wood may be preserved differentially because of their use prior to burial, primitive preservative techniques, impregnation by oils during use, or the presence of localized toxins. Moreover, different species and areas of wood succumb to decay at varying rates; heart oak full of tannins and resins is least attacked. All these conditions could preserve the *cellulose* of wood, but others, such as pseudomorphic replacement by iron corrosion products or charcoal, preserve the structure alone. More usually, wood in aerated deposits is broken down totally by bacteria, fungi, insects, and other soil organisms. A localized humification of the soil may be preserved, or simply a stain with no structural elements. The material excavated from aerated deposits, then, represents a very incomplete and eccentric archaeological record.

6.2.2.3   Wood from anaerobic land or marine deposits[14]

GOOD EXTERNAL APPEARANCE (plate 2.2).   The condition of much wood found in these types of deposits may appear extremely good; but unfortunately this can be extremely misleading. The waterlogged wood in fact will be very weak, unable to hold its own weight, and readily marked, even by a fingernail. This is because the cellulose, even though protected from fungal and most bacterial decay, will have undergone hydrolysis and anaerobic bacterial attack (section 6.1.2), leaving the cells composed mainly of lignin and held up by water, organic debris, and silt. Decay is less marked in wet, sealed, anaerobic deposits where hydrolysis is much lower, and so wet wood may be more sound than waterlogged wood. The degree of decay and waterlogging of a piece of wood is dependent also upon species and tissue type. Alder, beech, and maple, being porous wood, waterlog completely in a few hours and together with ash, birch, and willow have poor survival in water. However, oak heartwood and yew are virtually indestructible in these conditions (section 6.2.1), and even if the surface is decayed, a sound core will remain.

Just as fibres shrink when deprived of water, to some extent the cellulose and lignin swell when submerged. Thus the waterlogged oak timbers of the Swedish warship *Wasa*, after 333 years of submersion, had a 1 per cent increase in tangential dimension.

BLACKENING.   The dark appearance of most wood from these conditions is due in part to the formation of iron tannates, from an interaction between the wood and the deposit. Sulphides too, however, may be in part responsible, but more work is required here to determine the true cause.

6.2.2.4   Wood from aerated marine sites

MARINE BORER DAMAGE (plate 6.2).   Attack of wood in marine and some brackish water by a variety of animals results in wood riddled with passages of varying sizes. Ships, piers, etc. may suffer this decay during their useful life, but in general it occurs after deposition, before the wood sinks into anaerobic bottom deposits. An important animal here is the shipworm (*Teredo* spp. a mollusc) which makes channels up to 1 metre long and 20 millimetres in diameter that are often found still lined with the tube-like shell. It can survive in conditions of extremely low oxygen. The channels formed by the gribble (*Limnoria lignorum*, a crustacean) are much smaller, and often form an interconnecting network which leaves the wood soft, spongy, and easily damaged by erosion. It can live in very cold water as long as there is sufficient dissolved oxygen. Sometimes the full extent of marine borer damage may be disguised by an apparently well preserved surface, but in other cases much of the wood

Plate 6.2 Large tunnels in wood from marine sites caused by shipworm; the smaller holes are caused by the gribble

may have eroded, leaving only a remnant of the original object. In extreme cases the presence of calcareous shipworm tubes may be all that remains of decayed wood.

WOOD ENCASED IN FERROUS CONCRETION. Small pieces of marine wood, such as the handles of tools, may be preserved within a shell of ferrous concretion (section 5.2.2.2); these can usually be seen when the concretion is x-rayed.

SEMI-FOSSILIZED WOOD. In certain conditions under water, insoluble compounds (usually siliceous, calcareous, or ferruginous) precipitate within the wood itself, filling the cells so that the wood becomes semi-fossilized. This may start to happen within a few hundred years and is very common on marine sites. The colour of the wood varies from a stone grey to black or 'rusty', depending on how much iron or oxygen is present. The wood is characteristically very hard and stone-like. It presents interesting problems for conservation, most of which have up to now received only minimal attention.

6.2.3 Examination

Visual examination reveals construction and technological details including the grain direction, all of which should be recorded. Inks and pigments may be visible, but the use of IR or UV could be helpful. The examination of wet wood, especially that retaining delicate tool marks (plate 6.3), needs to be carried out as soon as possible after examination since these may become less distinct even after a few weeks of wet

Plate 6.3 Saw marks on a Roman plank; part of a well lining

storage.[15] Usually it is possible to identify oak from surface examination, but for other species it will be necessary to take a small sample or at least make a razor cut *across* an exposed grain face. Complete identification of species, part of tree, etc., is a specialist technique; some further information on its complexity is given by Dimbleby.[16]

For treatment purposes, it will be necessary not only to know tree species, but also the extent and type of decay. The presence of a sound core is detected by the use of fine probes, and damage by marine borer may be identifiable by the use of radiography. However, more precise measurements require a sample of perhaps 1 centimetre cube, from which the water content, and thus remaining cellulose and lignin, blocking and discolouring materials, etc., can be determined. Further histological studies are carried out with a light or scanning electron microscope.

Since the lifting of marine or wet structural timbers or hulls is so expensive and time-consuming, recording of technological and construction details can be made *in situ* by moulding[17] in polysulphide rubber. When a large artefact, such as a hull, is to be dismantled for lifting, reconstruction at a later date is greatly assisted if first moulds are taken.

6.2.4 Cleaning

To remove surface dirt, dry wood is not washed but is lightly brushed or gently swabbed with dilute alcohol; excess water could cause deleterious expansion or loss of paint, etc. For wet wood, great care is taken not to mark the soft surface, thereby introducing misleading 'tool marks'. Thus it is sprayed or hosed gently and the silt loosened with soft brushes.

The dark or black coloration of much waterlogged wood may be considered unsightly. However, before attempts are made to remove it, the following points should be noted: that it is difficult, if not impossible, to know what the colour of the wood was when in use, how dark it was then; that evidence such as food remains or original preservatives may also be removed in the process; that during such cleaning a certain degree of breakdown of wood is probable. Since it appears that blackening is caused by different factors from site to site, and that these remain uncertain, there is no reliable way of removing it. However, several chemicals have been used with some lightening effect, but care in their choice is essential to prevent weakening any remaining cellulose or lignin.[18]

6.2.5 *Deterioration after excavation*

6.2.5.1 Dry wood

Any alteration of the moisture content will be extremely deleterious to dry wood, since the whole structure of the artefact has probably weakened during burial/entombment. The post-excavation environment in all probability will be of a different humidity than that of the soil/tomb; unless steps are taken destructive movement of timber as described in section 6.2.2.1 is almost inevitable. The wood will continue to provide a useful substrate for insect larvae and fungus and so could become infested.

6.2.5.2 Wet wood

From its moment of exposure on an excavation, waterlogged wood is extremely susceptible to decay. If water begins to evaporate from the surface, part of the bulking agent of the decayed cells (section 6.2.2.3) is thereby removed. The walls of the cells collapse in on themselves, surface details are lost, and the timber begins to shrink. As more water is lost, the surface cracks, possibly spalls; later, cracks appear deeper in the timber, accompanied by considerable twisting and warping. In extreme instances the artefact diminishes in size, perhaps tenfold, and twists out of all recognition (plate 6.4). The seriousness of this cell collapse, even on a small scale, is compounded by the fact that it is irreversible. When the inner faces of the cells meet, they bond together in a manner which it is at present impossible to reverse without damaging the wood yet further. Wet wood which retains more of its cellulose collapses less, but it is subject to extensive shrinkage and warping if its moisture content falls. Most wet wood is so weak that much post-excavation damage is done by mishandling; often such material cannot be lifted without support.

Wood from wet or waterlogged deposits has been preserved anaerobically but on exposure to oxygen it can still provide a substrate for bacteria and fungi. Algal blooms on wet wood, debris, and water tanks are common, giving rise to areas of brilliant colour whilst bacteria, actinomycetes, etc. produce slimes (section 2.1.1.2).

Marine wood, such as a ship's timbers, which must be left exposed to sea-water during the course of an excavation, is especially vulnerable to secondary decay, not only in the form of attack by fungi and bacteria, but also renewed colonization by marine wood borers whose larvae may settle on any piece of exposed wood. Some borers can continue to channel in almost anaerobic conditions after the wood has been reburied at the close of a season's excavation.[20]

a

b

Plate 6.4 Deterioration of waterlogged wood after excavation. (a) Piece of round wood as excavated from a waterlogged deposit – only 14% of its weight is composed of wood, the remainder is water. (b) The same piece after drying in air has led to total distortion

6.2.6 *Stabilization*

6.2.6.1 Passive

DRY WOOD. At first the moisture content of the wood must be maintained at the same level as during burial. In the longer term, it may be possible to condition wood in reasonably good state to a moisture content which is in equilibrium with the RH of the ambient environment. This is carried out in a similar manner to seasoning (section 6.2.1) by very slow drying out or dampening of the wood under controlled conditions until the required RH surrounding the artefact is reached. For wood in poor condition and acclimatized to damp conditions, it may be impossible to reduce the moisture content low enough to enable it to come into equilibrium with the level of RH likely to be found in stores/display areas without the accompaniment of cracking. However, even more dangerous than over-desiccation is a fluctuating moisture content and thus the RH must be kept as stable as possible below the fungal growth point of 65 per cent.

The probability of insect attack is reduced by avoiding contamination from infected timber and by good housekeeping.

WET AND WATERLOGGED WOOD. It is absolutely essential that upon excavation wet wood is not permitted to lose any moisture. Waterlogged wood should actually be immersed in water, whilst wet wood may only require an environment with a RH of nearly 100 per cent. If it is impossible to provide such care then the wood must not be removed from the ground/water; it must be covered up again with clay, silt, etc. as soon as possible. Reburial of wet/waterlogged timbers in a different but similar anaerobic storage deposit could be considered. At present, work is being undertaken in Denmark[19] to determine the most appropriate burial environment used for this, since even slight alterations in conditions for long-term storage of wet/waterlogged wood could be extremely damaging. Deep freezing of wood for storage has been suggested (section 6.1.3) but before it can be recommended wholesale, further research is necessary. By immersion in water, especially in that which has been boiled, levels of oxygen are kept down; close-fitting lids assist in the prevention of resorption of oxygen. Wood simply stored wet in sealed containers is in great danger from attack by fungi, a danger which may be reduced by using close-fitting bags or even vacuum sealing. Exclusion of light from these wet conditions will help cut down on algal blooms and some bacterial growth. However, sometimes, for long-term storage of wet and waterlogged wood, biocides and even oxygen scavengers may be necessary. These not only preserve the wood, they also prevent the formation of noxious or toxic odours; material from urban sites is particularly liable to produce such unpleasant conditions. With less polluted material, success in the reduction of surface slime has been achieved by biological controls, with perch and with water snails.[21]

On occasion, success has been achieved in the stabilization of wet wood simply by extremely slow drying,[22] enabling the water loss to be uniform throughout the thickness of the timber (section 6.2.1) until the wood is in equilibrium with the ambient relative humidity (section 6.2.6.1). However, it appears that only wood in exceptionally good condition, as determined by a thorough programme of examination, can be dried slowly with success. This method is not suitable for poorly preserved or unevenly decayed timber.

6.2.6.2   Active

DRY WOOD. There have been several approaches to the dimensional stabilization of dry wood[23], including the application of mechanical restraints or moisture barriers, and the introduction of humectants (section 6.1.3.2). However, little success has been achieved with any of these methods and passive dimensional stabilization is much to be preferred.

Inactivation of fungi and insects can be effected by biocides of which there has been considerable development, as reviewed in Hickin.[24]

When choosing consolidants for badly decayed wood, care has to be taken to avoid causing surface darkening and surface cracking due to shrinkage of the consolidant. This has been achieved in the past by the use of low-viscosity thermosetting resins (section 3.4.2.2), but currently a more reversible thermoplastic acrylic is being used with success.[25]

Glues used to join hygroscopic wood must allow for the movement of the timber as RH levels change. Thus, soft emulsions or animal glue may be the preferred types.

WET WOOD.[26]   The addition of biocides to wet storage must be considered interventionist since they may well interfere with ^{14}C dating, analytical, or conservation procedures. Higher concentrations will be required to prevent fungal and algal growth on 'bagged' (rather than immersed) wood, where the oxygen levels are high. Biocides are discussed in section 3.4.2.2 and the range used on wet wood is wide. When wood is stored in tanks, algaecides to prevent discoloration may be required as well, but it should be remembered that with non-polluted wood, biological control may replace the need for any chemicals (section 6.2.6.1).

Stabilization of wet or waterlogged material by storage is relatively cheap but it may be unsatisfactory for several reasons: sufficient space and curatorial/environmental conservation care are not available; considerable handling for study purposes is required and this is awkward and damaging to soft wood; the material is required for display other than by immersion in water in a glass tank. The active stabilization of wood is one of the most widely studied fields in the whole of conservation. In part, this is because many wet wood finds, such as entire wrecks or intricate wooden carvings, are spectacular; and in part because the problem lends itself to scientific investigation. It should be noted, however, that it is virtually impossible to retain fine surface detail such as delicate tool marks or impressions left by a writing stylus, on degraded wood by active stabilization; these marks are best studied whilst wood is still wet.

There are three important approaches to stabilization in use at present:
1. *Replacement of water with bulking material.*   In this approach the wet wood is placed in a solution which gradually displaces the water and then

hardens within the tissue. This prevents the collapse of the wood both by the drag of the surface tension of water as the liquid front retreats (section 3.4.2.1) and from the weakness of the tissue once the water is removed. Early methods employed alum but now the main consolidant used is polyethylene glycol (PEG) (section 3.4.2.2), the use of which has been reviewed by Pearson.[27] PEG 4000 has been used with some success, producing strong heavy objects, stable up to comparatively high ambient RH at a reasonable cost, with low health risks, and with the possibility of using very simple equipment. Its drawbacks include the dark, waxy, blurred finish, the difficulty of removing excess wax from the preserved surface, and its slowness (taking up to nine months for 1 inch planks). Because of the size of the molecule it is unable to penetrate dense woods such as heart oak and sound beech; this leads to warping and cracking as the unreplaced water dries out. Attempts to avoid this failure have been made by choosing PEG of lower molecular weight, but when such hygroscopic PEG is present in the large quantities which are needed to bulk cells, it makes the wood appear dark and wet at high ambient RH.

Alternative methods to achieve better penetration by PEG 4000 have been studied. These aim to pre-treat the wood by removing materials such as tannins, resins, oils, silt, iron corrosion products, or partially decayed cellulose which may be blocking the cells. These pre-treatments include the use of acids, sequestering agents, bleaches, and solvents[28] but they often fail to work and could remove useful materials which are actually holding the cells up.

PEG has been used for some important conservation programmes, notably for the five Viking ships from the Roskilde Fjord, Denmark, lifted in 1962[29] (plate 6.5), and the seventeenth-century warship *Wasa*, lifted from Stockholm harbour in 1961;[30] also it is being used on the Graveney boat at Greenwich[31] and the Bremen Cog in Bremerhaven.[32]

Recently a search has been made for cheaper consolidants than PEG; bearing in mind that wood is basically a polymer of glucose, experiments have been carried out with sucrose[33] and other sugars.

2. *Replacement of water by a solvent with or without the introduction of a bulking agent.* Here the wood is placed in a solvent of low surface tension which gradually displaces the water. If the wet wood is not badly decayed, the object can now simply be air-dried without any damage.[34] However, normally for waterlogged wood, a consolidant is introduced into the solvent before air-drying.

Such methods as the acetone/rosin treatment[35] follow this plan; acetone/rosin after pre-treatment with acid has been found to be successful even on heart oak, producing light-coloured medium-weight articles with good surface detail (plate 6.6a). Against this, wood may look overbleached and be brittle; the technique is not successful on open

Plate 6.5 One of the Viking ships from the Danish fjord at Roskilde which has been stabilized with PEG 4000

structured woods such as willow and poplar and it involves considerable fire hazards.

A treatment which results in the deposition of silica in the decayed cell walls by the use of tetraethylorthosilicate (TEOS) has been suggested, but it is in no way reversible. It has had little success in heavy timber consolidation[36] but it can be used satisfactorily on lightweight basketry. TEOS reacts with water in the material to give silica and ethanol which evaporates from the delicate structure without causing any damage.

3. *Freeze-drying with introduction of fibre coating materials.*[37] By the use of freeze-drying (section 3.4.2.1), water is removed without incurring either the force of its surface tension on delicate structures or the drag of consolidant from the core to the surface of the wood. Since water expands on freezing, disrupting fragile surrounding material, before lowering the temperature, the wet wood is soaked in a solution which does not expand on freezing. Once the decayed wood is dry, it possesses numerous hydroxyl groups on the shortened cellulose molecules, which are extremely reactive, taking up moisture from the atmosphere and causing the wood to crack and warp. A material therefore must be added which masks the wood from moisture in the air but which at the same time allows it to retain moisture to prevent cracking if the RH falls; that

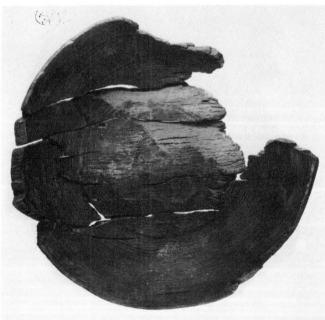

Plate 6.6 Stabilization of medieval waterlogged wooden bowls which were in different conditions of preservation.
(a) Using the acetone/rosin method.
(b) Using PEG 4000 pre-treatment followed by freeze-drying

is a humectant should be added (section 6.1.3.2). PEG 4000 performs all these functions preventing freezing damage and cracking and has been used quite widely in freeze-drying, producing lightweight articles with good surface detail (plate 6.6b); for more decayed wood where consolidation is also required, it is mixed with PEG 400.

Interesting use of the Arctic winter, that is, dry air and energy from bright sunlight with subzero temperatures, has been made for freeze-drying canoes, where the wood is not unduly degraded. By simply exposing the material on the roof of a Canadian laboratory[38] for one winter, it freeze-dried naturally much in the same way as snow 'disappears' on a clear day when the temperature does not rise above 0°C.

Finally, all three approaches to stabilization are combined in one technique which involves the replacement of water by the solvent tertiary butanol, the dissolution of PEG 4000 in this and subsequent freeze drying. Whilst this technique works for heart oak, and works quickly[39], it does involve health and fire risks which must be controlled.

It may be concluded that no method satisfies every criteria regarding safety, aesthetics, reversibility, cheapness, etc., nor is any one method suitable for all types of wood in all states of decay; it is ironic that the more decayed the wood (especially oak) the easier it is to stabilize.

6.2.7 Reshaping

A certain degree of warping of dry wood can be reversed by judicious application of water vapour to the concave surface. Cracks are much more difficult to close and always tend to reopen if the RH drops again. Reshaping of wet or waterlogged wood which has become misshapen during burial is occasionally successful. A template of the required curvature is constructed out of timber or plaster and the wet misshapen wood is gradually fitted to this. But the best results are achieved when the wood is full of warm consolidant, as at the end of some PEG treatments; but success is not guaranteed. Re-swelling of wet or waterlogged timber, which has shrunk and warped as a result of being allowed simply to air-dry is virtually impossible. As said before (section 6.2.5.2), the surfaces of the collapsed cells bond together; such links are difficult to break chemically, for example, by using acids, alkalis, or oxidizing agents, without destroying the weakened cell walls.

6.2.8 Summary

Conservation of wood, whether dry or wet, is centred on consideration of its moisture content. Thus upon exposure by excavation, wood is not allowed to lose water. At wet sites[40] this is particularly important where even 10 minutes' exposure to sun or drying wind will cause irreparable damage. Wood here has to be sprayed with water continuously or at least at regular intervals. Where this is impracticable the wood is covered with sodden plastic foam which is covered by polyethylene sheeting carefully weighted down to give a seal. At underwater sites, when wood embedded in silt is exposed by excavation to water either in estuaries or shallow seas, it has to be lifted as soon as possible since rapid decay from fungi and marine borers in the altered environment, containing high oxygen and light levels, is likely. There is less speed demanded in sites on anaerobic lake bottoms.

Before structural timbers are lifted, the rationale behind this is thoroughly examined and decisions are taken as to the extent of moulding, dismantling, and lifting required. This of course is even more important with submerged hulls. Lifting on a large scale is a specialist technique but when lifting small artefacts it must be remembered that they are much less able to bear their own weight and resist abrasion than they appear.

Large timbers are gently cleaned on site but small artefacts such as bowls and tools benefit from more controlled laboratory cleaning; this must be carried out within a few weeks if detail is not to be lost. The recording of structural timbers (shape, grain direction, tool marking, etc.) is carried out most easily on site before they are put into medium-term storage. For this a thin polyethylene sheeting is laid over the timber and a tracing made with waterproof markers.

Waterlogged wood has to be stored immediately upon lifting and immersed in water. For small objects, polypropylene boxes are ideal but for structural timbers temporary tanks have to be constructed on or near the site. Where immersion is impossible or where wood is wet rather than waterlogged, or where mud or silt is supporting or holding the artefact together, as in the case of wattle or basketry, damp storage (section 3.4.1.1) is used instead. In both methods it is essential that biological activity be controlled.

For publication purposes alone, wood may well not be actively stabilized, but prevention of damage by desiccation, handling, or fluctuating RH during study must be considered. Thus wet or waterlogged wood can be exposed for drawing or photography only for 5–10 minutes before it must be sprayed or re-immersed.

It is probably that most small artefacts will be actively stabilized for the long term; in this case the conditions of storage will depend upon the degree of decay of the wood and the type of consolidant, if any, used in its treatment. Generally, the more decayed the wood and the less humidity-sensitive consolidant used, the less rigorous will be the restrictions on the environment. However, details of requirements must be supplied by a specialist.

For structural timbers and hulls, questions of expense, time, and the unpredictability of success will influence the decision whether to stabilize actively, to store in a controlled environment, to select only wood demonstrating tool marks or joints, or else to dispose of all the wood.

6.3   Skin and gut products

6.3.1   Nature of artefacts

6.3.1.1   Collagen

These products comprising parchment, rawhide, leather, and catgut are based on the fibrous protein (section 6.1.1.2) collagen. Collagen is a polymer of only four different amino acids, one of which, hydroxyproline, is found uniquely in collagen and so can be used as an identifier. The collagen chains spiral together to form fibrils which are then made into bundles to form long fibres; tissue is formed from these fibres directly without first forming a cellular structure as do cellulose fibres. Collagen breaks down into smaller units by hydrolysis, to give gelatin, which is rapid at raised temperatures and pH > 6.5; if heated to 58–68°C, it deforms by shrinking to one-third its original length. Only some insects, such as carpet beetles and certain bacteria, can use collagen directly as a food source.

6.3.1.2   Structure and composition of skin products[41]

Skin products are made from the thickest of the three layers which form skin, namely the corium, which is made of a network of collagen fibres. *In vivo* these are surrounded by fats and blood vessels, but such putrescible materials, except in some rawhides, are removed during product manufacture. The outer or 'grain' surface of the corium has compact collagen fibres marked by fissures which once contained the hair follicles; the inner 'flesh' surface shows the loose ends of the less compact fibres (figure 6.6). The size, density, and direction of the fibres and the thickness of the corium varies with species, age of individual, and position on body, and thus, particular pieces of skin will be used for different artefacts: thick cattlehide for soles of shoes, goat and sheepskin for shoe uppers, and calfskin for tents. Skins can be slit laterally, producing two or more thinner sheets. During product manufacture, there is a degree of shortening of the collagen fibres by hydrolysis; the greater this is, the softer but weaker is the material.

Collagen fibres take up moisture, becoming flexible and able to move over one another, forming a pliable skin. During manufacture of leather, water is replaced by a less volatile material but one which still allows pliability. Leather may be made firmer by rolling or hammering to compact the fibres after manufacture.

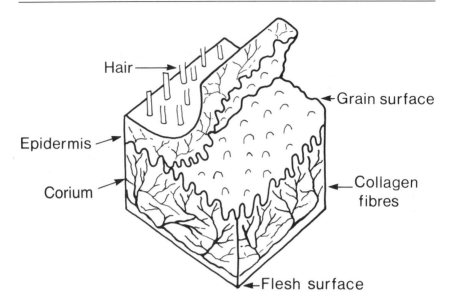

Hair
Grain surface
Epidermis
Corium
Collagen fibres
Flesh surface

Figure 6.6 Schematic section of skin

COMPOSITION OF RAWHIDE. If collagen is desiccated it becomes inflexible but also unaffected by bacteria and hydrolysis, the major agents of decay. Skin in this state can be used as 'rawhide' in dry climates or microclimates. It may be moulded whilst still wet around clay cores which are broken out after drying. The degree of removal of putrescible fats and blood vessels will vary widely and a coating of oil to provide a degree of flexibility and waterproofing may be applied.

COMPOSITION OF PARCHMENT. Parchment is made from skins, mainly of sheep with some goat and pig; vellum today is hard parchment made from calf. During manufacture, the collagen fibres are shortened considerably, those on the surface almost turning to gelatine. It is dried with some lime adsorbed into the fibres. The surface is then bulked with chalk for writing purposes or oil for a window dressing.

COMPOSITION OF SEMI-TANNED LEATHERS. Semi-tanning implies treating skin in such a way that it can withstand attack by water (section 6.3.1.1) to a greater degree than otherwise. There are two important ways of doing this. First, unsaturated fats such as tallow, egg yolk, or brains, can be rubbed into prepared skin which is then dried. The hydrophobic fats not only bulk the fibres in place of the water removed but also oxidize *in situ*, rendering the collagen less prone to decay;

chamois leathers are an example of this 'oil' tannage, being typically pale and soft.

Alternatively, if alum $(KAl(SO_4)_2.12H_2O)$ and salt $(NaCl)$ are introduced into skin, they replace the bound water, producing a stiff pale leather. Oil, egg yolk, and flour may then be rubbed in, bulking the fibres for flexibility, giving fine, pale, soft alum-tawed leathers sometimes used for sails.

COMPOSITION OF TANNED LEATHERS. Tanning preserves skin from water attack and raises the temperature at which it shrinks (section 6.3.1.1), by the formation of chemical bonds between the tanning agent and the collagen. Again there are two ways in which this can be carried out, the first being smoke tanning. Aldehydes in smoke cross-link with the collagen fibres, preventing shrinkage on drying and hydrolysis. A stiff dark leather is produced and it is usually softened with an application of fats.

However, in antiquity, vegetable tanning was perhaps the most common method in the west for preserving skins. Vegetable tans are complex polyphenols containing many hydroxyl groups, which bond onto positively charged collagen in an acid pH (section 6.1.1.2). The tans not only replace water within the fibres, they also deposit between them, leaving a pliable strong leather; even so, the leather contracts by between 5 and 10 per cent on drying during manufacture. There are two groups of vegetable tannins: the hydrolysable tannins (pyrogallols) found in oakwood and galls, in sumac leaves, etc., giving a pale brown leather; and the condensed tannins (catechols) found in mimosa and pine woods, in larch bark, etc., giving a redder leather.[42] Some sources such as oak bark have both types, giving a dark-red-brown leather. By heating to over 75°C in hot water, leather can be moulded, setting stiffly in shape, to give 'cuir-bouilli', which may be made more waterproof by a coating of wax and resin.

COMBINATION TANNING. Leather can be tanned in more than one of the ways described above. Thus buff leather is both semi-tanned with oil, and tanned with vegetable tannins, giving a strong but flexible material.

COMPOSITION OF FURS. Unlike leather, furs retain the hair follicles containing oils, cellular material, and the hair shafts embedded in the grain surface. But they may have a considerable quantity of the flesh surface removed. Furs are normally semi-tanned by both oiling and tawing or tanned by smoking.

COMPOSITION OF GUT PRODUCTS AND SINEW. Gut also is a network of collagen fibres but it is much thinner than skin. 'Catgut' is made from the tanned intestines of sheep, whilst sinew comes from tendons which are simply bundles of collagen fibres.

6.3.1.3 Dressings and finishings

Such a wide variety of fats and oils can be applied to finished leather either immediately or else during use to increase its flexibility and waterproofing that they cannot all be mentioned here. Dubbin (tallow plus cod oil) is a typical one; the working of this into wet leather is called currying. Leather may also be made more waterproof with pitch or given a shiny surface with albumin, casein, seaweed gum, waxes, shellac, etc. A smooth surface is also obtained by heating the surface with a hot metal tool; this and other more exotic finishes are described by Waterer.[43]

6.3.1.4 Associated materials[44]

Leathers and furs are frequently dyed using the types of vegetable dyes described in section 6.1.1.5; paint too has been found. Gold tooling or gilding using egg or glue size with either gold leaf, silver foil, or even tin sheeting varnished yellow, is possible. Decoration may include gold thread, whilst artefacts are constructed with leather thongs, or gut, hemp, or flax threads often waxed to allow a good grip. Riveting with metal rivets or joining with animal glues are other methods of construction. In an artefact, leather may be associated with a variety of other materials, for example wool fabric in shoe uppers.

6.3.2 *Nature of deteriorated materials*

During use, leather may become darkened and embrittled by the oxidation of the fats and oils applied to it, or from the alkaline pH of putrefying sweat. Soles and insoles especially become worn through, the wear patterns being of interest to medical studies.[45]

6.3.2.1 From dry sites

Where RH is less than 50 per cent, leather becomes embrittled, because of the loss of lubricating water; parchment is affected where RH is less than 40 per cent. Shrinkage, cracking, and exfoliation may follow. Oxidation of any fats/oils may also lead to stiffening and darkening. The larvae of carpet beetles bore holes in leather, whilst those of clothes moths destroy fur. Where the RH is slightly higher and the temperature warm, skin products may hydrolyse (section 6.3.1.1) leaving a black syrup which hardens on drying to a resinous lump; it may be difficult to recognize the remains of leather, if any, from such sites.[46]

6.3.2.2 From wet land and marine sites

GOOD APPEARANCE. Such leather is common from wet sites and in fact the collagen fibres may still be in extremely good condition. However, bulking oils and vegetable tannins may have been lost as a result of bacterial activity or leaching, their place being taken by water, silt, dissolved salts, organic debris, and polyphenols, etc., from the deposit. Where this detanning has been considerable, subsequent hydrolysis of the collagen will weaken the leather, creating more organic debris. If present, the hair on fur will no longer be fixed since the hair roots will have been destroyed by bacteria and hydrolysis.

FRAGMENTING/CRUMBLING. Detanning and hydrolysis is more acute and the fibre network begins to disintegrate.

SPLITTING. Leather may be found beginning to split laterally into two layers, or if it has been disturbed, already divided into what appears to be two deliberately split pieces. This phenomenon is caused by the natural discontinuity between the compact fibres of the grain layer and the looser fibres of the flesh layer (section 6.3.1.2), compounded by the lack of penetration of tanning agents to the centre of the skin during manufacture.

BLACKENING OR DARKENING. Common blackening is possibly due to the reaction of tannins in leather with iron in the deposit solution giving iron tannates, but further work on this is required. Tannins in leather act as pH indicators and therefore appear darker the higher the pH.

6.3.2.3   Presence or absence of skin products in a deposit

This depends on the nature both of the product and of the deposit. Rawhide/gut, parchment, and semi-tanned leathers will not normally survive wet conditions, for water will penetrate the fibres leading to hydrolysis and bacterial attack. Well-tanned leathers and the hair of furs stand a much greater chance of survival. Proximity to decaying copper or heart oak, which contains tannins, will assist in slowing down bacterial decay.

Desiccation or dry salty conditions will preserve rawhide/gut, tanned and semi-tanned materials, and sometimes even parchment, by preventing hydrolysis and bacterial attack; salt both desiccates and inhibits micro-organisms. Only tanned leather will withstand wet or waterlogged conditions and then only if the collagen remains tanned. A high pH extracts vegetable tannins and hydrolyses collagen more rapidly than a low pH; no leather survives in land deposits where the pH is above 6.4. However, leather from marine wrecks in an alkaline environment is often extremely well preserved. The precise reasons for this are unclear but a high concentration of tannins from nearby oak timbers may be a contributing factor. Here, and in other types of deposits where polyphenols are found, these may tan collagen *in situ* or replace tannins leached from the leather. It should be noted that not all polyphenols bond to collagen, and those in a deposit may be bacteriostatic rather than tanning in nature.

It is unlikely that skin products will survive burial in damp aerated soils except by some exceptional circumstance, such as impregnation by metal salts from decaying artefacts.

Burnt leather is much more difficult to characterize than charcoal, although some three-dimensional fibre network might be visible microscopically; this could then survive most burial environments.

6.3.3   Examination[47]

Low magnification and good lighting assist in identifying associated materials such as threads and paints. Dyes may well be obscured by discoloration but their presence or the traces of adhesives used for gold leaf etc. may be disclosed by UV or IR examination; the latter, for example, is used a great deal in the reading of documents on parchment. From the examination of the pattern of the follicles and the thickness of the skin, clues to its source are obtained but fine identification requires a sample to be taken and examined by an expert. It is possible chemically to determine whether the collagen has been oiled or tawed (given those materials have not been removed during burial) but the identification of the source of vegetable tannin is extremely difficult even though it has been attempted. Calculation of the shrinkage temperature (section 6.3.1.1) would give some indication of the degree of deterioration of skin, but this is usually done simply by examination.

At present, concern is being expressed about the problem of recording the dimensions of wet leather artefacts.[48] During manufacture, when leather is finally allowed to dry, it shrinks; when it is deposited in a wet or waterlogged environment, it swells, but it is possible that in certain circumstances it might then begin to shrink again. When wet, leather is actively stabilized; it shrinks to a lesser or greater extent (section 6.3.6.2) and details such as stitch holes tend to become blurred. It would seem that examination and measurement for comparative study (plate 6.7) are best carried out whilst the leather is still wet. But it remains unclear when the dimensions of a leather artefact are closest to those of its original state. However, in all cases, the condition which the leather is in when drawn should be noted, so that dimensions can be more usefully evaluated.

The unfolding of dry skin products[49], especially for examination, is a highly skilled task; important parchments, for example, require very carefully controlled dampening in water vapour. Good rawhide can be dampened and reshaped around or under wet sand, and well preserved oil-tanned leathers can be waterlogged for reshaping. Furs, untanned gut,

Plate 6.7 Recording the dimensions of fragments of Roman shoes whilst wet using a Melinex sheet and waterproof pen

and decayed leathers have to be first treated with humectants or oil emulsions to reintroduce flexibility (section 6.3.6.2) before reshaping is attempted.

Wet leather will be weakened along creases and unfolding is carried out under water, but a flexible consolidant may have to be introduced into the fibres before an attempt is made to straighten them without cracking.

6.3.4 Cleaning

6.3.4.1 Dry skin products

Non-absorbent artefacts in good condition can be cleaned with damp swabs, but great care is taken not to allow overdamping in discrete areas or else localized swelling, puckering, or staining results. Absorbent skins have to be cleaned dry using abrasion (air abrasion or powdered gum, described in section 3.3.2.1), but in all cases solvents alone are avoided for they tend to degrease the embrittled collagen even further.

6.3.4.2 Wet leather

Leather is supported on mesh trays and submerged in water where surface dirt is loosened with soft brushes; ultrasonics can be used to dislodge particles from within the fibre network of leather in good condition. Disagreement arises about the removal of the blackening from leather (section 6.3.2.2). Even though it is not possible to know exactly what colour the leather was when made or when abandoned, removal of blackening may help to display a 'truer' leather colour (plate 6.8). But chemicals used to lighten the colour of skins usually affect the artefact adversely; thus alkalis and strong acids extract tannins and dyes and hydrolyse collagen; sequestering agents remove dyes; whilst solvents, when mixed with water, are known for their ability to extract tannins. Since vegetable tannins act as visual indicators of pH, becoming paler as

Plate 6.8 Stabilized fragments of medieval shoes which have been treated to remove a degree of blackening

the pH falls, the colour of leather after treatment will in part depend on the reagents and washing procedures used.

6.3.5 *Deterioration upon excavation*

6.3.5.1 Dry skin products

These have usually survived by desiccation, and thus a sudden rise in ambient RH will cause movement of the fibres and possible damage. An RH of over 65 per cent will allow fungal growth on any remaining oils/fats, etc. (fungi do not attack collagen itself) leading to staining. At higher RH, bacteria may attack the collagen, especially in parchment, where the alkaline pH encourages growth and hydrolysis of the protein, resulting in a clammy, stained, weakened skin. Bacteria too attack the roots of hairs in furs, causing them to fall out.

Light, especially UV, will bleach dyes and some leathers, whilst also causing oxidation of the collagen and thus embrittlement. Sulphur dioxide from polluted air forms sulphuric acid, especially if iron is present in the leather to act as a catalyst; in historic, condensed, vegetable-tanned leather, the acid causes powdering of the skin and polymerization of the tannin to form brick-red phlobaphenes, a type of decay known as 'red rot'. Few insects attack skin products, but dermestid beetle larvae or woodworm may bore through it.

6.3.5.2 Wet leather

If this is allowed to dry out, the surface tension of the retreating water front drags the decayed collagen fibres together. Since tanning agents and oils have been lost during burial, the fibres are kept apart mainly by water, and so drying leads to severe shrinking. Strong bonds may form between the collapsed fibres, making the reintroduction of water extremely difficult, but perhaps not so impossible as in the case of shrunken wood (section 6.2.5.2). Shrunken leather is very brittle, not only because few oils remain, but also because the collagen fibres have been shortened by decay (plate 6.9). Impregnation with silt and salts causes internal abrasion of leather when it is flexed. If the salt content is high, as in leather from the sea, salt efflorescences (section 4.1.2) may appear on the surface.

If the leather is kept wet, fungal growth on decayed collagen and debris from the deposit within the fibres leading to weakening and staining is likely. If the pH of the storage solution is incorrect, further leaching of the tannins and hydrolysis of the collagen over time will result.

It should be noted that the temperature at which decayed collagen shrinks is lower than that for leather (section 6.3.1.1) and thus heat of any sort can cause deteriorated leather to shrink irreversibly.

Plate 6.9 Embrittlement of leather if allowed to dry out without treatment is shown by this fragment of a medieval shoe

6.3.6 Stabilization

6.3.6.1 Passive

DRY PRODUCTS. As with all moisture-containing materials, the RH has to be controlled to allow skin products to retain the optimum quantity of water but to prevent the growth of micro-organisms. For leather this is in the range of 50–60 per cent, for parchment 55–60 per cent; where the artefact is painted or gilded it is especially important that the RH does not fluctuate. If products come from an extremely dry RH, then they are dampened only gradually. Temperatures less than 18°C are advised, and much reduced temperatures discourage biological activity; this is often put to use with furs to prevent decay of the hair roots and loss of hair. Control of light levels (150 lux, or 50 lux for dyes, manuscripts, and furs) and elimination of UV and sulphur dioxide prevent further deterioration (section 6.3.5.1), whilst insect damage is prevented by good housekeeping.

WET LEATHER. Loss of water must be prevented; this is done simply by storage in sealed containers where growth of micro-organisms is discouraged by refrigeration. Again, deep freezing has been suggested and in fact seems to do no damage. Excessive leaching of tannins in storage solutions is avoided by use of a small quantity of water rather than by immersion.

6.3.6.2 Active

Since partially decayed skin products provide a valuable food source for micro-organisms, stabilization is often difficult to achieve by passive means alone. But extreme caution must be used when choosing a biocide for either wet or dry skins, since if it alters the pH of the product, detanning and hydrolysis could occur, dyes become bleached, or the skin colour altered. A problem too arises with the addition of lubricants or humectants to decayed skin products, described below; if care is not taken, their excess application can easily mask technological details such as stitch holes.

DRY SKIN PRODUCTS. Desiccated leather has usually been treated with oily lubricants,[50] emulsions often giving the best penetration. These lubricants are commonly based on lanolin and cedarwood oil. However, recently their over-use, or even their use at all, has been called into question.[51] In order to reintroduce flexibility into stiff skin products, it would be possible to use humectants such as glycerol, sorbitol, or low-molecular-weight PEGs (section 3.4.2.2); but care then has to be taken to prevent the RH falling too low when the humectant acts as a desiccant instead. Alternatively, desiccated archaeological leather could be water-logged and then treated as wet leather. At present there is no suitable method available to refix the hairs of furs once the roots have been destroyed.

WET LEATHER.[52] The aims of active stabilization of this material are as follows: to remove water so that the product is in equilibrium with the ambient RH; to do this without allowing the collagen fibres to collapse and the product to shrink; to prevent the cross-linking of collagen fibres on water removal; and to reintroduce flexibility of the fibres, either by maintaining a certain moisture content or by replacing this with a lubricant. Depending on the degree of degreasing, detanning, and degeneration of the collagen, these criteria will be more or less important for every piece of skin material – virtually no two pieces will respond identically or even predictably to treatment. Before these treatments are carried out, soluble salts, especially high in marine leather, are soaked out to prevent later efflorescence.

Since virtually all active stabilization treatments result in some measure of shrinkage (section 6.3.3), it is essential that for comparative purposes the shape and size of leather artefacts are recorded both before and after treatment (plate 6.7).

Broadly, there are three methods of stabilization. The first aims to replace the water with a less volatile material which coats the fibres, preventing cross-linking on drying. One group of reagents that can be used on leather which still contains oils and tannins is the humectants described in section 6.1.3.2. However, where oils and tannins have been lost, larger quantities of non-water-sensitive 'stuffing' reagents must be used. The second method involves solvent drying followed by the introduction of a bulking material. If water is replaced by a liquid of lower surface tension, there is less likelihood of collagen fibres collapsing and cross-linking, and so the product should dry softer. The leather is then treated as is dry leather (see above). It has been found that mechanical manipulation of the fibres, which happens if the dressing is rubbed in by hand, plays an important part in the reintroduction of flexibility. The third method of freeze-drying (section 3.4.2.1), is used for the same reason as is solvent drying. Before freezing, humectants (section 6.1.3.2), which bond to the decayed leather and help to prevent cross-linking on drying, are added to the water. Very often freeze-dried leather does not need further lubrication, but that in poor condition may require consolidation. The method is not labour intensive and, since adhering soil falls away during treatment, the cleaning process is also accelerated.

In conclusion it must be said that it is still unclear exactly how the added humectants, bulking agents, or lubricants are bonded to the leather. Further research is required to discover why this bonding sometimes fails, leading to excessive shrinkage and hardening. The shrinkage experienced in all the treatments is generally from 3 to 15 per cent; further study is required to determine the acceptable or even the desired (section 6.3.3) figure. A particular problem arises on wet or waterlogged sites where leather is excavated in bulk; it is not possible to treat each piece separately and yet each will respond to treatment differently. Mass freeze-drying looks promising here, with 'problem pieces' being lubricated or consolidated afterwards. If these masses of wet leather are simply allowed to air-dry with no treatment, rewetting and treating at a later date are not always possible, since poorly preserved pieces irreversibly shrink and embrittle.

6.3.7 Reshaping

See section 6.3.3

6.3.8 Summary[53]

Like wood, leather, the only skin product likely to be found on wet site excavations, is not allowed to dry out; but, unlike wood, immersion in water is not necessary. At the other extreme, parchment found in exceedingly dry environments has to be maintained initially at a very low RH. When lifted from the wet ground/sea-floor, a layer of deposit is retained adhering to leather artefacts to prevent loss of paint, gilding, textile, etc. Cleaning is a laboratory treatment since skin products are normally more frail than they appear and are likely to have important associated material. Since wet leather contracts when treated, drawings should always note in what state the artefacts were when measurements were taken.

In the long term it is important to store skin products, whether treated or not, at the correct RH; this must be neither too high nor too low, details being furnished by a specialist. Light levels should be minimal and temperatures as cool as possible.

6.4   Skeletal material (bony)

6.4.1   Nature of artefacts[54]

Like skin, vertebrate skeletal materials are based on the protein collagen (section 6.3.1.1), whilst shell depends on a similar protein, conchiolin. Unlike in skin, the scaffolding of collagen fibrils is made rigid by the deposition around and in them of a crystalline inorganic material, hydroxyapatite $Ca_{10}(PO_4)_6(OH)_2$. Both these constituents are associated with water, some of which is lost at death, leading to hardening. Bone, antler, and ivory differ in their ratio of hydroxyapatite to collagen and in their micro and macro structures. Individual bones, teeth, tusks, antlers, shells, etc., all have internal structures which are mechanically designed for their particular use/shape; when cut up to make artefacts, they lose this mechanical formulation, and therefore dimensional stability. Bone, antler and ivory are all, like wood, anisotropic (section 6.2.1). This means that they have different mechanical characteristics along the different planes of their structure. It results from the long collagen fibrils being laid out mainly in one plane, a feature exaggerated by the laminated structures of ivory and long bones. This text concentrates on the treatment of worked bone etc.; for discussion of the treatment of unworked human and animal bone, the reader should consult the numerous texts on this subject.[55]

6.4.1.1   Bone

The average content of bone from adult vertebrates is about 1:2 collagen:hydroxyapatite, with 5 per cent by weight of water. It has two major types of structure, namely the light cancellous tissues found in the interior of bones, and the heavier, dense, compact tissues found on the outside, and in the shafts of long bones; but density varies with species too, whalebone being particularly porous. Long bones tend to have a laminated structure on their external surface, particularly in young individuals. Bone is perforated by a network of tiny canals together with a number of larger holes which allow blood vessels etc. to enter the bone. Bone can be temporarily slightly softened for shaping into artefacts by soaking in water; more extensive softening by soaking in acid (vinegar, sour milk, etc.) impairs its mechanical properties.

6.4.1.2 Antler

Antlers are bony outgrowths of the skulls only produced by the even-toed ungulates (Artiodactyla). The tissue is more irregular than that of bone, having a compact surface and cancellous internal structure. It is significantly tougher than bone but responds to softening similarly.

6.4.1.3 Ivory

True ivory is from the upper incisors of elephants and mammoths. It is composed of dentine, which is approximately 1:3 collagen:hydroxyapatite, with 10 per cent by weight of water. Unlike bone, it has a marked laminated structure caused by growth rings, and does not have a canal system. It also has a remarkable structure of very fine tubules, whose gyratory pattern produces the 'engine turning' markings which identify true ivory. To some extent ivory can be softened by very hot water or vinegar but because of the specific size and shape of the raw material, many artefacts contain joins. The colour of ivory varies according to its origin; in light it bleaches but if much handled it develops a fine yellow/brown patina from the grease and other exudates of the hands. When burnt it becomes grey, a feature which may be used decoratively.

Walrus ivory, from the upper canines of this vertebrate, is chemically similar, but the inner zone appears much more translucent, with circular opaque markings; this results partly from a higher degree of crystallinity.

6.4.1.4 Teeth

Teeth are composed of a core of dentine (section 6.4.1.3) covered by a thick cap of enamel, a material which is 97 per cent by weight hydroxyapatite. Occasionally at their base a white area of cementum, a bone-like material, is seen. Like ivory, they have a degree of lamination, often with a void in the middle.

6.4.1.5 Associated material

Artefacts may be glued together, joined by bone pins, or riveted with iron or copper alloy rivets. Ivory is decorated by addition of a variety of materials such as gold leaf affixed with glue and paint, or stained green to resemble jade, or covered with wax and used as a writing tablet. Bone too may be dyed, inlaid with black materials, or coated in beeswax for decorative purposes.

6.4.2 Nature of deteriorated material[56]

6.4.2.1 Preservation of skeletal materials

These materials are preserved in almost all archaeological environments, but the condition in which they are found and their deterioration subsequently can vary enormously. This is because, unlike other materials, they are made up of two components which are preserved at opposing pH. Thus in acidic deposits the inorganic hydroxyapatite dissolves, leaving soft collagen which shrinks when it dries out, causing anisotropic structures to warp. In alkaline deposits the organic collagen hydrolyses and is attacked by bacteria, leaving brittle hydroxyapatite which crumbles on drying. At less extreme pH, there is a softening of the surface which may be due to a slight loss of collagen alone. Very dry environments or where there are high levels of calcium carbonate at a moderate pH, as is found in the sea, produce the best conditions for preservation. The environment which can lead to the total loss of skeletal material is an aerated, non-calcareous (i.e. acidic) through-draining gravel. Fossilization occurs in calcareous deposits when the organic fraction of skeletal material is replaced by inorganic calcium salts from the deposit, but since this process is extremely lengthy, fossilization of artefacts is not to be expected.

Artefacts made from both teeth and ivory suffer badly from splitting caused by physical factors including soluble salts (section 4.1.2). Since teeth have a protective enamel, they are found in good condition from a wider range of sites than is ivory. Where the environment does not favour any preservation, the non-destructible enamel coating may alone be found. A layer of patina/grease on an ivory object may well help prevent, at least initially, surface deterioration.

Burnt (calcined) skeletal material, because of its lack of organic material, survives burial extremely well; it still retains detail of structure for identification purposes.

6.4.2.2 Appearance

APPARENT GOOD CONDITION. Bone and antler can both appear and be in remarkably good condition upon excavation. This is usual in anaerobic non-acidic conditions, such as urban deposits or marine silts and even the sea itself. It will be slightly softer when wet than after drying since, in burial, it takes up water lost on drying after death of the animal (section 6.4.1). However, bone from slightly acidic anaerobic environments, such as peats, looks good, but splits or warps on drying (section 6.4.5).

SHAPE GOOD BUT SURFACE COARSENED OR EVEN ROUGHENED. In fine sands a degree of surface coarsening occurs, but more decay is revealed on drying when the surface cracks/flakes. In damp, more oxygenated deposits, such as coarser calcareous sand or loam, the surface is rougher and can be scratched easily. On drying, these materials appear chalky and warping/cracking/laminating of the surface (especially of ivory) may be considerable, and weight loss noticeable. Ivory and bone in this state may become difficult to differentiate, but the former is usually stronger than the latter.

SHAPE GOOD BUT SOFT AND ABRADED. Antler and bone from coarse calcareous gravels in this condition dry out with little dimensional change. But their nature has now changed to a powdery chalk because of the total loss of collagen. From chalk sites bone may be particularly eroded, fragile, and powdery. Overlying white encrustations of insoluble salts (section 2.2.1.5) can obscure the surface of this type of material.

FIBROUS SOFT BONE FROM PEATS (plate 6.10). Bone from these very acidic deposits appear as interwoven fibres like a kitchen scourer. It is pliable but hardens on drying. Here inorganic hydroxyapatite has been dissolved out by the acid and the collagen fibres preserved, having been 'tanned' by natural tannins.

DISCOLORATION. These materials, being pale and porous, are likely to become stained whilst buried; blackening/brown coloration from peat

Plate 6.10 Bone from a waterlogged peat deposit: whilst the shape is maintained, the texture which can be seen on the zygopophyses is fibrous and the bone is flexible

deposits or anaerobic silts/sludges is common, whilst iron staining, whether orange/brown oxide or blue/green phosphate (vivianite), may be found.

6.4.3 Examination

Before material, especially ivory, is 'cleaned', care should be taken to ensure that what is about to be removed are not the traces of glues, paints, etc. Whilst it may be difficult to differentiate poorly preserved material,[57] bone, antler, and ivory can usually be identified with the aid of a hand lens (details for the identification of well-preserved material must be sought in other texts[58]). Where bone, etc. is eroded, it may be difficult to distinguish worked from unworked material. X-radiography can assist in determining the construction and degree of decay of an object. These materials fluoresce in UV and the use of such a light source might help in identifying a badly broken up artefact when it is still in the ground.

6.4.4 Cleaning

It is much easier to clean damp/wet material before the soil on the outside dries out. Moreover, once ivory has dried out (or if it was excavated dry), it is very dangerous to apply even damp swabs in cleaning, because localized swelling can lead to cracking and exfoliation of the lamellae. In such cases, controlled swabbing with solvents is used, bearing in mind that certain of these will attack the surface of ivory.[59] But even with bone, care has to be taken in cleaning, for often the surface is much softer and more easily marked than is assumed.

Since encrusting insoluble salts are chemically very similar to hydroxyapatite, and since collagen is a sensitive material, removal of these may not be as simple as it is from pottery (section 4.5.4). Often only mechanical methods can be used and it may be preferable to leave the encrustation *in situ*. For similar reasons, stains are very difficult to remove and so usually must be left untouched.

6.4.5 Deterioration upon excavation

To some extent the changes which this group of materials undergo on drying have already been discussed (section 6.4.2). In general, some bone, soft in the ground, hardens on drying, which can be beneficial. Bone and antler which are extremely well preserved, or which contain very little organic material, usually do not change shape on drying. However, that material which still contains a certain level of collagen fibrils, cracks and warps as these shrink (plate 6.11); this damage is exacerbated over time,

Plate 6.11 Shrinkage and warping on drying fragments of bone and antler which still contain considerable quantities of collagen

if the ambient RH rises and falls. The surfaces of long bones are particularly prone to lamination. Ivory, in any condition, because of its fully laminated structure is particularly likely to crack and exfoliate when dried and when the RH is allowed to fluctuate. Furthermore, material which, to make an artefact, has been softened and deformed, (sections 6.4.1.1–3), may revert to its natural shape when it is dried out after excavation.

Bone and ivory from extremely dry environments will have equilibrated to that RH; on excavation, a sudden rise in RH can cause swelling of the collagen and disruption exacerbated if the RH fluctuates. Ivory is particularly susceptible to disruption by soluble salts (section 4.1.2), since it readily laminates (plate 3.3).

Shell in storage has long been known to suffer occasionally from efflorescences; this is probably the result of reaction with organic acids in the environment (section 2.4.6).[60]

6.4.6 Stabilization

6.4.6.1 Passive

Dimensional stability of bone etc. is readily achieved by control of the ambient RH. Like wood (section 6.2.6.1), slow drying (or wetting) of material can sometimes bring it into equilibrium with a different RH than that in which it was found (plate 6.12). Some material, antler for example, was deliberately shaped wet (section 6.4.1.2); it may be prevented from reverting to its natural shape on drying by weighting down with sand. However, other material, especially ivory, will not equilibrate by slow drying. Here, the only hope of preventing cracking and warping is to maintain the moisture content of the material at initial levels by careful control of the ambient RH indefinitely; there is little hope of active stabilization.

Deep freezing of all wet material may not be suitable for, like frost, it may cause structural damage (section 2.2.1.1); this has yet to be fully investigated.

For ivory, light/UV levels must be kept low to prevent embrittlement; temperatures should be cool and even.

6.4.6.2 Active[61]

Dimensional stabilization of these materials remains difficult to attain. In the case of dense material, such as ivory, it is difficult to achieve penetration of stabilizing agents whilst for all materials where substantial quantities of collagen survive it is not easy to mask reactive groups against RH changes. Certainly use of PVAC and polyethylene glycol

Plate 6.12 A medieval antler comb, damp on excavation, which retained its shape on drying. The storage RH can favour the antler since no iron remains in the rivets

cannot be relied upon to prevent shrinkage, but some success with bone has been achieved with a polyvinyledene chloride emulsion. Where cracking does not occur, wet skeletal material may be air-dried or dewatered in solvents before it is consolidated.

Consolidation of powdering/crumbling material presents less of a problem since polymers can penetrate the porous structure and, as little collagen remains, internal stresses on RH alteration are less extreme.

Before drying marine material, salts are removed by soaking in fresh water; salt removal from dry ivory is not such a straightforward process. Soaking is not possible, and a very laborious method of desalting using damp swabs followed by drying in a series of solvents has to be followed.

Even with active stabilization, control of the ambient RH of skeletal material is essential in the long term. Where it is impossible to control the ambient RH adequately, sheet ivory could be mounted onto a flexible backing which would at least hold the pieces together.

6.4.7 Summary

In general, skeletal artefacts are prevented from drying after excavation; the exception is soft material which does not crack on losing moisture. Cleaning is a laboratory problem. Certain material, especially ivory, can only be stabilized by rigorous control of the ambient RH but, in general, none will withstand low RH, even if it has been consolidated.

6.5 Horn, tortoiseshell, and feathers

6.5.1 Nature of artefacts[62]

Together with hair, wool, claws, hooves, and whalebone (baleen), these materials are all based on the protein keratin.

6.5.1.1 Keratin

Keratin is composed of a number of different amino acids (section 6.1.1.2), some of which contain sulphur. Keratin can exist both as a long fibrillar molecule and as an amorphous matrix. The molecules are held together to form fibrils by the cross-linking of the sulphur-containing groups in what is known as disulphide bridges. In hot water or steam these disulphide bridges rupture, allowing movement of the molecules, and reform, possibly in new positions, on drying. Hydrolysis of keratin is generally slow except at high pH, where the disulphide bridges are destroyed, with weakness and brittleness resulting. Unlike collagen, keratin is not found as extracellular fibres; more like cellulose, it is found as the material of cells which, on becoming fully keratinized, are no longer living. Keratin tissues can be coloured by pigments (black, brown, or yellow granules), whilst their optical properties provide further visual effects. Like collagen, keratin can take up water.

6.5.1.2   Horn

This material comes from the outer sheath of the bony horn core outgrowths of bovids and antelopes. It is made of keratinized cells arranged in layers with a distinct striated structure giving anisotropic mechanical properties (section 6.2.1). Horn can be flattened by soaking and boiling in water, disrupting the disulphide bridges; it is then dried flat under weights. Horn may be joined by similar techniques, and split into thin sheets. These can be made more elastic by soaking in acids, or rendered more transparent with fats or oils. Alternatively, artefacts can be made from the thick horn tip. The horn of the rhinoceros, however, is made of compressed hairs: see section 6.6.1.2.

6.5.1.3   Tortoiseshell

Layers of keratinized cells build up into the scales of the reptile group, Chelonia. Like horn, it can be flattened, split, and joined after soaking in salted water. It fluoresces yellow-brown under UV.

6.5.1.4   Feathers

Here the cells are made of fibrils of keratin embedded in a keratin matrix. The feathers themselves consist of a hollow rachis from which branch barbs; smaller barbules branch from these. Much of the visual effect of feathers is given by optical properties of the material as well as by pigment granules.

6.5.2   Deterioration of materials

AGENTS OF DETERIORATION.   The only significant insect to attack keratin is the larva of the clothes moth; even this can only utilize very thin sheets of the protein, like the barbules of feathers. Certain species of fungi and bacteria can utilize keratin especially in conjunction with chemical hydrolysis. Except in alkaline conditions hydrolysis is slow with the break-down of fibrils being slower than of matrix. Water enhanced by heat causes softening, and thus artefacts may become misshapen under heavy deposits, or they may simply revert to the original shape of the horn or shell before it was deformed in manufacture. In regions of very low humidity, the water associated with keratin fibrils is lost, leading to possible shrinkage and warping. Complete horns split longitudinally from the base upwards and exfoliate, the layers often curling.

In the ground horn becomes opaque and begins to laminate as more of the matrix hydrolyses, a fibrillar structure becomes apparent. Fibering continues until the horn simply becomes a fibrous pulp. On drying out, the pulp falls to dust.

Feathers survive a remarkable range of burial deposits. On drying out after excavation, they can appear dull because of deterioration of the surface and could suffer attack by the clothes moth.

6.5.3 Conservation

Wet horn and tortoiseshell is not immediately dried out; lamination or powdering may result. Little work has been carried out on the active stabilization of wet material, but it is probable that it, and dry material, would be treated in a similar manner to amber or jet (section 6.7), perhaps with the addition of humectants. Reshaping when wet or by judicious dampening might be feasible. Feathers suffer the least from drying out, but the barbules tend to stick together; this is overcome by blow-drying in cool air, sometimes with the addition of an inert oil/wax to the surface to restore the optical properties. Fragile dry featherwork is best cleaned with a carefully chosen mixture of detergent and solvent.[63]

6.6 Fibres

Fibres are used, either as part of an artefact such as threads and bindings, or as ropes and fabrics, when they are wound, looped, woven, or beaten together. The sources of suitable fibres are countless, deriving both from plants and animals, being either cellulosic or proteinaceous; only a selection of common ones will be discussed here. If a long thread is required, normally the individual fibres must be spun into long elements which in their turn can be strengthened by spinning together to give yarns. All the fibres have water in their structure (section 6.1.1), animal fibres tending to have a higher moisture content than plant fibres.

6.6.1 Nature and use

6.6.1.1 Cellulosic fibres

The purest cellulose fibres come from the single hair cells on the tips of cotton seeds having a natural spiral form which can be readily spun into threads. An important source of material is the bast fibres of a wide variety of plants. These are the lignified dead cells running up plant stems, giving them support, and thus are not unlike wood. Examples are those of the linseed plant *Linum* which give true linen when spun, and those of the nettle family which give a similar material. Woven baskets made from grasses, reeds, sedges, etc., being flexible in nature, are discussed here; whilst these stems are unlignified, they contain some silica.

6.6.1.2   Proteinaceous fibres

Strands of keratin (section 6.5.1.1), derived as is horn from the outer layers of the skin, comprise wool, hair, kemp, etc., the distinction between these being one of size. Wool is generally fine and short, whilst hair or kemp is thicker and longer. These fibres are formed from cells of keratin fibrils comprising a cortex, and an outside layer of flattened scale cells (figure 6.7). The scale cells or 'bracts' act as hooks holding the fibres together on spinning.

Silk is non-cellular, being composed of two absolutely continuous filaments of the protein fibroin. The filaments, produced by the cultivated silkworm *Bombyx mori* to create a cocoon, are simply unwound, but in the wild the emerging adult bites through the filaments, reducing their length.

6.6.1.3   Fabrics[64]

Fabrics can be made from certain fibres by matting them together. Shortened cellulose fibres held together by a size (gelatin, starch, or synthetics) give paper; fibrous leaves held together by a natural gum give papyrus, whilst felt can be made by compressing wet wool (often together with heat and alkali to break and reset the disulphide bridges) causing the individual shafts to mat (section 6.5.1). Weaving requires the interlocking of two distinct groups of parallel threads at right angles to each other; it produces both textiles and basketry. Knitting implies the looping of a single thread. Other methods of construction include coiling and binding, to make basketry, and twisting and plaiting to make ropes.

Finishing techniques used on textiles include deliberate surface felting (see above) of woven and knitted woollens, and compaction of linen fabrics by rubbing with smoothers often made of glass.

6.6.1.4   Associated materials

Dyes[65] are organic molecules which are either bonded onto fibres or else simply deposited in them. In order to make dyes fast, strong bonding is

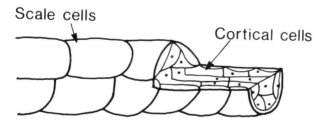

Scale cells

Cortical cells

Figure 6.7   Scheme of cellular structure of hair

needed; the fibre molecule should possess a charge opposite to that of the dye molecule. Protein fibres in acid or alkaline pH have a charge so, unlike cellulose fibres, may bond strongly to dyes. There are no naturally occurring dyes which bond directly to fibres and so, in antiquity, the use of mordants was common. These are chemicals which combine with dye molecules to give a 'lake' and which form a bridge between the fibre and the dye. So, for example, madder (section 6.1.1.5) forms a lake with alum which will bond onto wool and even cellulose giving a brick-red colour. A third group of dyes are the developed or vat dyes, such as woad (indigotin) which are chemically precipitated into intrafibrillar spaces; they are especially useful for cellulosics. Other associated materials include metallic threads, gold leaf, and construction or sewing threads.

6.6.2   Nature of deteriorated material

6.6.2.1   Appearance

DETERIORATION DURING USE. Wear and tear will be considerable, as will any amount of staining, soiling, and natural bleaching. Decaying sweat with an alkaline pH causes considerable weakening of clothing.

DULL APPEARANCE. As the surfaces of fibres, especially wool, decay, they lose their sheen.

LOSS, BRITTLENESS, WEAKENING, AND INSECT ATTACK. As fibres lose their bound water in dry environments (section 6.1.1) they lose their flexibility. In such environments, insect attack is likely, the most noteworthy being moth larvae on wool, silverfish on thin papers, and woodworm larvae (section 6.1.2.1) on woody basketry; cellulosic textiles are not likely to be attacked. However, for a fuller discussion of insect pests in fabrics, other texts[66] must be consulted. Weakening results from oxidation enhanced by iron in dyes or stains as well as from slow hydrolysis.

GOOD CONDITION FROM WET/WATERLOGGED DEPOSITS. Wool can be found looking extremely well preserved; but weakening by slow hydrolysis will have occurred; silk is found likewise. Woody basketry will be preserved as for wood (section 6.2.2.3), whilst other fibres such as hemp which are highly ligneous, will also be preserved.

DISCOLORATION. In wet deposits, dyes may become leached out, especially where the pH does not favour the bond to the fibres, or they may remain *in situ*, but change colour because of a change in pH or in the nature of the mordant. Fibres may become stained by corroding metal salts, and especially by iron tannates in the deposit which virtually dye the fibres. Alternatively, blackening may be due to iron sulphide and browning to iron oxide.

6.6.2.2   Presence or absence of materials in a deposit

The retrieval of fibres is dependent partly on intrinsic and partly on extrinsic factors. Thus cotton and paper will hydrolyse and decay completely except in *very* dry environments, whilst linen and other cellulosics combined with lignin will survive longer; linens may even survive much longer in anaerobic conditions where the pH is not too low. Wool is much less readily hydrolysed and, like silk, is found in many wet anaerobic environments. Dyes may assist preservation by acting as biocides, unless, as shown in section 6.6.2.1., they speed up decay. Either contamination by copper salts or dry salty conditions can lead to preservation, even of cellulosic fibres. However, in most damp aerated deposits, because of fungal, bacterial, and hydrolytic deterioration combined, loss of fibres within a few years is almost inevitable.

6.6.3   Examination[67]

Visual examination to determine the construction of the fabric or yarn and presence of dyes is essential. With all the discoloration described in section 6.6.2.1, it is often impossible to see any remaining dye; it can only be found through analysis. IR may help in the location of ornamenting materials, and x-radiography, metallic threads. The weave of a fabric is recorded using a series of conventions. To identify fibres, one or more is extracted and examined with a transmitted light microscope, or where opaque, scanning electron microscope; this will also show the state of deterioration of the fibres. To confirm the identity of dyes, these must be extracted and analysed, usually by spectrophotometry, which requires only very small samples.

6.6.4   Cleaning

6.6.4.1   Dry fibres[68]

The cleaning of historical textiles is a speciality in its own right and the cleaning of archaeological textiles, when found dry, may be given over to these textile specialists. Some points of interest concerning this work are given here. Water is always the best cleaning agent for fibres and is used wherever possible: it not only cleans but also plumps up fibres, reintroducing lost flexibility to some extent. Folded textiles are unwrapped either when totally immersed or after dampening by spraying. If it is found that dyes run in water, attempts to fix them are of little value, and so the fabric is cleaned using carefully selected solvents to prevent the removal of absorbed water and dyes. Bleaching of ancient textiles is to be avoided, for more damage than conservation results. Frail textiles are not brushed but are freed from loose dirt by puffer brushes. Brittle basketry is usually cleaned by barely damp swabs of water or alcohol. It can only be reshaped after flexibility has been reintroduced; this may simply be by a water spray or high RH, but it may require the addition of a consolidant (section 6.6.6.2) first.

6.6.4.2   Wet fibres

These must always be cleaned before air-drying, for if the soil dries and contracts, it can rupture delicate fibres. Wet cleaning is always done by supporting the textile on a synthetic net frame (plate 6.13). This is placed in a water bath and the fabric unfolded whilst immersed. Soft brushes and sponges alone are used to help remove the dirt but ultrasonics could be useful. Great care is taken with the pH of the washing water to prevent removal of dyes and enhanced hydrolysis of fibres. Because of this, chemicals are rarely used; attempts to remove blackening do not avoid these dangers. However, where it is clear that dyes are absent and the exact nature of the fibres is known, chemicals to remove stubborn clay or iron concretions have been used.[69]

6.6.5   *Deterioration upon excavation*

Crumbling and fragmentation are the most immediate dangers upon excavation owing to the fragility of the material. If dry, this is enhanced by brittleness and if wet, by the weight of water. Also, soil particles within fabrics will act as internal abrasives. If mud is allowed to dry on wet fabrics, it shrinks, pulling fibres away from the threads. Waterlogged woody baskets may collapse like wood (section 6.2.5.2) on dehydration, but this is less of a problem with fabrics. In the long term the worst enemy to fibres is light. Energy, especially from the UV region, is absorbed by the material, and in the presence of oxygen and water oxidizes the polymer molecules; the absorption of energy is greatest where impurities, especially yellow or iron stains/dyes, are present. Silk is especially sensitive to this type of decay. Further embrittlement arises in excessively dry environments where lubricating moisture is lost, or in excessively wet environments when hydrolytic decay continues. Cellulosics are embrittled by acids present, either as a result of pollution or, as in some cheap papers, from their method of manufacture (plate 6.14).

Moulds grow readily on cellulose fibres which take up moisture as the RH rises, and finally lead to their destruction. Actinomycetes and bacteria alone attack woollens at high humidities, leading to a rank smell

Plate 6.13 Washing a fragment of blackened fragile woollen textile from a waterlogged deposit sandwiched between two layers of fine net

and destruction of the fibres. Insect attack is described in section 6.6.2.1.

Light, of course, plays an important role in the discoloration of fabrics, resulting in the fading of dyes, especially yellows, since they absorb the most dangerous blue/UV wavelengths. Papers brown noticeably because of oxidation of lignin if this is present, but browning of cottons and papers can also be by the formation of oxycelluloses. Fabrics have surfaces full of crevices and so readily pick up dirt and soot, which can prove very difficult to remove.

6.6.6 Stabilization

6.6.6.1 Passive

Wet woody baskets or uncleaned fabrics must be kept damp until conserved; with textiles, biocides should be avoided for they may interfere with dyes and even fibres. Textiles should be kept refrigerated or even frozen, and conserved as soon as possible.

After removal of surface and internal soils, wet fabrics can usually be stabilized by air-drying, the type of collapse found in cellular wood or

Plate 6.14 Poor packaging leading to continued deterioration of a fragment of textile: note acidic card backing, pressure tape losing adhesion, and unsecured fragment

collagenous skin products, not occurring. Further decay is prevented by extremely careful packaging and handling (figure 6.8). Light is excluded or kept to extremely low levels, and dirt and dust prevented from access to fibres. Micro-organisms are controlled by maintaining a RH of less than 65 per cent and insects by good housekeeping or, where infected, by fumigation. Dimensional stability is maintained by preventing the RH from fluctuating and keeping within a range of 50 to 65 per cent.

6.6.6.2 Active

If fibres have become only slightly embrittled, addition of a humectant (section 6.1.4.2) may restore some flexibility if the RH drops too low again, but once decayed it is difficult to 'rejuvenate' fibres since the addition of strengthening consolidants simply stiffens the fibres. However, some success has been found using cellulose derivatives.[70] Alternatively, decayed textiles can be strengthened by the labour-intensive method of sewing with a multitude of tiny stitches onto a backing fabric, a process known as 'couching' (plate 2.1). Controversy still surrounds the speedier method of strengthening textiles by sticking them onto a backing fabric with adhesive[71] (plate 6.15). Where degradation is much advanced, individual fibres pull away from the threads; a satisfactory means of

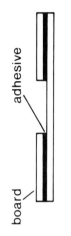

ii Cross-section of boards

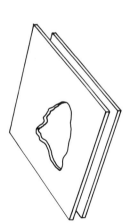

i Acid-free board with cut-out shape placed on sheet of acid-free board

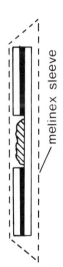

iii

Figure 6.8 Packaging for textile fragments[72]

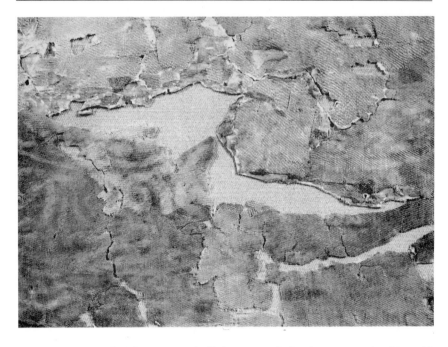

Plate 6.15 Very frail fragments of silk from a tomb fixed to a paper backing with adhesive

preventing this loss whilst allowing the textile to remain flexible is not yet available. For extremely decayed flat artefacts, total encapsulation in a hard resin has been used.[73] When treating a mass of fragments of textile, funds often allow no more than storing the textiles horizontally in perforated polyethylene bags.

Some flexibility has been reintroduced to dry basketry using humectants,[74] and some strength by use of tetraethylorthosilicate (TEOS).[75] This is particularly suitable for fibres containing silica, for the strengthening material deposited is also silica (section 6.2.6.2).

6.6.7 Summary

Excavated textiles are extremely fragile and should always be lifted together with surrounding silt, mud, etc. They must be well supported, packed extremely carefully, and any cleaning left entirely to the laboratory. Dry material is kept dry and wet material wet, with special care taken to avoid the growth of micro-organisms (section 3.4.1.7).

After conservation, again careful handling and packing are essential;

vertical display of frail material is not usually possible. Control of environmental conditions is important, with attention being paid to all aspects, especially those of light and dust/dirt.

6.7 Minerals of organic origin

6.7.1 Amber[76]

Amber is the fossilized resin exuded by certain extinct conifers. During fossilization, volatile fractions are lost, leaving a complex mixture of polymers of resin acids and esters. The source of the amber may be identified by analysis of the constituents. It is an amorphous, transparent, pale to dark red-brown material, which softens at 150°C and has a green fluorescence under UV light and a conchoidal fracture. Some constituents are soluble in solvents in which it softens. Amber may be stable in an opaque form which is due to the presence of microscopic bubbles.

DETERIORATION. Amber darkens over time by oxidation, and can obtain a greyish opaque weathering crust as the more soluble fractions become leached out. Oxidation also leads to deep cracking and increased solubility of the resin acids. Soil becomes lodged in these cracks. When waterlogged, the cracks and weathering may not be visible (plate 6.16), but on dehydration the extent of decay is revealed. It appears that excavated amber continues to become more cracked and less translucent for several years after drying out from the ground.

CONSERVATION. Very little work on the conservation of amber has been carried out, but it is suggested that upon excavation even amber which is apparently in extremely good condition should be prevented from drying out, and sent as soon as possible to a laboratory. Water may cause clear amber, once dried out, to become opaque.

By filling cracks in a weathering crust, impregnation with a consolidant could help to reintroduce translucency. For this, amber oil (if amber is heated to 300°C it decomposes to an oil) and waxes have been used, as have synthetic resins in the least aggressive solvent. However, provenance studies could well be affected by any introduction of consolidants.[76]

6.7.2 Jet, cannel coal, and bitumens

These are the compressed, more or less altered, remains of old land vegetation, transformed by slow chemical changes into a material rich in carbon. Jet is a resinous, hard, coal-black form of lignite capable of taking a high polish. Cannel coal is a variety of coal without lustre, whilst

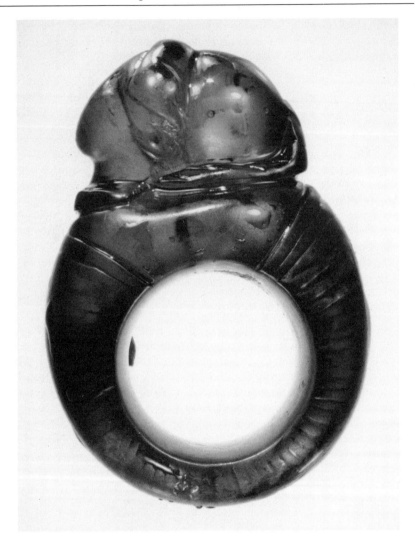

Plate 6.16 Roman amber ring from Carlisle, from a waterlogged deposit before treatment shows no visible signs of deterioration

bitumens are essentially hydrocarbons, used either as hard glass-like solids which have a conchoidal fracture, or as adhesives. Jet can contain hygroscopic alumina inclusions.

The deterioration and conservation of these materials have not been studied in depth. Jet can appear on excavation at damp/wet sites to be in extremely good condition, but on drying the true extent of decay is revealed as the surface crazes and spalls. This type of material then is best stored damp until it reaches a laboratory, when it can either be dried under controlled conditions or impregnated with a consolidant such as PEG 4000 (section 6.2.6.2).

Archaeological conservation: a guide to organizations, training, and literature

Uniting all specialisms of conservation there exists the International Institute for Conservation (IIC). It is open to all, but Fellows are elected. It publishes the main conservation journal *Studies in Conservation*, and, in association with The Getty Conservation Institute, the essential abstracts *Art and Archaeology Technical Abstracts*, and a bulletin. It holds a biennial conference, the proceedings of which are published as preprints, and helped to initiate what is intended to be a series of fundamental texts in conservation published by Butterworths (Sevenoaks, England).

A second international organization, the International Council of Museums (ICOM), has a Committee for Conservation which organizes a triennial conference whose proceedings are also published as preprints, based on the research of working groups in particular specialisms within conservation. The Committee also publishes a newsletter, as do some of the working groups.

In Britain, the United Kingdom Institute for Conservation (UKIC), open to all at present, publishes a journal *The Conservator* and the bulletin *Conservation News*, as well as holding numerous meetings where proceedings may be published in a series of Occasional Papers. Amongst the specialist sections of UKIC is the Archaeology Section open to all those with an interest in the treatment of archaeological materials; this section publishes a series of Guidelines and organizes occasional meetings and courses. In Scotland, the Scottish Society for Conservation and Restoration (SSCR) publishes a bulletin and holds a number of meetings each year, occasionally publishing the proceedings. In 1987, the Museums and Galleries Commission (MGC) set up a Conservation Unit to look after the interests of conservation as a whole in England and Wales, including keeping a register of practitioners.

Elsewhere there are regional conservation groups, some of which are affiliated to the IIC and many of which publish journals or bulletins. Amongst the most flourishing are the American Institute for Conservation

(AIC), the Canadian Group of IIC (IIC–CG), the Nordic group of IIC (IIC–Nordic), and the Australian Institute for the Conservation of Cultural Materials (ICCM).

Based in Rome, the International Centre for the Study and the Preservation and Restoration of Cultural Property (ICCROM) is particularly involved with conservation problems outside Europe and North America. It runs courses and occasional conferences, publishes a newsletter and a number of paperback books, and has a growing library, the listings of which are available.

In 1985, the J. Paul Getty Trust established The Getty Conservation Institute in California, to further scientific knowledge and professional practice in conservation. Apart from undertaking research and coordinating the Conservation Information Network offering a number of databases which in Britain are accessed through the Conservation Unit, the Institute assists with training and on-site conservation projects and with conferences.

Entry to the practice of archaeological conservation today requires a recognized training. Amongst other attributes, such training demands a good understanding of chemistry, evidence of practical skills, and sympathy with archaeology, and thus is of great interest to those who wish to combine the sciences and the humanities. In Britain, there are three training courses, two at undergraduate level at the Universities in London and Cardiff, and one at graduate level at the University of Durham; details of these and courses in other areas of conservation are available from UKIC. Archaeological conservators, once trained, can expect to find employment in conservation, some of which are permanent; it is more difficult to find suitable posts for mid-career development. Jobs are advertised in the *Museums Bulletin* published by the Museums Association and *Conservation News*, whilst international posts may be advertised in the IIC Bulletin.

Elsewhere in Europe and in North America and Australia courses exist, but they are on the whole more committed to the conservation of historic material. A full list of training opportunities is available from ICCROM.

References

Guide to references

Almost all the literature cited is in English. This is not felt to limit the usefulness of the references or the bibliography since there are only one or two major texts in other languages which have relevance, and even these concentrate on the conservation of objects in museums rather than freshly excavated material. Chapter references have been chosen either because they sum up an aspect or they will lead the reader further into the literature should he or she choose to delve deeper. When reference is made to a large text or a conference, page numbers will guide the reader to the more reliable and relevant areas of such items.

1 Introducing archaeological conservation

1. Young, R. and Welfare, A. T. (1978) 'Excavations at Crawley Edge in Weardale', *Archaeological Reports for 1977*, Durham, Universities of Durham and Newcastle, pp. 8–10.
2. Cramp, R. J. (1982), 'Excavations at the Hirsel, Coldstream, Berwickshire', *Archaeological Reports for 1981*, Durham, Universities of Durham and Newcastle, pp. 33–7.
3. ICOM (1984b).
4. UKIC (1983).
5. D of E (1978).
6. *The publication of archaeological excavations* (1983). Report of joint working party of the Council for British Archaeology and the Department of the Environment, chaired by B. W. Cunliffe.
7. *Selection and retention of environmental and artefactual material from excavations* (1983). Report of British Museum working party, chaired by I. H. Longworth.
8. Leigh (1982).
9. UKIC Archaeology Section (1982).
10. Keene (1980).
11. Brown, D., 'Conservation and the study of finds', in Keene (1980), pp. 10–12.
12. Cronyn and Horie (1986).
13. Unesco (1982).

2 Agents of deterioration and preservation

1. Limbrey, S. (1975), *Soil Science in Archaeology*, London: Academic Press.
2. Alexander, M. (1977), *Introduction to Soil Microbiology*, 2nd edn, New York: Wiley; Fairbridge, R. W. and Finkl, C. W. (eds) (1979), *Encyclopedia of Soil Science: Part I*, Stroudsberg, PA: Dowden, Hutchinson & Ross; Weier (1973).
3. Biek (1963); Robinson (1981b).
4. Zeuner, F. E. (1955), 'Notes on the Bronze Age tombs at Jericho I', *Palestine Exploration Quarterly* October: 118–28.
5. Biek (1963).
6. Bethell, P. H. and Carter, M. O. H., 'Detection and enhancement of decayed inhumations at Sutton Hoo' in Böddington *et al.* (1987), pp. 10–21.
7. Agrawal, O. P. *et al.* (1982), 'Stop dangerous practices', *Museum* 34: 44–64; Thomson (1986).
8. Baynes-Cope, A. D. (1981), *Caring for Books and Documents*, London: British Museum; Fleming, A. E., 'Conservation and storage: photographic materials', in Thompson (1986), pp. 362–7; Mitchelmore, D. J. H., 'The storage of archaeological records', in Partington-Omar and White, pp. 25–6.
9. de Guichen (1984); Thomson (1986).

3 Techniques of conservation

1. Pye (1986); Pearson (1988); Sease (1988).
2. Robinson (1981a); Sease (1988); Spriggs (1980); Tubbs, K. W. (1985), 'Preparation for field conservation in the Near East', *The Conservator* 9: 17–21; Watkinson (1987); Pearson (1988); Hodges (1987).
3. Roberts, F. and Andreasen, T. V., 'The retention of extremely degraded organic material from excavations', in Black (1987), pp. 249–52.
4. Dowman (1970), pp. 98–180.
5. Newey, H., Dove, S., and Calver, A., 'Synthetic alternatives to plaster of Paris on excavation', in Black (1987), pp. 33–6.
6. Anon. (1981), 'Expanded polyurethane', *Conservation News* 15: 7; Watkinson, D. and Leigh, D. (1978), 'Polyurethane foam: a health hazard in conservation', *Conservation News* 6: 7.
7. Jones, J. M. (1980), 'The use of polyurethane foam in lifting large fragile objects on site', *The Conservator* 4: 31–3; Price, J., 'Some field experiments in the removal of larger fragile archaeological remains', in IIC (1975), pp. 153–64; Van Geersdaele, P. (1975), 'The 13th century tile-kiln from Clarendon Place: its removal and reconstruction', *Studies in Conservation* 20: pp. 158–68.
8. Watkinson (1987).
9. Arrhenius, B. (1973), 'Teknisk verksamhet', *Kungliar Vitterhets Historie och Antikvitets Akademiens Arsbok*, pp. 176–82.
10. Clogg, P. W. (1987), *The Use of Freezing for the Lifting of Archaeological Remains*, B.Sc report, Institute of Archaeology, University College, London.
11. Robinson (1981a).
12. Brown, C. and Peacock, E. (1981), 'Flexible mould components for wet sites', *Conservation News* 15: 8–9; Newey, H. (1985), 'On-site casting', *Conservation News* 27: 23–4; Van Geersdaele, P., 'Plaster moulding of waterlogged wood', in Oddy (1975), pp. 109–11.
13. Bryce, T. and Caldwell, D. (1981), 'Scottish medieval sculpture – the making of reproductions and their uses', *Museums Journal* 81: 67–72; Larsen (1981);

Watkinson, D. (1982), 'Making a large scale replica: The Pillar of Eliseg', *The Conservator* 6: 6–11.

14. Jones, A. K. K., Jones, J. M., and Spriggs, J. A. (1985), 'Results of second marker trial', *Conservation News* 24: 37–8.
15. Graham and Eddie (1984); Goffer (1980), pp. 38–40; Tite (1972), pp. 252–4.
16. Gottlieb, B. A. and Roberts, J., 'Panoramic x-rays of cylindrical objects', in ICOM (1984a), pp. 84.1.65–8.
17. Reimers, P. and Riederer, J., 'The examination of works of art by means of x-ray computer tomography (CAT)', in ICOM (1984a), pp. 84.1.77–9; Hall (1984), pp. 38–42.
18. Jett, P., Sturman, S., and Drayman Weisser, T. D. (1985), 'A study of the Egyptian bronze falcon figures at the Walters Art Gallery', *Studies in Conservation* 30: 112–18.
19. Goffer (1980); Mairlinger, F. and Schreiner, M., 'New methods of chemical analysis – a tool for the conservator', in IIC (1982), pp. 5–15; Tite (1972).
20. Crafts Council (1983a).
21. See Refs 1 and 2; UKIC Archaeology Section (1983).
22. Thomson (1986); de Guichen (1984); Staniforth (1986); Turner, I. K. (1980), *Museum showcases; a design brief*, Occasional Paper No. 29, London: British Museum; Stolow (1987); Harding (1985).
23. Gregson, C. (1980), 'A flexible tank storage system', *Conservation News* 27: 24; Spriggs (1980).
24. Knight, B. (1982), 'A note on the storage of freshly excavated iron objects', *Conservation News* 17: 19.
25. UKIC Archaeology Section (1984).
26. Lafontaine, R. H. and Michalski, S., 'The control of relative humidity – recent developments', ICOM (1984a), pp. 84.17.33–7.
27. Rainer, B., 'The design and construction of two humidity-controlled display cases', ICOM (1984a), pp. 84.17.46–9.
28. Daniels, V. D. and Wilthew, S. E. (1983), 'An investigation into the use of cobalt salt-impregnated papers for the measurement of relative humidity', *Studies in Conservation* 28: 80–4; Ramer, B. (1981), 'The use of colour change relative humidity cards', *Conservation News* 16: 10.
29. Watkinson (1987).
30. Spriggs, J. A., 'The Coppergate helmet: a holding operation', in Keene (1985), p. 33.
31. Blackshaw, S. N. and Daniels, V. D. (1979), 'The testing of materials for use in storage and display in museums', *The Conservator* 3: 16–19; Hopwood, W. R. (1979), 'Choosing materials for prolonged proximity to museum objects', *Preprints of the AIC 7th Annual Meeting*, Washington, DC: AIC, pp. 44–7.
32. Thomson (1986).
33. Horie (1986).
34. Ref. 2; Lucas, D. A., 'On-site packing and protection of wet and waterlogged wood', in Grattan and McCawley (1982), pp. 51–5; UKIC Archaeology Section (1983).
35. Walker, K. (forthcoming), *Guidelines for the Choice and Storage of Archaeological Archive Materials*, London: UKIC Archaeology Section.
36. UKIC Archaeology Section (1982).
37. Evenson, J. (1980), 'Freeze-drying', in *Konservering og Restaurering af Laeder Skind og Pergament*, Copenhagen, Konservatorskolen: Kongelige Danske Kunstakademi, pp. 226–39.
38. Hodges, H. W. M., 'Conservation treatment of ceramics in the field', in

Hodges (1987), pp. 144–9; MacLeod, I. D. and Davies, J. A., 'Desalination of glass, stone and ceramics from shipwreck sites', in ICOM (1987), pp. 1003–8.

39. Stansfield, G. (1985), 'Pest control: a collections management problem', *Museums Journal* 85: 97–100.

40. Baynes-Cope, A. D., 'Fungicides and the preservation of waterlogged wood', in Oddy (1975), pp. 31–3; Dawson, J., 'Some considerations in choosing a biocide', in Grattan and McCawley (1982), pp. 269–77 and preceding discussion on pp. 267–8.

41. Dersarkissian, M. and Goodberry, M. (1980), 'Experiments with non-toxic anti-fungal agents', *Studies in Conservation* 25: 28–36; Hickin, N. E., 'Insect damage in the decorative arts: a world problem', in IIC (1978), pp. 19–22; Stansfield (1985) (op. cit., ref. 39).

42. Crafts Council (1983b); Dewitte, E., 'Resins in conservation: introduction to their properties and application', in Tate *et al.* (1983), pp. 1–6; DeWitte and Goessens-Landrie (1976); Horie (1987); IIC (1984); Torraca (1975).

43. Torraca (1982), p. 117.

44. Feller *et al.* (1985).

45. Sease, C. (1981), 'The case against using soluble nylon in conservation work', *Studies in Conservation* 26: 102–10.

46. Horie (1987), pp. 117–22.

47. Koob, S. (1981), 'Conservation with acrylic colloidal dispersions', in *Preprints of the AIC 9th Annual Meeting*, Washington, DC: AIC, pp. 86–94.

48. Grissom and Weiss (1981); Dinsmore, J. (1987), 'Considerations of adhesion in the use of silane-based consolidants', *Conservator* 11: 26–9.

49. Ref. 42; Davison, S., 'A review of adhesives and consolidants used on glass antiquities', in IIC (1984), pp. 191–4.

50. Koob, S. P. (1982), 'The instability of cellulose nitrate', *The Conservator* 6: 31–4.

51. Koob, S. P. (1986), 'The use of Paraloid B72 as an adhesive: its application for archaeological ceramics and other materials', *Studies in Conservation* 31: 7–14.

52. Shorer, P. H. T., 'Interpretation through reconstruction of a rusted 10th century Viking iron sliding key', in ICOM (1984a), pp. 84.22.33–40.

53. Bradley, S. (1983), 'Conservation recording in the British Museum', *The Conservator* 7: 9–12; Corfield, M. (1983), 'Conservation records in the Wiltshire Library and Museum Service', *The Conservator* 7: 5–8.

4 Siliceous and related materials

1. Stambolov and Van Asperen der Boer (1976 and following); Torraca (1982); Winkler, E. M. (1975), *Stone: Properties and Durability in Man's Environment*, 2nd edn, New York: Springer.

2. Rosenfeld, A. (1965), *The Inorganic Raw Materials of Antiquity*, London: Weidenfeld & Nicholson; Shackley, M. (1977), *Rocks and Man*, London: Allen & Unwin.

3. Plenderleith and Werner (1971), pp. 299–333.

4. Shepard, W. (1972), *Flint; its Origins, Properties and Uses*, London: Faber & Faber.

5. Amoroso, C. G. and Fassina, V. (1983), *Stone Decay and Conservation: Atmospheric Pollution, Cleaning, Consolidation and Protection*, Amsterdam: Elsevier; Larson, J. (1982), 'A museum approach to the techniques of stone

conservation', in K. Gauri and J. A. Gwinn (eds), *Proc. 4th Int. Congr. on Deterioration and Conservation of Stone*, Louisville, KT: University Press, pp. 219–38; Domaslowski, W. (1982), *La Conservation Préroutine de la Pierre*, Paris: Unesco.

6. Bradley, S. M. and Hanna, S. B., 'The effect of soluble salt movements on the conservation of an Egyptian limestone standing figure', in IIC (1986), pp. 57–61.

7. Ashurst, J. (1984) 'The cleaning and treatment of limestone by the lime method: Part I', *Monumentum* 47: 233–52; Price, C. A. and Ross, K. D. (1984), 'Part II', *Monumentum* 47: 301–12.

8. Bradley, S. M., 'Evaluation of organo silanes for use in consolidation of sculpture displayed indoors', in Felix (1985), pp. 759–69; Larson (1982) (op. cit., ref. 5).

9. Oddy, W. A. and Lane, H. (1976), 'The conservation of waterlogged shale', *Studies in Conservation* 2: 63–6.

10. Plenderleith and Werner (1971), p. 325.

11. Blake, N. E. (1947), *Ancient Roman Construction in Italy from the Prehistoric Period to Augustus*, Washington: Carnegie Institute; Davey, N. A. (1961), *A History of Building Materials*, London: Phoenix House.

12. Davey, N. and Ling, R. (1982), *Wallpainting in Roman Britain*, Gloucester: A. Sutton; Mora *et al.* (1984); Gettens, R. and Stout, G. (1966), *Painting Materials*, New York: Dover; Thompson, D. V. (1956), *The Materials and Techniques of Medieval Painting*, New York: Dover

13. ICCROM (1983); Neal, D., 'Floor mosaics', in Strong and Brown (1976), pp. 241–52.

14. Warren, S. E., 'Buildings in the raw: an analytical approach to the study of raw materials', in Phillips (1985), pp. 13–16.

15. Mora, P., 'Conservation of excavated intonaco, stucco and mosaics', in Stanley Price (1984), pp. 97–108.

16. Torraca, G. (1984), 'Environmental protection of mural paintings in caves', in *Proc. 7th Int. Symp. on Conservation and Restoration of Cultural Property – conservation and restoration of mural paintings I*, Tokyo: National Research Institute of Cultural Properties, pp. 1–18.

17. Stubbs, J., 'Protection and presentation of excavated structures', in Stanley Price (1984), pp. 79–86; ICCROM (1983); ICCROM (1985).

18. Mora *et al.* (1984); Barov, Z., 'Recent developments in mosaic lifting techniques and new supports for removed floor mosaics', in ICCROM (1985), pp. 163–83; International Committee for Mosaics (1980); Pye, E. (1984), 'The treatment of excavated fragmentary wall plaster', in *Proc. 7th Int. Symp. on Conservation and Restoration of Cultural Property – conservation and restoration of mural paintings I*, Tokyo: National Research Institute of Cultural Properties, pp. 179–95; ICCROM (1983); Sturge, T. (1986), 'The reassembly and display of fallen Roman wallplaster from Leicester', *The Conservator* 10: 37–43; Sturge, T. (1987), 'Polyester based supports for mosaics', *Conservation News* 32: 18–19; Miller, E., Lee, N., and Ellam, D., 'Remounting and conservation of archaeological wallpaintings', in Black (1987), pp. 289–96; Tubb, K., 'The lime plaster figurines from 'Ain Ghazal', in Black (1987), pp. 387–92.

19. Pye (1984) (op. cit., ref. 18).

20. Mora (1984) (op. cit., ref. 15).

21. Newton and Davison (1989).

22. Frank, S. (1982), *Glass in Archaeology*, London: Academic Press; Vose,

R. H. (1986), *Glass*, London: Collins.

23. Newton, R. G. (1980), 'Recent views on ancient glass', *Glass Technology* 21: 173–83.
24. Hughes, M., 'Enamels: materials, deterioration and analysis', in Bacon and Knight (1987), pp. 10–12.
25. Biek, L. and Bayley, J. (1979), 'Glass and other vitreous materials', *World Archaeology* 11: 1–25; Tite, M. and Bimson, M., 'Identification of early vitreous material' in Black (1987), pp. 81–6.
26. Newton and Davison (1989); Newton, R. G. (1985), 'The durability of glass: a review', *Glass Technology* 26: 21–38.
27. Gwinnet, J. and Gorelick, L. (1983), 'An innovative method to investigate the technique of finishing an ancient glass artefact', *Journal of Glass Studies* 25: 249–56.
28. Frank (1982) (op. cit., ref. 22); Hughes (1987) (op. cit., ref. 24).
29. Hunter, K. and Foley, K., 'The Lincoln hanging-bowl', in Bacon and Knight (1987), pp. 16–18.
30. Plenderleith and Werner (1971), p. 345.
31. Hunter, K., 'The Friars' Park Window: excavation and reconstruction of a 13th century window', in ICOM (1987), pp. 989–96.
32. Newton and Davison (1989); Fisher, P. and Norman, K., 'A new approach to the reconstruction of two Anglo-Saxon glass claw beakers', *Studies in Conservation* 32 (1987), 49–58.
33. Hodges (1976), p. 21; Lawrence, W. G. (1972), *Ceramic Science for the Potter*, Radnor, PA: Chilton; Shepard, A. O. (1965), *Ceramics for the Archaeologist*, 6th printing, Carnegie Institute: Washington, DC.
34. Davison, S. and Harrison, P. (1987), 'Refiring archaeological ceramics', *The Conservator* 11: 34–7.
35. Biek (1963), p. 168.
36. Evans, J. (1983–4), 'Identification of organic residues in ceramics', *Experimental Firing Group Bulletin* 2: 82–5.
37. Olin, J. and Franklin, M. (eds) (1982), *Archaeological Ceramics*, Washington, DC: Smithsonian Institution; Tite, M. S., Freestone, I. C., Meeks, N. D., and Craddock, P. T., 'The examination of refractory ceramics from metal production and metalworking sites', in Phillips (1985), pp. 50–5.
38. Olive, J. and Pearson, C., 'The conservation of ceramics from marine archaeological sources', in IIC (1975), pp. 63–8; Hodges, H. W. M., 'Conservation treatment of ceramics in the field', in Hodges (1987), pp. 144–9.
39. Larsen, J. (1980), 'The conservation of terracottas', *The Conservator* 6: 38–45.
40. Taylor, S. (1987), 'Consolidation of earthenware', *Conservation News* 33: 24–5.
41. Plenderleith and Werner (1971), p. 327.
42. Larney, J. (1978), *Restoring Ceramics*, 2nd edn, London: Barrie & Jenkins; Mibach, E., 'Restoration of coarse archaeological ceramics', in IIC (1975), pp. 55–62; Williams, N. (1983), *Porcelain Repair and Restoration*, London: British Museum.
43. Plenderleith and Werner (1971), pp. 341–2.

5 Metals

1. Tylecote, R. (1986), *The Prehistory of Metallurgy in the British Isles*, London: Institute of Metals; Tylecote, R. (1976), *A History of Metallurgy*, London: The Metals Society.
2. France-Lanord, A. (1980), *Ancient Metals: Structure and Characteristics*, Rome: ICCROM; Norton, J. T. (1970), 'Metallography and the study of art objects', in W. Young (ed.), *Application of Science to the Examination of Works of Art II*, Boston: Museum of Fine Arts, pp. 13–19; Stanley Smith, C., 'The introduction of microstructures of metallic artefacts', ibid., pp. 20–52; Scott (1987).
3. Lechtman, H. and Steinberg, A. (1970), 'Bronze joining: a study of ancient technology', in S. Doeringer, D. G. Mitten, and A. Steinberg (eds), *Art and Technology: a Symposium on Classical Bronzes*, Cambridge, MA: MIT Press, pp. 5–36; Fell, V. (1982), 'Ancient fluxes for soldering and brazing', *MASCA Journal* 2: 82–5.
4. Untracht, O. (1968), *Metal Techniques for Craftsmen*, London: Robert Hale.
5. Oddy, W. A. (1977), 'Gilding and tinning in Anglo-Saxon England', in W. A. Oddy (ed.), *Aspects of Early Metallurgy*, London: Historical Metallurgy Society and British Museum, pp. 129–34.
6. Oddy (1977) (op. cit., ref. 5); Scott, D. A. (1976), 'Gold and silver alloy coatings over copper – an examination of some artefacts from Ecuador and Colombia', *Archaeometry* 28: (1): 33–50.
7. Oddy, W. A., Bimson, M., and LaNiece, S. (1983), 'The composition of niello decoration on gold, silver and bronze in the antique and medieval periods', *Studies in Conservation* 28: 29–35.
8. Bateson, J. D. (1981), *Enamel-working in Iron Age, Roman and Sub-Roman Britain*, Oxford: British Archaeological Reports 93.
9. Evans, U. R. (1981), *Introduction to Metallic Corrosion*, 3rd edn, London: Arnold; Scully, J. C. (1975), *The Fundamentals of Corrosion*, 2nd edn, Oxford: Pergamon; Stambolov (1985).
10. Pourbaix, M., 'Electrochemical corrosion and reduction', in Brown *et al.* (1977), pp. 1–16.
11. Fabrizi, M. and Scott, D. A., 'Unusual copper corrosion products and problems of identity', in Black (1987), pp. 131–4.
12. Cronyn, J., Pye, E., and Watson, J., 'Recognition and identification of organic materials in association with metal artefacts', in Phillips (1985), pp. 24–7; Edwards, G., in Janaway and Scott (1989), pp. 3–7.
13. Plenderleith and Werner (1971), pp. 197–200.
14. Skerry, B., 'How corrosion inhibitors work', in Keene (1985), pp. 5–12; Turgoose, S., 'Corrosion inhibitors for conservation' in Keene (1985), pp. 13–17.
15. Tylecote (1986) and (1976) (op. cit., ref. 1).
16. Tylecote, R. and Black, J. (1980), 'The effect of hydrogen reduction on the properties of ferrous materials', *Studies in Conservation* 25: 87–96; Ehrenreich, R. and Strahan, D., 'Effects of boiling on the quenched steel structure of martensite', in Black (1987), pp. 125–31.
17. Manning, W. H., 'Blacksmithing', in Strong and Brown (1976), pp. 143–54; Tylecote, R., 'The medieval smith and his methods', in Crossley (1981), pp. 42–50.
18. Corfield, M., 'Tinning of iron', in Miles and Pollard (1986), pp. 40–3.
19. Cronyn *et al.* (1985) (op. cit., ref. 12); Edwards (1989) (op. cit., ref. 12).
20. Keepax, C. (1975), 'Scanning electron microscopy of wood replaced by iron

corrosion products', *Journal of Archaeological Science* 2: 145–50.

21. Organ, R. M., 'The current status of the treatment of corroded metal artefacts', in Brown *et al.* (1977), pp. 107–42.

22. Robinson (1981b).

23. Fell, V. (1985), 'Examination of an Iron Age metalworking file from Gussage', *Dorset Proc.* 107: 176–8.

24. Corfield, M., 'Radiography of archaeological ironwork', in Clarke and Blackshaw (1982), pp. 8–12.

25. Scott, B., 'The retrieval of technological information from corrosion products in early wrought iron artefacts', in Janaway and Scott (1989), pp. 8–14; Tylecote and Black (1980) (op. cit., ref. 16).

26. Hamilton, D. L. (1976), *Conservation of Metal Objects from Underwater Sites: a Study in Methods*, Austin, TX: Memorial Museum.

27. Watkinson, D. (1983), 'Degree of mineralisation: its significance for treatment and stability of excavated ironwork', *Studies in Conservation* 28: 185–90.

28. Turgoose, S., 'The nature of surviving iron objects', in Clarke and Blackshaw (1982), pp. 1–7.

29. Gilberg, M. R. and Seeley, N. J. (1981), 'The identity of compounds containing chloride ions in marine iron corrosion products: a critical review', *Studies in Conservation* 26: 50–6.

30. Knight, B., 'Why do some iron objects break up in store?', in Clarke and Blackshaw (1982), pp. 50–1.

31. Stambolov, T., 'Introduction to the conservation of ferrous and non-ferrous metals', in SSCR (1979), pp. 10–14.

32. Turgoose, S. (1982), 'Post-excavation changes in iron antiquities', *Studies in Conservation* 27: 97–101.

33. Rinuy, A. and Schweizer, F., 'Application of the alkaline-sulphite treatment to archaeological iron: a comparative study of different desalination methods', in Clarke and Blackshaw (1982), pp. 44–9; Gilberg, M. (1985), 'The storage of archaeological iron under deoxygenated conditions', *ICOM Committee for Conservation, Metal Working Group Newsletter* 1: 3.

34. Spriggs, J., 'The Coppergate helmet: a holding operation', in Keene (1985), p. 33.

35. Turgoose, S. (1985), 'The corrosion of archaeological iron during burial and treatment', *Studies in Conservation* 30: 13–18.

36. Pearson, C. (1977), 'On the conservation requirements for marine archaeological excavations', *International Journal of Nautical Archaeology* 6: 37–46.

37. McCawley, J. C., 'Current research into the corrosion of archaeological iron', in ICOM (1984a), pp. 84.22.25–7; Gilberg and Seeley (1981) (op. cit., ref. 29); Turgoose (1982) (op. cit., ref. 28).

38. Scott, B. A. and Seeley, N. J. (1987), 'The washing of fragile iron artefacts', *Studies in Conservation* 32: 73–6.

39. Argo, J. and Turgoose, S., 'Amines for iron: a discussion', in Keene (1985), pp. 31–2; McCawley (1984) (op. cit., ref. 37).

40. North, N. A. and Pearson, C., 'Alkaline sulfite reduction treatment of marine iron', in ICOM (1975), pp. 75/13/3, 1–14.

41. Gilberg, N. R. and Seeley, N. J. (1982), 'The alkaline sodium sulphite reduction process for archaeological iron: a closer look', *Studies in Conservation* 27: 180–4.

42. Wihr, R., 'Electrolytic desalination of archaeological iron', in IIC (1975), pp. 189–93.

43. North, N. A. and Pearson, C. (1978), 'Washing methods for chloride removal from marine iron artefacts', *Studies in Conservation* 23: 174–86.
44. Ankner, D. (1982), 'Entsalzen von Eisenfunden mit organischen Lösungsmitteln', *Arbeitsblätter für Restauratoren* 19: (1): 212.
45. Turgoose (1985) (op. cit., ref. 14).
46. Barker, B. O., Kendell, K., and O'Shea, C. 'The hydrogen reduction process for the conservation of ferrous objects', in Clarke and Blackshaw (1982), pp. 23–7; Barkman, L., 'Conservation of rusty iron objects by hydrogen reduction', in Brown *et al.* (1977), pp. 155–66; Jakobsen, T., 'Iron conservation at the National Museum of Denmark – past and present', in ICOM (1984a), pp. 84.22.8–10.
47. Tylecote and Black (1980) (op. cit., ref. 16).
48. Duncan, S. and Ganiaris, H., 'Some sulphide corrosion products on copper and lead alloys from London waterfront sites', in Black (1987), pp. 109–18.
49. Turgoose, S., 'The corrosion of lead and tin: before and after excavation', in Miles and Pollard (1986), pp. 15–26.
50. Lane, H., 'Some comparisons of lead conservation methods including consolidative reduction', in SSCR (1979), pp. 50–60; Organ (1977) (op. cit., ref. 21).
51. Watson, J., 'Conservation of lead and lead alloys using EDTA solutions', in Miles and Pollard (1986), pp. 44–6.
52. Mattias, P., Maura, G., and Rinaldi, G. (1984), 'The degradation of lead antiquities from Italy', *Studies in Conservation* 29: 87–92.
53. Brown, D., 'The making of pewter tableware in Roman times', in Miles and Pollard (1986), pp. 9–14.
54. Leidheiser, H. (1971), *Corrosion of Copper, Tin and their Alloys*, New York: Wiley.
55. Organ (1977) (op. cit., ref. 21).
56. Charles, J. A. (1975), 'Where is the tin?', *Antiquity* XLIX: 19–24.
57. Plenderleith, H. J. and Organ, C. (1952), 'Decay and conservation of museum objects of tin', *Studies in Conservation* 1: 63–72; Turgoose (1986) (op. cit., ref. 49).
58. Coghlan, H. H. (1975), *Notes on the Prehistoric Metallurgy of Copper and Bronze in the Old World*, Occasional Papers on Technology no. 4, 2nd edn., Oxford: Pitt Rivers Museum; Lewin, S. and Alexander, S. (1967), 'Composition and structure of copper and copper alloys: a bibliography', *Art and Archaeological Technical Abstracts* 6: 4: 201–83 and 7: 1: 278–370; Tylecote (1986) (op. cit., ref. 1).
59. Oddy, A. W. and Bimson, M., 'Tinned bronze in antiquity', in Miles and Pollard (1986), pp. 33–9.
60. Weil, P. D., 'A review of the history and practice of patination', in Brown *et al.* (1977), pp. 77–92.
61. Chase, W. T. (with others), 'Structural questions 1–11', in Brown *et al.* (1977), pp. 191–216; Oddy, W. M. and Meeks, N. D., 'Unusual phenomena in the corrosion of ancient bronzes', in IIC (1982), pp. 119–24; Organ, R. M., 'The conservation of bronze objects', in Doeringer *et al.* (1970) (op. cit., ref. 3), pp. 73–84; Gettens, R. J., 'Patina: noble and vile', in Doeringer *et al.* (1970) (op. cit., ref. 3), pp. 57–72.
62. Duncan and Ganiaris (1987) (op. cit., ref. 48).
63. Borrelli, L. V., 'Les alterations des bronzes antiques en milieu marin' in ICOM (1975), pp. 75/13/1, 1–8; Campbell, H. S. and Mills, D. J. (1977), 'Marine treasure trove; a metallurgical examination', *Metallurgist and Materials Technologist* 9: 551–7; MacLeod, I. D. (1982), 'Formation of

marine concretions on copper and its alloys', *International Journal of Nautical Archaeology* 11: 131–63.
64. Chase, W. T. (1978), 'Solid samples from metallic antiquities and their examination', in *Proc. Int. Symp. on the Conservation and Renovation of Cultural Property*, Tokyo: National Research Institute of Cultural Properties, pp. 73–109; Organ (1970) (op. cit., ref. 3).
65. Oddy and Meeks (1982) (op. cit., ref. 61); Scott, D. A. (1985) 'Periodic phenomena in bronze antiquities', *Studies in Conservation* 30: 48–57.
66. Leidheiser (1971) (op. cit., ref. 54).
67. Tylecote (1986) (op. cit., ref. 1), p. 40.
68. Jakes, K. A. and Sibley, L. R. (1985), 'An examination of the phenomenon of textile fabric pseudomorphism', in J. B. Lambert (ed.), *Archaeological Chemistry*, Washington, DC: American Chemical Society, pp. 404–24.
69. Seeley, N. J., 'Aims and limitations in the conservation of coins', in Casey and Cronyn (1980), pp. 5–9.
70. Meek, L. E. (1978), 'A study of reagents used for the stripping of bronzes', *Studies in Conservation* 23: 15–22.
71. Casey and Cronyn (1980).
72. Organ (1970 and 1977) (op. cit., refs 61 and 21).
73. Madsen, H. B. (1967), 'A preliminary note on the use of benzotriazole for stabilising bronze objects', *Studies in Conservation* 12: 163–7; Sease, C. (1978), 'Benzotriazole: a review for conservators', *Studies in Conservation* 23: 76–85; Walker, R., 'The role of benzotriazole in the preservation of antiquities', in SSCR (1979), pp. 40–9.
74. Weisser, T. D., 'The use of sodium carbonate as a pre-treatment for difficult-to-stabilize bronzes', in Black (1987), pp. 105–8.
75. Erhardt, D., Hopwood, W., and Padfield, T., 'The durability of Incralac', in ICOM (1984a), pp. 84.22.1–3.
76. Weisser, T. D., 'The dealloying of copper alloys', in IIC (1975), pp. 207–14.
77. Knauth, P. (1974), *The Metalsmiths*, The Netherlands, Time–Life; Maryon, H. (1971), *Metalwork and Enamelling*, 5th edn, New York: Dover.
78. Hedges, R. E. M. (1976), 'On the occurrence of bromine in corroded silver', *Studies in Conservation* 21: 44–6; Plenderleith and Werner (1971), pp. 219–41; Spriggs (1980).
79. MacLeod, I. D. and North, N. A. (1979), 'Conservation of corroded silver', *Studies in Conservation* 24: 165–70.
80. Bradley, S., 'Testing anti-tarnish preparations', in Keene (1985), pp. 21–2.
81. Organ, R. M. (1965), 'Reclamation of wholly mineralised silver in the lyre from Ur', in *Application of Science in the Examination of Works of Art*, Boston: Research Laboratory, Museum of Fine Arts, pp. 126–44.
82. Knauth (1974) (op. cit., ref. 77).
83. Craddock, P. (1982), 'Corinthian bronze: Rome's purple sheen gold', *MASCA Journal* 2: 40–1.
84. Scott, D. A. (1983), 'The deterioration of gold alloys and some aspects of their conservation', *Studies in Conservation* 28: 194–203.

6 Organic materials

1. Brown, C. H. (1971), *Structural Materials in Animals*, London: Pitman; Dimbleby (1978); Mills (1987).
2. Grattan, D. W. (1980), 'The oxidative degradation of organic materials and

its importance in the deterioration of artefacts', *Journal of IIC–Canadian Group* 4: 1: 17–26.

3. Ambrose, W. R. (1978), 'Natural causes in the deterioration of buried archaeological material', in F. McCarthy (ed.), *Aboriginal Antiquities in Australia*, *Australian Aboriginal Studies* 22: 109–13.

4. Brothwell, D. (1980), *The Bogman and the Archaeology of People*, London: British Museum; Boddington *et al.* (1987).

5. *Frozen Tombs: the Culture and Art of the Ancient Tribes of Siberia* (1978), London: British Museum.

6. Reed (1972), pp. 187–97.

7. Hall (1984).

8. Millett, M. and McGrail, S. (1987), 'The archaeology of the Hasholme logboat', *Archaeological Journal* 144: 69–155.

9. Seaward, N. (1976), *The Vindolanda Environment*, Haltwhistle: Barcombe.

10. French, C. and Taylor, M. (1985), 'Desiccation and destruction: the effect of dewatering at Etton, Cambs.', *Oxford Journal of Archaeology* 4: 139–56.

11. Cronyn, J., Pye, E., and Watson, J., 'Recognition and identification of organic materials in association with metal artefacts', in Phillips (1985), pp. 24–7.

12. Taylor, M. (1981), *Wood in Archaeology*, Princes Risborough: Shire; Hodges (1976); Edlin, H. L. (1973), *Woodland Crafts in Britain*, Newton Abbot: David & Charles.

13. Stamm, A. J., 'Wood deterioration and its prevention', in IIC (1971) 2: 1–12; Brommelle, N. and Werner, A. E. A., 'Deterioration and treatment of wood', in ICOM (1969), pp. 69–118.

14. Barkman, L., 'The preservation of the warship Wasa', in Oddy (1975), pp. 65–106; Florian, M.-L. E. and McCawley, J. C. (1977), 'Microscopic analysis of some woods from marine wrecks', in *Papers from 1st Southern Hemisphere Conf. on Maritime Archaeology*, pp. 128–43; Levey, J. F. (1977), 'Degradation of wood', in S. McGrail (ed.), *Sources and Techniques in Boat Archaeology*, Oxford: British Archaeological Reports suppl. ser. 29: 15–22.

15. French and Taylor (1985) (op. cit., ref. 10); Orme, B. J. (1982), 'Prehistoric woodlands and woodworking in the Somerset Levels', in S. McGrail (ed.), *Woodworking Techniques before 1500 AD*, Oxford: British Archaeological Reports int. ser. 129: 79–94.

16. Dimbleby (1978), p. 103.

17. Murdock, L. D., Newton, C., and Daley, T., 'Underwater moulding techniques on waterlogged ships' timbers employing various products including liquid polysulphide rubber', Abstract in Grattan and McCawley (1982), pp. 39–40; Oddy, W. A. and Van Gearsdaele, P. C. (1972), 'The recovery of the Graveney boat', *Studies in Conservation* 17: 30–8.

18. Blackshaw, S. (1976), 'Comments on the examination and treatment of waterlogged wood based on work carried out during the period 1972–1976 at the British Museum', in G. Grosso (ed.), *Pacific Northwest Wet-site Wood Conservation Conf.*, Neah Bay, WA, vol. I, pp. 27–36.

19. Jespersen, K. (1985), 'Extended storage of waterlogged wood in nature', in CETBGE (1985), pp. 39–54.

20. Watson, J., 'Suitability of waterlogged wood from British excavations for conservation by freeze-drying', in Black (1987), pp. 273–6.

21. Dawson, J., Ravindra, K., and Lafontaine, R. H., 'A review of storage methods for waterlogged wood', in Grattan and McCawley (1982), pp. 227–35, including discussion.

22. Schweizer, F., Houriet, C., and Mas, M., 'Controlled air drying of large

Roman timber from Geneva', in CETBGE (1985), pp. 327–38.
23. Stamm (1971) (op. cit., ref. 13).
24. Hickin, N., 'Insect damage to wood in the decorative arts: a world problem', in IIC (1978), pp. 19–22.
25. Serck-Dewaide, M., 'Deinfestation and consolidation of polychromed wood at the Institut Royal du Patrimoine Artistique, Brussels', in IIC (1978), pp. 81–4.
26. McCawley, J. C. (1977), 'Waterlogged artefacts: the challenge to conservation', *Journal of Canadian Conservation Institute* 2: 17–26.
27. Pearson, C., 'The use of polyethylene glycol for the treatment of waterlogged wood: its past, present and future', in de Vries-Zuiderbaan (1981), pp. 51–6.
28. Blackshaw (1976) (op. cit., ref. 18).
29. Christensen (1970).
30. Barkman (1975) (op. cit., ref. 14).
31. Clarke, R. W. and Gregson, C., 'A large-scale polyethylene glycol conservation facility for waterlogged wood at the National Maritime Museum', in ICOM (1987), pp. 301–8.
32. Hoffman, P. (1986), 'On the stabilization of waterlogged oakwood with PEG II: designing a two-step treatment for multi-quality timber', *Studies in Conservation* 31: 103–13.
33. Parrent, J. M. (1985), 'The conservation of waterlogged wood using sucrose', *Studies in Conservation* 30: 63–72.
34. Hillman, D. and Florian, M.-L. E. (1985), 'A simple conservation treatment for wet archaeological wood', *Studies in Conservation* 30: 39–41.
35. Bryce, T., McKerrell, H., and Varsanyi, A., 'The acetone–rosin method for the conservation of waterlogged wood', in Oddy (1975), pp. 35–44.
36. Jespersen, K., 'Some problems using TEOS for conservation of waterlogged wood', in Grattan and McCawley (1982), pp. 203–7.
37. Ambrose, W. R. (1976), 'Sublimation drying of degraded wet wood', in G. Grosso (ed.), *Pacific Northwest Wet-site Wood Conservation Conf.*, Neah Bay, WA, vol. I, pp. 7–16; Rosenqvist, A. M., 'Experiments in the conservation of waterlogged wood and leather by freeze-drying', in Oddy (1975), pp. 9–24; Watson (1987) (op. cit., ref. 20); Watson, J., 'Research into aspects of freeze-drying hardwoods between 1982 and 1984', in CETBGE (1985), pp. 213–18.
38. Grattan, D. W., McCawley, J. C., and Cook, C. (1978 and 1980), 'Potential of the Canadian winter for freeze-drying wood, Parts I and II', *Studies in Conservation* 23: 157–67 and 25: 118–36.
39. Christensen (1970).
40. Coles (1984); Lucas, D. A., 'On-site packing and protection of wet and waterlogged wood', in Grattan and McCawley (1982), pp. 51–5; Spriggs (1980).
41. Haines, B. M. (1981), *The Fibre Structure of Leather*, London: Leather Conservation Centre; Reed (1972); Stambolov (1969); Waterer, J. W., 'Leatherwork', in Strong and Brown (1976), pp. 179–94.
42. Dimbleby (1978), p. 49.
43. Waterer, J. W. (1972), *A Guide to the Conservation and Restoration of Objects made Wholly or in Part of Leather*, London: Bell, p. 8.
44. Doughty, P. S. (ed.) (1973), 'Excavated Shoes to 1600', *Transactions of the Museums Assistants Group*, no. 12; Reed (1972); Stambolov (1969).
45. Swallow, A. W., 'Interpretation of wearmarks seen in footwear', in Doughty (1973) (op. cit., ref. 44), pp. 28–32.
46. Biek (1963), p. 249; Plenderleith and Werner (1971), p. 29.

47. Goubitz, O. (1984), 'The drawing and registration of archaeological footwear', *Studies in Conservation* 29: 187–96; Gritten, P. (1975), *Hides and Leather under the Microscope*, Egham: British Leather Manufacturers' Association; Haines (1981) (op. cit., ref. 41); Reed (1972).

48. Van Dienst, E. (1985), 'Some remarks on the conservation of wet archaeological leather', *Studies in Conservation* 30: 86–92; Goubitz (1984) (op. cit., ref. 47).

49. Schaffer, E. (1974), 'Properties and preservation of ethnographic semi-tanned leather', *Studies in Conservation* 19: 66–75; Vandyke-Lee, D. J. (1976), 'The conservation of tandu', *Studies in Conservation* 21: 74–8.

50. Stambolov (1969); Tuck, D. H. (1985), *Oils and Lubricants used on Leather*, Northampton: Leather Conservation Centre.

51. Morrison, L. (1986), 'The conservation of seal-gut parkas', *The Conservator* 10: 17–24; Raphael, T. and McGrady, E., 'Leather dressing – a misguided tradition?', in ICOM (1984a), pp. 84.18.6–8; Van Soest, H. A. B., Stambolov, T., and Hallebeck, P. B. (1984), 'Conservation of leather', *Studies in Conservation* 29: 21–31.

52. Ganiaris, H., Keene, S., and Starling, K. (1982), 'A comparison of some treatments for excavated leather', *The Conservator* 6: 12–23; Van Dienst (1985) (op. cit., ref. 48).

53. Peacock, E. E., 'Archaeological skin material', in Hodges (1987), pp. 122–31.

54. Macgregor, A. (1985), *Bone, Antler, Ivory and Horn: the Technology of Skeletal Materials since the Roman Period*, London: Croom Helm; Penniman, T. K. (1971), *Pictures of Ivory and other Animal Teeth, Bone and Antler*, Occasional Papers on Technology no. 5, Oxford: Pitt Rivers Museum; Penderleith and Werner (1971), pp. 148–51; O'Connor, T. P., 'On the structure, chemistry and decay of bone, antler and ivory' in Starling and Watkinson (1987), pp. 6–8; Creep, S. J., 'Use of bone antler and ivory in the Roman and medieval periods', in Starling and Watkinson (1987), pp. 3–5.

55. Brothwell, D. R. (1981), *Digging Up Bones*, 3rd edn, London: British Museum, Natural History; Chaplin, R. E. (1971), *The Study of Animal Bones from Archaeological Sites*, London: Seminar Press; Coy, J. (1978), *First Aid for Animal Bones*, Hertford: Rescue.

56. O'Connor, S., 'The identification of osseous and keratinaceous materials at York', in Starling and Watkinson (1987), pp. 9–21; O'Connor (1987) (op. cit., ref. 54); Beeley, J. G. and Lunt, D. A. (1980), 'The nature of the biochemical changes in softened dentine from archaeological sites', *Journal of Archaeological Science* 7: 371–7; Refs 55.

57. O'Connor, S. (1987) (op. cit., ref. 56).

58. Penniman (1971) (op. cit., ref. 54).

59. Matienzo, L. and Snow, C. E. (1986), 'The chemical effects of hydrochloric acid and organic solvents on the surface of ivory', *Studies in Conservation* 31: 133–9.

60. Tennent, N. H. and Baird, T. (1985), 'The deterioration of mollusca collections', *Studies in Conservation* 30: 73–85.

61. Koob, S. P., 'The consolidation of archaeological bone', in IIC (1984), pp. 98–102; Plenderleith and Werner (1971), p. 152; Snow, C. E. and Weisser, T. D., 'The examination and treatment of ivory and related material', in IIC (1984), pp. 141–5; Bunn, M., 'SARAN as a treatment for bone', in Starling and Watkinson (1987), pp. 28–33.

62. Macgregor (1985) (op. cit., ref. 54); O'Connor, S. (1987) (op. cit., ref. 56).

63. Petersen, K. S. and Sommer-Larsen, A., 'Cleaning of early feather garments

from South America and Hawaii', in ICOM (1984a), pp. 84.'3.13–16.

64. Geijer, A. (1979), *A History of Textile Art*, London: Pasold Research Foundation, Sotheby Parke Bernet; Landi (1985); Lewis, N. (1974), *Papyrus, in Classical Antiquity*, Oxford: Clarendon; Wild, J. P., 'Textiles', in Strong and Brown (1976), pp. 167–8.

65. Diehl, J. M., 'Natural dyestuffs', in Leene (1972), pp. 23–31.

66. Hueck, H. J., 'Textile pests and their control', in Leene (1972), pp. 76–97; Vigo, T. L., 'Protection of textiles from biodeterioration', in Pertegato (1980), pp. 18–26.

67. Taylor, G. W. (1983), 'Detection and identification of dyes on Anglo-Scandinavian textiles', *Studies in Conservation* 28: 153–60; Walton, P. and Eastwood, G. (1983), *The Cataloguing of Archaeological Textiles*, York: Walton and Eastwood.

68. Rice, J. W., 'Principles of fragile textile cleaning', in Leene (1972), pp. 32–72; Geijer (1979) (op. cit., ref. 64).

69. Bengtsson, S., 'Preservation of the Wasa sails', in IIC (1975), pp. 33–6.

70. Hofenk de Graaff, J. H., 'Hydroxypropyl cellulose; a multi-purpose conservation material', in ICOM (1981), pp. 81.14.9.1–7; Geijer (1979) (op. cit., ref. 64).

71. Finch, K., 'Changing attitudes – new developments – full circle', in Pertegato (1980), pp. 82–6; Geijer, A., 'Preservation of textile objects', in IIC (1963), pp. 185–9; Masschelein-Kleiner, L. and Bergiers, F., 'Influence of adhesives on the conservation of textiles', in IIC (1984), pp. 70–3.

72. Morrison, L., 'The treatment, mounting and storage of a large group of archaeological textile fragments', in ICOM (1987), pp. 391–6.

73. Bengtsson (1975) (op. cit., ref. 69).

74. Schaffer, E. (1976), 'Preservation and restoration of Canadian ethnographic basketry', *Studies in Conservation* 21: 129–33.

75. Irwin, H. T. and Wessen, G. (1976), 'A new method for the preservation of waterlogged archaeological remains', in G. Grosso (ed.), *Pacific Northwest Wet-Site Wood Conservation Conf.*, Neah Bay, WA, vol. I, pp. 49–59; Jespersen (1982) (op. cit., ref. 36).

76. Beck, C., 'Authentification and conservation of amber: a conflict of interests', in IIC (1982), pp. 104–7.

Bibliography

The literature devoted to archaeological conservation is not extensive; there are no existing textbooks specifically on this subject. The Bibliography aims to list those items which are of special relevance to conservation in archaeology in terms of technology, deterioration, and treatment. It incorporates key papers and conference proceedings wholly devoted to archaeological conservation as well as texts and proceedings which contain substantial reference to this topic. As noted in the Preface, conservation is a subject which is rapidly developing, which means that, sadly, much material published a number of years ago contains ideas and methods which have now been superseded. New developments are often only published in articles and some may not even have reached this stage. Thus it is essential to exercise extreme caution when consulting older texts which includes some published no earlier than 1982.

Ambrose, W. R. (1973) 'Conservation in field archaeology. Does it exist?', in C. Pearson and G. L. Pretty (eds) *Proc. National Seminar on Conservation of Cultural Materials*, Perth: ICCM, pp. 221–2

Bacon, L. and Knight, B. (eds) (1987) *From Pinheads to Hanging Bowls: the Identification, Deterioration and Conservation of Applied Enamel and Glass on Archaeological Objects*, Occasional Paper no. 7, London: UKIC

Biek, L. (1963) *Archaeology and the Microscope*, London: Lutterworth

Black, J. (compiler) (1987) *Recent Advances in the Conservation and Analysis of Artefacts*, Jubilee Conservation Conference Papers, London: Summer Schools Press, University of London, Institute of Archaeology

Boddington, A., Garland, N., and Janaway, R. (eds) (1987) *Death, Decay and Reconstruction*, Manchester: Manchester University Press

Brown, B. F., Burnett, H. C., Chase, W. T., Goodway, M., Kruger, J., and Poubaix, M. (eds) (1977) *Corrosion and Metal Artefacts*, Special publication 179, Washington, D.C.: National Bureau of Standards

Casey, P. J. and Cronyn, J. M. (eds) (1980) *Numismatics and Conservation*, Occasional Paper 1, Durham: University of Durham, Dept. of Archaeology

CETBGE (1985) *Waterlogged Wood: Study and Conservation, Proc. 2nd ICOM Waterlogged Wood Working Group Conf.*, Grenoble: Centre d'étude et de traitement des bois gorgés d'eau

Christensen, B. B. (1970) *The Conservation of Waterlogged Wood in the National Museum of Denmark*, Studies in Museum Technology, no. 1, Copenhagen: The National Museum of Denmark

Clarke, R. W. and Blackshaw, S. N. (eds) (1982) *Conservation of Iron*, Maritime Monographs and Reports 53, London: National Maritime Museum

Coles, J. (1984) *The Archaeology of Wetlands*, Edinburgh: Edinburgh University Press

Corfield, M. and Foley, K. (eds) (1982) *Microscopy in Archaeological Conservation*, Occasional Paper no. 2, London: UKIC

Crafts Council (1982) *An Introduction to Materials*, Science for Conservators, Book 1, London: Crafts Council

Crafts Council (1983a) *Cleaning*, Science for Conservators, Book 2, London: Crafts Council

Crafts Council (1983b) *Adhesives and Coatings*, Science for Conservators, Book 3, London: Crafts Council

Cronyn, J. M. and Horie, C. V. (1986) *St Cuthbert's Coffin: its History, Technology and Conservation*, Durham: Dean & Chapter, Durham Cathedral

Crossley, D. W. (ed) (1981) *Medieval Industry*, CBA Research Report 40, London: CBA

de Guichen, G. (1984) *Climate in Museums*, 2nd edn, Rome: ICCROM

D of E (1978) *The Scientific Treatment of Materials from Rescue Excavations*, a report by a working party of the Committee for Rescue Archaeology of the Ancient Monuments Boards for England, chaired by G. Dimbleby, London, Department of Environment

de Vries-Zuiderbaan, L. H. (ed) (1981) *Conservation of Waterlogged Wood: Proc. Int. Symp. on the Conservation of Large Objects of Waterlogged Wood*, The Hague: Ministry of Education and Science

Dewitte, E. and Goessens-Landrie, M. (eds) (1976) 'The use of synthetic polymers in conservation: an annotated bibliography', Supplement *Art and Archaeological Technical Abstracts* 13: 1: 201–81; 2: 279–354, London: IIC

Dimbleby, G. (1978) *Plants and Archaeology*, rev. edn, St Albans: Granada-Paladin

Dowman, E. A. (1970) *Conservation in Field Archaeology*, London: Methuen

Feller, R., Stolow, M., and Jones, F. H. (1985) *On Picture Varnishes and their Solvents*, rev. enlarged edn, Cleveland, OH: Case Western University

Felix, G. (ed) (1985) *Proc. 5th Int. Congr. on Deterioration and Conservation of Stone*, Lausanne: Presses Polytechnique Romandes

Foley, K. (1984) 'The role of the conservator in field archaeology', in N. Stanley-Price (ed) *Conservation on Archaeological Excavations*, Rome: ICCROM, pp. 11–20

Goffer, E. (1980) *Archaeological Chemistry: Chemical Analysis*, vol. 55, New York: Wiley

Graham, E. and Eddie, T. (1984) *X-ray Techniques in Art Galleries and Museums*, Bristol: Adam Hilger

Grattan, D. W. and McCawley, J. C. (1982) *Proc. ICOM Waterlogged Wood Working Group Conf.*, Ottawa: ICOM Committee for Conservation, Waterlogged Wood Working Group

Grissom, C. A. and Weiss, N. R. (eds) (1981) 'Alkoxysilanes in the conservation of art and architecture: 1961–1981, an annotated bibliography', Supplement *Art and Archaeological Technical Abstracts*, 18: 1: 150–200

Grosso, G. (1978) 'After excavation – then what?' *Occasional Paper on Method and Theory in Californian Archaeology*, Society for Californian Archaeology, part 2, pp. 53–6

Hall, R. (1984) *The Viking Dig*, London: Bodley Head

Harding, E. (ed) (1985) *A Guide to the Storage, Exhibition and Handling of Antiquities, Ethnographia and Pictorial Art*, London: British Museum Dept. of Conservation

Hodges, H. W. M. (1976) *Artefacts*, rev. edn, London: Baker

313

Hodges, H. W. M. (ed) (1987) In situ *Archaeological Conservation, Proc. Meetings, 6–13 April 1986, Mexico*, Instituto Nacional di Antropologiá e Historia, Mexico and J. Paul Getty Trust: Mexico and Century City, CA

Horie, C. V. (1986) 'Conservation and storage: decorative art', in J. Thompson (ed.), *Manual of Curatorship*, Sevenoaks: Butterworths

Horie, C. V. (1987) *Materials for Conservation*, London: Butterworths

ICCROM (1983) *Mosaics No. 2: Safeguard*, Rome: ICCROM

ICCROM (1985) *Mosaics No. 3: Conservation* in situ, Rome: ICCROM

ICOM (1965) *Problems of Conservation in Museums, Proc. Meeting ICOM Committee for Museum Laboratories and Care of Paintings*, Washington and New York, Paris: Eyrolles (1969)

ICOM (1969) *Preprints 2nd Triennial Meeting, ICOM Committee for Conservation, Amsterdam, 1969*, Paris: ICOM

ICOM (1975) *Preprints 4th Triennial Meeting, ICOM Committee for Conservation, Venice, 1975*, Paris: ICOM

ICOM (1978) *Preprints 5th Triennial Meeting, ICOM Committee for Conservation, Zagreb, 1978*, Paris: ICOM

ICOM (1981) *Preprints 6th Triennial Meeting, ICOM Committee for Conservation, Ottawa, 1981*, Paris: ICOM

ICOM (1984a) *Preprints 7th Triennial Meeting, ICOM Committee for Conservation, Copenhagen, 1984*, Paris: ICOM

ICOM (1984b) *The Conservator–Restorer: a Definition of the Profession*, Conservation Committee, Paris: ICOM

ICOM (1987) *Preprints 8th Triennial Meeting, ICOM Committee for Conservation, Sydney, 1987*, Paris: ICOM

IIC (1963) *Recent Advances in Conservation: Contributions to the Rome Conf.*, 1961, G. Thomson (ed), London: Butterworths

IIC (1971) *Conservation of Stone and Wooden Objects: Preprints of New York Conf., June 1970*, G. Thomson (ed), 2nd edn, Vol. I Stone, Vol. II Wooden Objects, London: IIC

IIC (1975) *Conservation in Archaeology and the Applied Arts: Preprints of the Stockholm Congress, June 1975*, D. Leigh, A. Moncrieff, W. A. Oddy, P. Pratt, N. Brommelle, and P. Smith (eds), London: IIC

IIC (1978) *Conservation of Wood in Painting and the Decorative Arts: Preprints of Oxford Congress, September 1978*, N. Brommelle, A. Moncrieff, and P. Smith (eds), London: IIC

IIC (1982) *Science and Technology in the Service of Conservation: Preprints of Washington Congress, September 1982*, N. Brommelle and G. Thomson (eds), London: IIC

IIC (1984) *Adhesives and Consolidants: Preprints of Paris Congress, September 1984*, N. Brommelle, E. M. Pye, and G. Thomson (eds), London: IIC

IIC (1986) *Case Studies in the Conservation of Stone and Wallpaintings: Preprints of Bologna Congress, September 1986*, N. Brommelle and P. Smith (eds), London: IIC

International Committee for Mosaics (1980) *Mosaics No. 1: Deterioration and Conservation*, Rome: International Committee for Mosaics–ICCROM

Janaway, R. and Scott, B. (eds) (1989) *Evidence Preserved in Corrosion Products*, Occasional Paper no. 8, London UKIC

Keene, S. (ed) (1980) *Conservation, Archaeology and Museums*, Occasional Paper no. 1, London: UKIC

Keene, S. (ed) (1985) *Corrosion Inhibitors in Conservation*, Occasional Paper no. 4, London: UKIC

Kuhn, H. (1986) *Conservation and Restoration of Works of Art and Antiquities*, (part I) trans. A. Trone, Sevenoaks: Butterworths

Landi, S. (1985) *The Textile Conservator's Manual*, Sevenoaks: Butterworths

Larsen, E. B. (1981) *Moulding and Casting of Museum Objects*, Copenhagen: School of Conservation, Royal Danish Academy

Leene, J. E. (ed) (1972) *Textile Conservation*, Sevenoaks: Butterworths

Leigh, D. (1982) 'The selection, conservation and storage of archaeological finds', *Museums Journal* 82: 115–6

Miles, G. and Pollard, S. (eds) (1986) *Lead and Tin: Studies in Conservation and Technology*, Occasional Paper no. 3, London: UKIC

Mills, J. S. (1987) *The Organic Chemistry of Museum Objects*, Sevenoaks: Butterworths

Mora, P., Mora, L., and Phillipot, P. (1984) *Conservation of Wallpaintings*, Sevenoaks: Butterworths

Newton, R. and Davison, S. (eds) (1989) *Conservation of Glass*, Sevenoaks: Butterworths

Oddy, W. A. (ed) (1975) *Problems of the Conservation of Waterlogged Wood*, Maritime Monographs and Reports no. 16, London: National Maritime Museum

Partington-Omar, A. and White, A. J. (eds) (1981) *Archaeological Storage*, Lincoln: Society of Museum Archaeologists

Pearson, C. (1988) *Conservation of Marine Archaeological Objects*, Sevenoaks: Butterworths

Pertegato, F. (ed) (1980) *Conservation and Restoration of Textiles*, Milan: Centro Italiano per lo Studio della Storia Tessuto

Phillips, P. (ed) (1985) *The Archaeologist and the Laboratory*, CBA Research Report 58, London: CBA

Plenderleith, H. J. and Werner, A. E. A. (1971) *The Conservation of Antiquities and Works of Art*, 2nd edn, Oxford: Oxford University Press

Pye, E. M. (1986) 'Conservation and storage: archaeological material', in J. Thompson (ed), *Manual of Curatorship*, Sevenoaks: Butterworths, pp. 203–38

Reed, R. (1972) *Ancient Skins, Parchments and Leathers*, London: Seminar Press

Robinson, W. S. (1981a) *First Aid for Marine Finds*, Handbooks in Maritime Archaeology no. 2, London: National Maritime Museum

Robinson, W. S. (1981b) 'Observations on the preservation of archaeological wrecks and metals in marine environments', *International Journal of Nautical Archaeology*, 10: 3–14

Scott, D. A. (1987) *Metallography of Ancient Metallic Objects*, London: Summer Schools Press, Institute of Archaeology

Sease, C. (1988) *A Conservation Manual for the Field Archaeologist*, Los Angeles: UCLA

Singer, C., Holmyard, E. J., Hall, A. R., and Williams, T. J. (eds) (1956) *A History of Technology*, vol. II, Oxford: Claredon

Spriggs, J. A. (1980) 'Recovery and storage of materials from waterlogged deposits at York', *The Conservator* 4: 19–24

SSCR (1979) *The Conservation of Metals: Proc. Symp. Edinburgh, 1979*, Edinburgh: SSCR

Stambolov, T. (1969) 'Manufacture, deterioration and preservation of leather: a literature survey of theoretical aspects and ancient techniques' in ICOM (1969) *Preprints 2nd Triennial Meeting, ICOM Committee for Conservation, Amsterdam, 1969*, Paris: ICOM

Stambolov, T. (1985) *The Corrosion and Conservation of Metallic Antiquities and Works of Art*, (literature survey), enlarged edn, Amsterdam: Central Research Laboratory for Objects of Art and Science

Stambolov, T. and Van Asperen der Boer, J. R. J. (1976 and following) *The Deterioration and Conservation of Porous Building Materials in Monuments: a Literature Review*, 2nd edn, Rome: ICCROM (1976); Supplements in ICOM (1978) 78.10.11, ICOM (1981) 81.10.1, ICOM (1984a) 84.10.23–24

Staniforth, S. (1986) 'Environmental conservation' in J. Thompson (ed) *Manual of Curatorship*, Sevenoaks: Butterworths

Stanley Price, N. (ed) (1984) *Conservation on Archaeological Excavations*, Rome: ICCROM

Starling, K. and Watkinson, D. (eds) (1987) *Archaeological Bone, Antler and Ivory*, Occasional Paper no. 5, London: UKIC

Strong, D. and Brown, D. (eds) (1976) *Roman Crafts*, London: Duckworth

Stolow, N. (1987) *Conservation and Exhibitions*, Sevenoaks: Butterworths

Tate, J. D., Tennent, N. H., and Townsend, J. H. (eds) (1983) *Resins in Conservation: Proc. Symp. Edinburgh, 1982*, Edinburgh: SSCR

Thomson, G. (1986) *The Museum Environment*, Sevenoaks: Butterworths

Thompson, J. (ed) (1986) *Manual of Curatorship*, Sevenoaks: Butterworths

Tite, M. (1972) *Methods of Physical Examination in Archaeology*, London: Seminar Press

Torraca, G. (1975) *Solubility and Solvents for Conservation Problems*, Rome: ICCROM

Torraca, G. (1982) *Porous Building Materials – Materials Science for Architectural Conservation*, 2nd edn, Rome: ICCROM

UKIC (1983) *Guidance for Conservation Practice*, London: UKIC

UKIC Archaeology Section (1982) *Excavated Artefacts for Publication: U.K. Sites*, Guidelines no. 1, London: UKIC

UKIC Archaeology Section (1983) *Packaging and Storage of Freshly-Excavated Artefacts from Archaeological Sites*, Guidelines no. 2, London: UKIC

UKIC Archaeology Section (1984) *Environmental Standards for the Permanent Storage of Excavated Material from Archaeological Sites*, Guidelines no. 3, London: UKIC

Unesco (1982) (various authors) 'Conservation: a challenge to the profession', *Museum* 34: 1

Watkinson, D. (ed) (1987) *First Aid for Finds*, 2nd edn, Hertford/London: Rescue/UKIC Archaeology Section

Weier, L. (1973) 'The deterioration of inorganic materials under the sea', *Bulletin of the Institute of Archaeology* 11: 131–63

Index

Bold type indicates definition or major entry
Italic type indicates plate

317